THE NEW UNEMPLOYMENT HANDBOOK

By Guy Dauncey
and
Jane Mountain

I am born to win!
I am born to win!
I've been rejected, considered dead,
I've been accused and been refused
but the stone that the Builder refused
shall be the Head Cornerstone,
I cannot fail, 'cause I'm not alone,
I am born to win!

(Jimmy Cliff)

This Handbook is dedicated to YOU, the reader,
in the hope that together, we can win.

NATIONAL EXTENSION COLLEGE

FOREWORD TO THE 1987 EDITION

In 1979, when unemployment first became a major national problem, many people believed that it would be just a temporary matter. By 1981, when the first edition of The Unemployment Handbook was published, people were just beginning to realise that something different might be happening, which would require some fundamental rethinking.

In the years since 1981, practical local initiatives have sprung up all over Britain to tackle the problems. It is hard now to find anyone outside the south-east who seriously believes that unemployment will go away in the near future. The need for personal support for individual unemployed people, and for positive, life-affirming advice is as great today as it ever was.

Two-thirds of the Handbook is completely new. The rest has been revised and updated from the 1982 edition. Even as we update it, things are changing, and we know that we have not been able to do a perfect job. To begin preparing for the fourth edition, we are including a *Freepost feedback sheet* at the back of the book, which we hope you will use to give us information, ideas and corrections. We are going to set up a system of 'contributing authors' for the fourth edition, drawing on the experience of people out in the field, who are up to their neck in unemployment activities. If you would like to help in this way, please write to us at the National Extension College.

The authors hope that this contribution towards the massive problems of unemployment will bring hope, encouragement and practical advice to many people.

Guy Dauncey and Jane Mountain
June 1987

CONTENTS

Questions

EASYFINDER: LOCAL ADDRESSES AND PHONE NUMBERS

A do-it-yourself directory! Spend 30 minutes with the telephone directory now and fill in these pages. You will find it very helpful as you work through the Handbook.

	Address	Tel.
Jobcentre: Under 'Manpower Services Commission, Employment Division'		
Unemployment Benefit Office: Under 'Employment, Department of'		
Department of Health and Social Security: Under 'Health and Social Security, Dept. of'		
Careers Office: Under 'Careers Service' or name of City or County Council, then 'Careers Service'		
Social Services: Under name of County or City Council, then under 'Social Services Dept.'		
Youth Service*: Under 'Youth Officers' or under City or County Council (Inner London Education Authority in London) and then 'Youth Service' or 'Youth Office'		
Employment Agencies: Yellow Pages		
Area Education Office: Under name of City or County Council (ILEA in London), then 'Education Dept.'		
Adult Education Centre*: as above		

Further Education Adviser*: as above (see also p. 00)		
Local College of Further Education, or Technical College*: as above, or under 'Schools and Colleges in Yellow Pages		
Adult Training Centre/Skillcentre: Under 'Manpower Services Commission, Skillcentre Training Agency'		
Council for Voluntary Service or Volunteer Bureau*: Yellow Pages, under 'Social Service and Welfare Organisations'		
Citizens Advice Bureau: Under 'Citizens Advice Bureaux'		
Information/Advice Centre: Ask the Citizens Advice Bureau		
Library: Under name of City or County Council, then 'Library Services'		
Unemployment Centre*: Ask the Citizens Advice Bureau		
Community Centre*: Ask the Citizens Advice Bureau		
Community Programme Agency: Go via 'Manpower Services Commission, Employment Division, Community Programme Offices'		

Sports/Leisure Centre: Yellow Pages, under 'Leisure centres' or under name of City or County Council, then 'Leisure Services Dept.'	
Enterprise Agency: Under 'Business Enterprise Agencies'	
Co-operative Development Agency: Under 'Business Enterprise Agencies'	
Disabled Advice Projects: Yellow Pages, under 'Disabled, amenities and information'	
Member of Parliament: Ask the Citizens Advice Bureau	
Local Councillor(s): Ask the Citizens Advice Bureau, or phone your City or County Council and ask directly	
Other Unemployment Projects or Initiatives: As you learn about them	

*** If you find these hard to locate, try Directory Enquiries (192, or 142 in London), or ask at your local Citizens Advice Bureau or Library.**

CHAPTER 1: DESPAIR, ANGER and ACTION

'Me? What do I say when people ask me that question, 'What do you do?' I tell them I haven't got an alibi any more. I'm simply me, myself, me. That shuts them up.'

A woman at the Camden Over-40s
Unemployed Group, 1984

This is a book of hope.

- Does being unemployed make you feel hopeless?
- Does it make you feel you are a 'failure'?
- Does it make you feel bloody angry?

Or does it make you feel happy to be out of the world of 9 — 5
working, at least temporarily,
and free at last to explore your own life
and follow your own heart?

If you react in any of the first three ways, you are not alone. (You are not alone if you belong to the fourth group, either.) You might *feel* alone, but you are in good company. Millions of other people feel the same. But be clear on one thing, even if much else confuses you:

You are NOT a failure.
You are NOT a number on the scrap heap.
You are a whole and a wonderful human being.
You are blessed and loved in the sight of God, or Krishna,
or Mohammed, or the Universe, or your own
inherent integrity as a human being,
whichever way you like
to see these things

'Why?', you may ask, 'why is this all happening? Surely, they can't let it go on for ever?' 'Don't the folks down south know that more than 1 in 4 of all the men of working age in Manchester, for instance, are out of work?' 'Don't they know what this does to our morale, to our skill, to our ability to play a useful part in the building of a different and perhaps a better Britain?'

Anger is a healthy reaction, if it then leads on to action. Anger leads people to *do* things, whereas apathy and despair lead to nothing. Depression is often caused by the suppression of our feelings. We bottle them up, and then they poison us from within. If more unemployed people were willing to let their feelings be heard (creatively and non-violently, not with the ugliness of hatred), more energy would be released to start improving things. The reaction which is painful to see is when people turn their feelings in on themselves.

Anger is *always* there somewhere, hidden underneath, when people are mistreated and oppressed. It is bound to be there, if you are mistreated, as all unemployed people are today. But if you don't express your anger, it will come out internally, bringing headaches, restless nights, and aching backs; it will come out within the family, cutting great wounds in people's marriages; and it will come out sideways against people of other races, adding new misery where there is already enough.

So let your anger be heard, and then begin to do something with it, so that its energy is used constructively, so that we begin to end this appalling state of affairs.

'So what can we do?', you ask.

'What magic action will suddenly give me
a job, an income,
and some reasonable hope in life?'

Britain is going through a huge upheaval. No easy answers are going to bring solutions. We have to work our way out of this one. A new vision, a new dream to pursue, the willingness to create new businesses, new ways of working and new ways of sharing work, a willingness to renew our own lives, gaining new skills and new abilities, a willingness to recreate our whole communities, and the persistence to see it all through, over 25 years at least — these are the things which will bring an end to the miseries.

Alone, you will always suffer. There is no relief to the pain as long as you keep it all to yourself. But shout it out, find people to share it with, find other people to help, to support, to love, to work with, to protest on the streets with, and your pain can turn to laughter, to struggle, to creative action and to hope.

This book preaches. It bears no shame in doing this. We know how much pain there is out there, and we want to help you transform it. There is so much that can be done when people get together and start to help each other. We can support each other, have parties together, hunt for jobs together, establish local workshops together, set up arts and music groups together, organise festivals together, establish community projects together, set up co-operatives together, set up community businesses together, organise holidays together, plant trees together, petition city hall together, protest together.

This book is a book of encouragement. The authors believe in the excellence and beauty of everyone. They also believe in our ability to achieve miracles, when we put our mind to it.

Is it possible that people who up until now have been so isolated, so depressed, and frequently so defeated, can turn all that around, and begin to follow a different tune?

Our answer is yes — it has already proven itself to be possible in the lives of many unemployed people, and it has to go on being possible — for we have work to do: the transformation of our own lives, and the transformation of our society. And it is not just our cities and communities which are in trouble — the whole world is in trouble too, with its nuclear missiles, its hunger, its slaughtered rainforests and its people's unwillingness to accept that we are all part of this small, fragile, incredibly beautiful planet. When it comes to transformation, we have a little work to do.

The belief that a tiny minority has held may become the belief of many:

that unemployed people,
through their discovery of new concepts of 'work'
and new ways of helping each other,
through their exploration of new possibilities for their lives,
can be the pioneers of a new,
a different
and a better future.

Every one of us is a miracle, waiting to happen.

And now, on with the practical stuff. . .

CHAPTER 2: AN UNEMPLOYMENT SURVIVAL KIT – BUILDING NEW SUPPORTS

OUR BASIC SUPPORTS – REBUILDING THE SUPPORTS – Purpose and direction – Regular daily activity – Identity and self-respect – Companions and friends – Money – Unemployment and your marriage – Family life

OUR BASIC SUPPORTS

Many people feel depressed and 'down' when they are unemployed. When you are in a job (or in regular training or education) your job gives you several important supports. If you lose your job, or just don't have one, you may lose some or all of these supports. If you don't rebuild them, the result may be depression.

This short survival kit therefore aims to:

IDENTIFY WHAT THESE SUPPORTS ARE → DECIDE WHICH ONES YOU HAVE LOST → PLAN HOW YOU CAN REBUILD THEM YOURSELF

These are the five basic supports:

1. A job brings a sense of *purpose and direction.*
   When people lose their job, they often feel they have lost their sense of purpose and direction. They feel they are drifting, unsure of where they are going.

   How true is this for you? 0 1 2 3 4 5 6 7 8 9 10
   (Circle whichever is appropriate.)

2. A job brings *regular daily activity*. It gives us regular work, regular hours, regular meal-breaks and regular holidays. Take the job away, and every day tends to become the same, week in, week out.

   How true is this for you? 0 1 2 3 4 5 6 7 8 9 10

3. A job provides a personal sense of *identity and self-respect.* You can say, 'I am a steel-worker', 'I am a nurse', or 'I am a student'. You know who you are, and you can tell other people who you are. It feels good (unless you hate the job). Take away the job, and you take away this identity. 'I am unemployed' just doesn't sound so good, somehow, and most people hate saying it.

   How true is this for you? 0 1 2 3 4 5 6 7 8 9 10

4. A job provides us with *companions and friends.* This is so obvious that we take it for granted. But take the job away, and you quickly realise how much you miss them.

Without these friends, many unemployed people are alone for much of the time, which can get depressing.

How true is this for you? 0 1 2 3 4 5 6 7 8 9 10

5. A job provides *money*. For most people, a job brings in more money than they get from state benefits.

How true is this for you? 0 1 2 3 4 5 6 7 8 9 10

These supports are very important to us.

If we lose them, it is no wonder we feel down.

In **Exercise 1** below, ask yourself how much support you felt you were getting from each of the five supports in your last job (or school, college, at home, etc) on the same scale, from 0 to 10. Write your scores in line A. Then write your scores from above in line B.

	Purpose and direction	Regular daily activity	Identity and self-respect	Companions and friends	Money	Total
Line A: Last job etc.						
Line B: Being unemployed						

Exercise 1: Personal supports
Your scores can tell you two things:

1. By comparing your totals in lines A and B, you can find out how much being unemployed has thrown you off balance by taking away or weakening your supports. (You might find your overall sense of support has *increased* in unemployment.)

- Points lost or gained in unemployment: . . . . lost/gained

2. You can see which particular supports need rebuilding. This is the basis of survival. You should pay serious attention to any support where you scored 4 or less in line B, and plan how you can rebuild these supports (see below).

   - Supports which I need to rebuild:

REBUILDING THE SUPPORTS

1. A sense of purpose and direction

The key to rebuilding this support is to begin to set your own goals and to make your own plans.

You may be lucky and find a new job quite soon. When unemployment is so high, however, the time it takes to find new work or training can be quite long, and it is possible you might be out of work for several months, or more.

If you tell yourself, 'Oh, I'll have a job by next week', you will not be able to make any plans for activities that last more than a day or two. If you recognise that you *might* be out of work for several months, you can say to yourself, 'I have got several months all to myself. What can I do with this time?' and make your plans accordingly.

It is important to spend time on this planning. Take a sheet of paper (or a page in your job-hunting file - see Chapter 4) and ask yourself, 'What would I most like to do in this time?'

Here are some suggestions:

- spend regular time every day/every week job-hunting
- learn a new skill ....
- join in local community activities
- spend more time with my family
- become involved in a sport, and get fit
- join a voluntary group
- explore possible self-employment
- read some books, to educate myself
- join a Jobclub (see p. 45)
- take over more of the housework
- become actively involved in something I believe in
- learn another new skill ....
- do something creative — art, music, sculpture, writing
- take some time to explore my inner world, to discover more about myself
- join an exam course at the local college
- learn to drive*
- join a 'Wider Opportunities' course (see p. 109)

*Puzzled that some things you'd love to do require money you haven't got? There are some 'dole queue secrets' it is useful to learn. (See Chapter 5.)

Exercise 2: Setting goals

1. On your sheet of paper, create your own list of activities that you would like to achieve in the next six months.
2. Choose your 'top seven', marking them with stars.
3. Place them in order of importance. Create a *goals list*, as in the example below:

March – July 1988: GOALS

1. 2 hours a day thorough jobhunting
2. Join a computing class at the local college
3. Work as a volunteer in a playgroup
4. Train for the marathon, with Jim
5. Start reading some books, to get some sense into my head
6. Learn to cook, clean and change little Polly's nappy
7. Do a sponsored hitch-hike to John o' Groats to raise funds for the local Unemployed Centre.

2. Regular daily activity

By planning your day *in advance* the night before, you will be able to get a lot more done during the day. Figure 1 gives a couple of sample daily timetables.

8.00 am — Get up, help get the kids off to school.
9.00 — Clean the kitchen floor.
9.30–11.30 — Work through the job advertisements in the daily papers, magazines, etc, and write off any application letters.
11.30 — Phone the Jobcentre, to check if anything has come in. (New jobs arrive every day, and have been sorted by mid-morning.)
Until lunch — working on the allotment, or taking the dog for a good walk.
1.30 — Lunch.
2.00–3.30 — Helping out on the neighbourhood housing action project, on the rota.
3.30 — Collect kids from school, have tea.
4.30–6.00 — Helping with gym/football/netball coaching at the school.
6.30 — Cook the family supper. Time with the children.
***9.25 — Miami Vice

7.30 am — Get up, take cup of tea back to bed, read good book in bed, and plan the day.
8.30 — Get up, breakfast.
9.30 — Go to the library to check through the papers, making a note of any suitable jobs. Call in at the Jobcentre.
10.30 — Swimming pool with Kate.
11.30 — With Kate to visit Pete and Jenny. Lunch with them.
2.15 — Commerce class, at Tech.
4.15 — Home, tea, sit down to write off any application letters, etc. Make any phone calls to ask for further info on any advertised jobs.
7.30 — Meeting of local chess club.

Fig. 1: Two daily timetables

3. Identity and self-respect

How can you restore your self-confidence and pride, if you haven't got a job? You can do so by building up your own life, so that you are busy doing what you want to do. This will restore your identity and self-respect.

If in the past you have based a lot of your self-respect on your job, you may understandably feel fairly low now. Remember that *we are all beautiful, unique people.* Having no job is no shame. You are still a beautiful, unique person, and you are still full of talents, abilities and special qualities. You may simply have to start expressing them in new ways. In time you may come to see this period without full-time work as a gift, which allowed you to explore new avenues in your life.

Exercise 3: Areas of life

The circles in Figure 2 have six segments, representing six areas of life. Circle A is an example. Take a coloured pen, and draw a line across each segment in Circle B showing how much you feel fulfilled in each area.

Now take a different coloured pen, and on the same circle draw a second line showing how much of each segment you would *like* to be filled.

After a while, when someone asks you the old question 'What do you do?' you may be able to answer, 'Well, I teach swimming to the cubs on Fridays, I'm learning welding at the Tech on Tuesdays, I'm involved in our local tenants' committee, I'm learning to play the Hawaiian bagpipes, and I'm helping out at the City Farm in the neighbourhood! How about you?'

By doing this kind of thing you can say to yourself, and to the world, that just because you are unemployed does not mean life will get you down. Like hell it will!

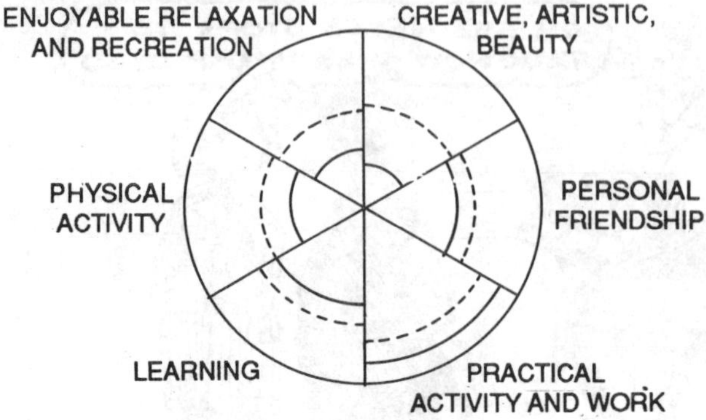

Circle A: Example:
——— = current
------- = future, ideal

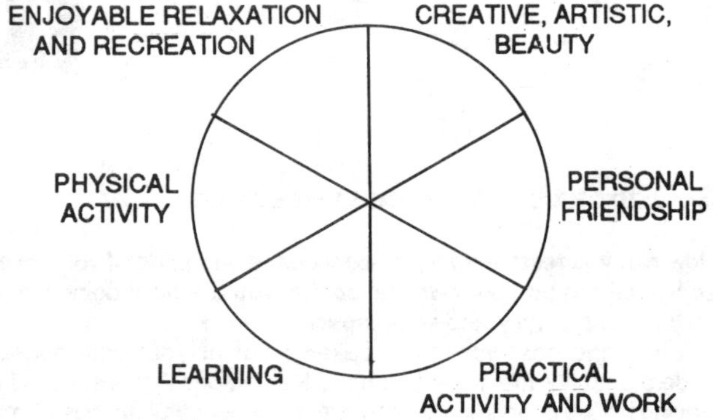

Circle B: Yourself, current and future ideal.

Figure 2. Areas of life.

4. Companions and friends

Companions and friends *are* important. One of the really depressing things about being unemployed can be not meeting enough people and spending too much time on your own, or just with the family at home (which can also cause extra worries and tensions).

The more things you do with your time, the more people you will meet. And remember, many jobs are found on the grapevine. The more people you get to know and see regularly, the greater your chance of hearing about something.

If you are a rather shy person who prefers to do things alone, such as reading or gardening, you might need to make a deliberate effort to take up some new kind of activity where you *will* meet people, even if it makes you uncomfortable at first.

Make a special point of calling in to see your friends, just to keep in touch.

Exercise 4: Companions and friends
Make a list (A) of the friends you currently see a lot of, and then a scond list (B) of friends you would like to see more of:

List A (Example)	**List B**	**List A**	**List B**
Marcie	Joan	....	....
Pete	Grant	....	....
Duncan		....	....
Hughie		....	....

Do you need to meet some new people, to enjoy some new friendships? yes.... maybe.... no....

Ways to meet new friends (Tick which ones interest you.)

...... Evening classes
...... Community activities
...... Sports
...... Local dramatic group
...... Local 'Save Earthworms' group
...... A self-help/support group

5. Money

This is obviously the hardest support to rebuild. How difficult is it to get by on your fortnightly giro?

Very difficult.........
Fairly difficult.........
I'll manage..........
Where I grew up, we used to stew the sheets for soup.........

You may be able to do more about financial difficulty than you think. Chapter 12 will help you.

6. Unemployment and your marriage

Many couples find that being at home too much puts a heavy strain on their marriage or relationship. Men often feel depressed at not being the breadwinner any more and women often feel confused by having their husband around the house all the time, disturbing the daily routines.

This situation *can* make a marriage grow, if you allow it to — you have got time together, for once, perhaps with the children out at school. If you are willing to change your routines, and talk openly about what is happening to you both, you might be able to reach a new level of personal sharing and trust.

It also allows you to have time with your children — time to go out to the park or the country with them, to share in their play, and to involve them in any activities or hobbies you are doing.

If being unemployed is putting a big strain on your relationship, what can you do? This Handbook *is* the advice. If you follow its suggestions you ought soon to become active again and the pressures will lift of their own accord. Recognise that your marriage is under strain because you have lost the important personal supports that your job gave you. Rebuild those supports, and you will almost certainly find that things get better.

If things remain bad, don't wait until they fall apart altogether, but seek help. Get in touch with the Marriage Guidance Council and make an appointment to see somebody. He or she will offer to see you either singly or together, and to listen to your problems intelligently. You will be helped to reach a clearer understanding of your relationship, and a clearer idea of what you need to do. Find their address in the phone book or contact their head office at Little Church Street, Rugby, Warwickshire.

Exercise 5: Your marriage

1. Do you find yourselves shouting at each other more than you used to?
   (a) yes ...... (b) about the same ...... (c) less than before ......

2. Do you talk together about the worries that unemployment brings?
   (a) no ...... (b) only a little ...... (c) yes ......

3. Do you develop practical ideas and activities to help reduce those worries?
   (a) no ...... (b) sometimes ...... (c) yes ......

4. Do you get out together doing something you enjoy, such as walking and enjoying the countryside?
   (a) no ...... (b) not enough ...... (c) yes ......

5. Are you making love less often than you used to before you were unemployed?
   (a) yes ...... (b) about the same ...... (c) more often ......

6. Do you feel your partner is helping you with your worries?
   (a) no...... (b) a bit ...... (c) yes ......

7. Do you feel you are helping your partner enough with his/her worries?
   (a) no ...... (b) a bit ...... (c) yes ......

8. Do you find yourself thinking 'This will have to end'?
   (a) yes, often ...... (b) occasionally ...... (c) no ......

Scores: (a) 2 (b) 1 (c) 0

11–16: It's tough — yes? If you know that things have got worse since you were unemployed, then ACT. Use this book to help you. Don't sit and watch your marriage being destroyed when there is lots that you could do.
6–10: There's a lot that could be improved — yes? See below.
0–5: If you take the book back to bed with you, you might get on even better!

Some of the ideas listed below might help your marriage. Sit down together, and think of things you could add to the list. Give each suggestion two scores from 0 to 10 (one from each of you), and make some decisions.

- read this Handbook together, and share in some of the exercises ....../......
- plan some small outings and excursions together ....../......
- sit down together and spend 30 minutes each in turn, just talking about how you feel, while your partner simply listens, without interrupting ....../......

- arrange an evening each week when you switch off the TV and spend time talking together about problems and possibilities ....../......
- swap some of the things you have each traditionally done — e.g. housework, shopping, childcare, finances ....../......
- arrange a session with the Marriage Guidance Council together ....../......
- give each other a surprise 'special day', as a reward for getting this far ....../......

A book which helps many people understand what goes on in marriages and families is *Peoplemaking* by Virginia Satir, published by Souvenir, £5.95. (With this, and all books referred to, always ask at the local library, and if it is not available, place an order for it.)

The Open University's short course on 'Family Relationships' is available to unemployed people at a special discount price of £5 (see p. 108).

See also *The Couple's Journey,* by Susan Campbell, which is a guide to 'the five-stage path of growth travelled by every intimate relationship — romance, power struggle, stability, commitment and co-creation' (Impact/Airlift). See also *Women who love too much* by Robin Norwood (Arrow).

7. Family life

It is not difficult to list the extra difficulties unemployment can bring to family life. So what about the positive possibilities? You can use this time to create something very special — so that the kids, when they are older, say, 'You remember the time when mum and dad were out of work? That was the happiest period of my childhood'.

Here are fifteen ideas which might help to create that happy time:

1. Make a kite together, and take it flying.
2. Go camping together — if you haven't got a tent, see below under 'Things, Toys and Equipment'. You could form a holiday group with other people who are on low incomes, and take the kids away together (see p. 165).
3. Take a greater interest in your children's hobbies, encourage and support them. Get them involved in *your* hobbies and find new ones to do together — borrow a good children's hobbies book from the library.
4. All go out for a midnight feast, sleep outside under the stars, let your hair down and have fun.
5. Start going out for a daily jog or swim together.
6. Turn off the TV three nights a week, and do things together instead.
7. Revive the old art of storytelling, both from books, and making your own stories up, by candlelight.
8. Teach your children to cook, and cook some meals together.
9. Go out and discover museums, castles and parks together. Take some of your friends' or neighbours' kids along with you — it'll add to the fun. (Well, it *could*).
10. Get together with other parents to put on a kids party, and let the kids help organise it (see books below).
11. Learn to make your own clothes together.
12. Make a deliberate choice to say at least three positive, encouraging things to each child, and to your partner, every day.
13. Move everything breakable, and have a really good pillow fight once a week.
14. Go to an evening class on massage, and start giving each other regular massages.
15. Get together with other kids, ask for assistance from the local community centre or youth service, and create a local kids magazine, and sell it or give it away door-to-door (if you can get advertising).

This list could have 30 things on it. Sit down and add a further 15, and then ask yourself 'Does unemployment really have to mean cutting back on family life?' You may have less money to go on expensive outings and to buy ice creams, but instead, you can start having more fun, more sharing, and more meaningful time together.

Things, toys and equipment

Even the smallest things cost money, not to mention kites, but it is possible to earn a tiny amount of additional money each week before your benefit is affected (see p. 150). Maybe on Saturday morning you could go out with your kids and wash a few cars together, or find something to make, such as cakes, which you could sell to your neighbours on your street. For collective activities such as parties and children's outings, organise a jumble sale or a bring-and-buy, to raise funds.

If you know other parents who are unemployed, single parents, or people simply willing to share, you can swap, lend and share things among each other. The more things that you start doing locally, whether it is going to an evening class or helping out in the youth club, the more people you will meet.

The Open University runs excellent short courses concerning children and family life at special discount prices for unemployed people (see p. 108).

Great books for having fun together

Ask your local library to order these books for you: you'll find them full of games, ideas and activities offering hundreds of hours of enjoyment:

- *The Youth Games Book,* from the IT Resource Centre (£3.95), 19 Elmbank St, Glasgow G2 4PB (ISBN 0 9506951 06)
- *Over 30 Games for All Occasions,* by Patrick Goodland (Scripture Union, £2.75)
- *Something to Do — 300 games, hobbies and pastimes for all the year round,* by Septima (Penguin, £1.25)
- *The Puffin Book of Indoor Games,* by Andrew Pennycock (£1.50).
- *Revolting Recipes,* (cookery for over 8's) by Nigel Roberts (Dragon Grafton, £1.95)
- *Kids' Britain,* by Betty Jerman (Pan, £2.95)
- *Kids' London* (Pan £2.95)
- *Sharing Nature with Children,* by J. B. Cornell (Interaction Imprint)
- *Co-operative Sports and Games Books 1 and 2,* by Terry Orlick (Writers and Readers).
- *The New Games Book,* out of print, sadly, but may be in some libraries (Sidgwick and Jackson).

The time has come to move on, to create new rules, more in tune with the times, games in which there are no spectators and no second-string players, games for a whole family and a whole day, games in which aggresssion fades into laughter — New Games.

George Leonard, in *The Ultimate Athlete*

Further reading

- *How to Survive Unemployment,* by Robert Nathan and Michel Syrett (Penguin)
- *Living with Unemployment,* by Ann Warren (Hodder and Stoughton). A personal account about being unemployed by a woman who went through it with her family
- *Taking Stock — Being Fifty in the Eighties,* by Charles Handy (BBC)
- *What Color is Your Parachute?* by Richard Bolles (Ten Speed/Airlift)

CHAPTER 3: BUT WHAT SHALL I DO? DISCOVERING YOUR NATURAL SKILLS: A PRACTICAL EXERCISE

INTRODUCTION – In your wildest dreams – WHAT ARE YOUR NATURAL SKILLS? – RELATING YOUR SKILLS TO POSSIBLE WORK – IN CONCLUSION: THE INNER WISDOM OF UNEMPLOYMENT

INTRODUCTION

- Do you know what kind of job you would like to do? Yes ..... No .....
- Do you know what kind of training might help? Yes ..... No .....
- Do you know what you are good at doing? Yes ..... No .....

If you can answer 'Yes' to all these questions, you might want to skip this chapter. However, it might tell you something about yourself and your abilities that you did not realise.

In the past, many of us had to build our working lives on false foundations, never able to do the things we loved doing, or perhaps dreamed of doing. We had to work in the factories, down the mines, or in the fields. Our lives were sacrificed to the demands of the Industrial Age.

Today, although the Industrial Age has ended, many schools still deliberately prepare children to live dull lives, because in the past they would have had dull jobs. Dreams are still being suppressed, and our natural skills and abilities — the things we love doing — not encouraged. There is as much tragedy in this now as there was then.

When people do not work in jobs they enjoy, they find it difficult to base their lives when unemployed on things they enjoy.

Why? Because they do not know what their own natural skills and abilities (the things they love doing) are. For one reason or another, they have not developed their birthright.

This chapter is focused around a single exercise, the 'Achievements Exercise'. It will give you information about your birthright. It will tell you what your own natural skills are, and help you to make them the foundation of your life from now on. You can do the exercise (1) alone, (2) with a friend, or (3) in a group. You will need a notebook or a few sheets of clean paper.

In your wildest dreams . . .

Before starting, take five minutes to ask yourself if you have already some private ideas about what you would *really* like to do. They may be ideas about which you feel, 'Oh, but that is ridiculous' — well, that doesn't matter. Try to think of four or five jobs that you would love to do if you had all the skills, money or whatever else was needed. Write them down and then forget about them for the time being.

WHAT ARE YOUR NATURAL SKILLS?

Exercise 6: The achievements exercise

The exercise in this chapter has been adapted from the book *Job Power Now!*, by Bernard Haldane (published by Acropolis Books, Washington), a careers counsellor in the USA. His

In your wildest dreams. . . .

work is acknowledged with thanks. Further useful self-assessment exercises can be found in *The Book of Tests,* by Michael Nathanson (Fontana, £3.95).

The following steps will help you identify your own natural skills and abilities. They will do this by referring you to things you have already done in your life that gave you a special sense of satisfaction, well-being and achievement.

Step 1

On page 1 of your notebook make a brief year-by-year diary of your life so far. Write down the important things that happened to you, the important things you have done, the jobs you have held and the schools you went to. The purpose of this is simply to re-awaken your memory. (Approx. 15 minutes.)

Step 2

Go through your life again, more slowly, year by year. On the next few pages of your notebook write down *the things you have done that you feel proud of, the things that gave you a special sense of satisfaction and the things that gave you (or give you) a specially deep sense of enjoyment.* Take it slowly. You will begin to remember things you had completely forgotten. Carry on until you reach the present. You might end up with a list of 10–15 items, depending on how able you are to admit you were proud to have done something, or that some experience meant a great deal to you. Many people find this hard, because they find it difficult to believe they have done *anything* to be proud of — which is never true. (Approx. 30-60 minutes.)

If you think of something, but then think, 'Oh, but that doesn't count', don't squash the idea. Write it down. Don't only measure your experiences by the things school or society normally counts as an 'achievement'. It is what *you* feel to have been an achievement or an important experience that matters, not what others think.

The following are typical achievements and good experiences people might feel especially proud of:

- laid a crazy paving terrace on my own;
- raised two children and was a good mother;

- fixed old bikes and made up new ones when I was 14;
- overcame my fear of cooking and now share cooking with my wife;
- planned and completed a five-day hike with my friends;
- supported a friend for a month when she was feeling very low;
- worked successfully as a foreman for a year;
- passed my school exams;
- settled in Britain, got used to the rain and became fluent in English language;
- wrote my own poems;
- ran a successful sales campaign;
- overcame illness and lack of schooling;
- successfully gave up smoking;
- organised help and looked after people when there was a car crash outside my home;
- learnt how to play with my sister's little children.

(*Note:* Some people find it hard to think what to list. Others list 20 things in no time at all. Don't worry — just take your time.)

Step 3

Look through your list when it is complete and choose the seven achievements which you feel mean the most to you. Place them in order of importance, numbering them from 1 to 7.

Now pause a minute. What you have got here is *evidence* of things you have done which have meant a lot to you. *Every one of us is brilliant.* We are all full of the most remarkable skills, gifts and qualities. Many of us live without ever really discovering what these abilities are, so we are not able to build our lives on true foundations. We have been (up until now) prevented from blossoming into our true selves — by our schooling, our parents, our employers, by racist or sexist attitudes, by our own husbands or wives. We have learnt to be much *less than we are.*

The challenge this book gives you is the challenge to build your life on *your own foundations*: on the skills, gifts and abilities which are truly yours. You may have

- a special skill with wood, or electronics;
- a natural ability at organising;
- an inborn 'way' with plants or animals;
- a natural eye for beauty, colour and design;
- a natural ease with other people, or an instinct to care.

What are your own natural skills and abilities? The evidence you need is in front of you.

Step 4

Using the list of skills in Figure 3, take each of your seven achievements in turn, and tick off the skills which you think you were using. Give your first three achievements double ticks. This is a very good exercise to do with someone else, since you could help each other. Use the spaces at the bottom to add in extra skills that you think of.

Step 5

When you have finished, add up the number of times you used each skill in the TOTAL column. Then take the *seven* skills with the highest scores, and copy them down into your notebook under the heading 'My Natural Skills and Abilities'.

This information is exceptionally valuable to you. It tells you some of the things you have done, which you really enjoyed doing, as evidence of where your heart's interests lie. It also tells you the skills and abilities which you have. But what do you do with the information? How can you use it to build yourself *new foundations*? Read on!

Skills	1	2	3	4	5	6	7	Total
Animals/plants	....	....	....	....	....	....	....	....
Artistic skills	....	....	....	....	....	....	....	....
Caring	....	....	....	....	....	....	....	....
Communication	....	....	....	....	....	....	....	....
Constant hard work	....	....	....	....	....	....	....	....
Co-ordination	....	....	....	....	....	....	....	....
Courage	....	....	....	....	....	....	....	....
Creativity	....	....	....	....	....	....	....	....
Dealing with people	....	....	....	....	....	....	....	....
Decision-making	....	....	....	....	....	....	....	....
Design skills	....	....	....	....	....	....	....	....
Determination	....	....	....	....	....	....	....	....
Diplomatic	....	....	....	....	....	....	....	....
Efficiency	....	....	....	....	....	....	....	....
Energy/drive	....	....	....	....	....	....	....	....
Figures	....	....	....	....	....	....	....	....
Foresight	....	....	....	....	....	....	....	....
Friendship	....	....	....	....	....	....	....	....
Human relationships	....	....	....	....	....	....	....	....
Humour	....	....	....	....	....	....	....	....
Ideas	....	....	....	....	....	....	....	....
Imagination	....	....	....	....	....	....	....	....
Initiative	....	....	....	....	....	....	....	....
Intuition	....	....	....	....	....	....	....	....
Inventive	....	....	....	....	....	....	....	....
Leadership	....	....	....	....	....	....	....	....
Listening	....	....	....	....	....	....	....	....
Loving	....	....	....	....	....	....	....	....
Management	....	....	....	....	....	....	....	....
Memory	....	....	....	....	....	....	....	....
Money skills	....	....	....	....	....	....	....	....
Observation	....	....	....	....	....	....	....	....
Organising	....	....	....	....	....	....	....	....
Outdoors/travel	....	....	....	....	....	....	....	....
Patience	....	....	....	....	....	....	....	....
Performance	....	....	....	....	....	....	....	....

Skills	1	2	3	4	5	6	7	Total
Persistence	....	....	....	....	....	....	....	....
Persuasive	....	....	....	....	....	....	....	....
Planning	....	....	....	....	....	....	....	....
Practical	....	....	....	....	....	....	....	....
Problem-solving	....	....	....	....	....	....	....	....
Production	....	....	....	....	....	....	....	....
Promotion/sales	....	....	....	....	....	....	....	....
Repair skills	....	....	....	....	....	....	....	....
Research	....	....	....	....	....	....	....	....
Responsibility	....	....	....	....	....	....	....	....
Self-discipline	....	....	....	....	....	....	....	....
Speaking	....	....	....	....	....	....	....	....
Stamina	....	....	....	....	....	....	....	....
Teamwork	....	....	....	....	....	....	....	....
Tolerance	....	....	....	....	....	....	....	....
Training	....	....	....	....	....	....	....	....
Trust	....	....	....	....	....	....	....	....
Work with hands	....	....	....	....	....	....	....	....
Writing	....	....	....	....	....	....	....	....
....	....	....	....	....	....	....	....	....
....	....	....	....	....	....	....	....	....

Fig. 3: Natural skills

RELATING YOUR SKILLS TO POSSIBLE WORK

Take a break. If you can, go for a walk to let your mind have a rest. Let it quietly mull over what you have just done.

The problem now is this: which kind of work would give you a chance to develop your natural skills? There are thousands of different kinds of work, some of which you may never even have heard of, let alone know what they involve.

From now on you need to ask yourself constantly over several weeks, 'What kind of work?' If you search constantly and persistently enough, your answer will come.

It might be that you are not able to find an actual job which gives expression to your skills at all. Not everyone is able to. This need not matter. It *does* matter, however, that you find *some* way to develop and express your skills.

Figure 4 shows ways to use your knowledge about your skills to make a creative leap, and to develop your life:

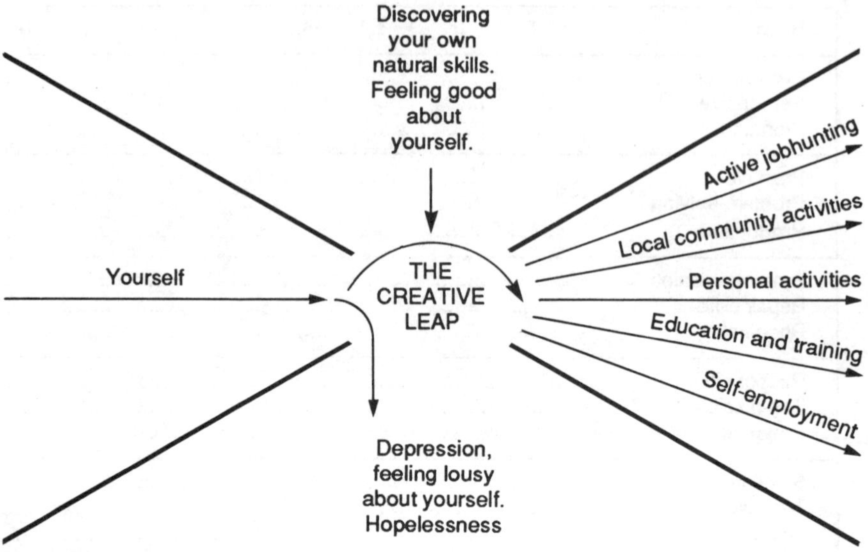

Fig. 4: Developing your life

Once you have discovered for yourself what your ENTHUSIASMS, SKILLS and LOVES are, ask yourself:

> What can I do with them?
> How can I express them and develop them?
> How can I use them to enjoy my life while I am 'out of work'?

1. If you decide that *jobhunting* is the choice that matters most, then approach it energetically. Turn Chapter 4 inside out, and make every effort to get yourself into a Job Club (see p. 45).
2. You may choose to get involved in *local community activities* — Chapters 5 and 10 are full of suggestions.
3. You may want to explore and expand your own *personal activities*. Chapters 9 and 10 will help.
4. You may want to use some time to learn, through *education and training*. Chapter 8 will set you on your path.
5. 50,000 people in Britain are using the *enterprise allowance scheme* every year to move from unemployment to self-employment, or to help set up a new co-operative. You may be one of them. Chapter 11 gives you the low-down.

Get this right — life need not be dull while you are out of work. You are a unique and very special person, with a combination of skills, talents and abilities that nobody else on the planet possesses. There may be no suitable jobs available today, or even tomorrow, but the world is still full of possibilities.

Suggestions to help you build up a 'possible jobs' list

1. Join one of the 'Wider Opportunities' courses, run by the MSC. These courses are run in order to help you find out what kind of work you would like to do. Ask at the Jobcentre (see p. 109). Scan the papers regularly, and ask yourself if the jobs being advertised might fit your skills. Then phone to find out more about them.

2. Read *What Color is Your Parachute?* This is full of good exercises relating skills to jobs. (See p. 48)
3. Spend some time browsing through three books in the library which are full of information about jobs and careers:
   Equal Opportunities: A Careers Guide for Women and Men, by Ruth Miller (Penguin, £5.95)
   Unqualified Success, by Juri Gabriel (Penguin, £3.95). A guide to over 100 careers which need no advance qualifications.
   An A-Z of Careers and Jobs, ed. Diane Burston (Kogan Page)
4. The local Careers Service may not be able to give you personal help unless you are under 19. However, in their offices you will find a wide range of books and magazines. You can also ask to see the *Careers in Focus* video list, distributed by COIC. Once you have been into the Careers Office, and made their acquaintance, you may also get some personal attention.
5. Talk to your friends about your search:
   - The friends who are eager to help you with ideas and suggestions.
   - The friends who are good at listening. If you can find just one person who will listen to you while you talk about what you might like to do, you may find that you discover new ideas yourself.
6. Try to ignore any voice inside that says:
   - 'But no one is ever paid to do that.' (You never know.)
   - 'Oh, I could never do that, it needs a certificate in fire-eating and competent Arabic.' (You could learn fire-eating from a travelling theatre-group, and Arabic by a correspondence course.) (See Chapter 8)
   - 'Oh, but women don't do that kind of work.' (Oh yes they do.)
   - 'Oh, but men don't do that kind of work.' (Oh yes they do.)

Coming up bump against reality

You may find that some of your ideas, either for jobs or for personal activities, are not possible for one reason or another. Don't give up altogether, but ask yourself (and the Careers Office staff) what other similar kinds of work or activity you could pursue. It is possible that if you can't do anything about an idea *now* , you may be able to in a year or two.

Coming up bump against reality

IN CONCLUSION: THE INNER WISDOM OF UNEMPLOYMENT

Two important pieces of wisdom can help you make your way on to the path which will be *your path*. The first is simply

FOLLOW YOUR HEART

Among the many possible kinds of work, classes, courses, community activities and interests you could pursue, your heart will secretly know which ones are for you. Some will have 'more energy' than others. These are the ones to follow.

When people are happy in life, it is often because they have given themselves permission to follow their own hearts. If you start doing this, you will discover the second piece of wisdom, which is that

ONE THING LEADS TO ANOTHER

For example

You join a body-fitness class or a mother and toddler group, you meet someone who belongs to a local community centre, you go along to one of their meetings and you find yourself involved in a discussion about the problems of one-parent families. So you join a working group that is making a video about the problem — and suddenly you discover you love making videos. You enrol in a video class, and learn that it is possible to do a full-time degree course in the visual arts. Five years later . . .

You ask if you can help at the City Farm which is not too far away. You find that the cheese-making group needs some help, and after a while you realise they could be making and selling much more than they do. This gets you interested in the processes of selling, and you read some books on small business techniques. At a City Farm conference, you hear a speaker talking about something called a 'community business', and you realise the City Farm needs to establish such a business to market and sell some of its products. Three years later . . .

You offer to help with benefits problems at an advice centre and you discover that no-one there can speak Urdu. You become a volunteer and after a while, you apply for a job as a multilingual advice worker. Three years later, you are being proposed as a candidate for a seat on the local council. . .

And so it goes on.

Maybe there is more to this unemployment business than meets the eye?

CHAPTER 4: PRACTICAL JOBHUNTING MADE EASY

PREPARATIONS – Personal Information chart – Curriculum Vitae – Jobhunting file – A good diary/notebook – FINDING OUT ABOUT JOBS – Careers Service – Jobcentre – Employment agencies – Newspapers, magazines and journals – Writing letters 'on spec' – Visiting – The grapevine – Local noticeboards – Local radio – Specialist information centres – Jobsharing – APPLICATION LETTERS AND FORMS – THE INTERVIEW – TELEPHONE TECHNIQUE – JOBCLUBS – THE COMMUNITY PROGRAMME – OBSTACLES TO JOBHUNTING – Sex discrimination – Criminal record – Transport problems – IN CONCLUSION – Booklist

It is much easier to put enthusiasm into hunting for a job if you know what you are hunting for:

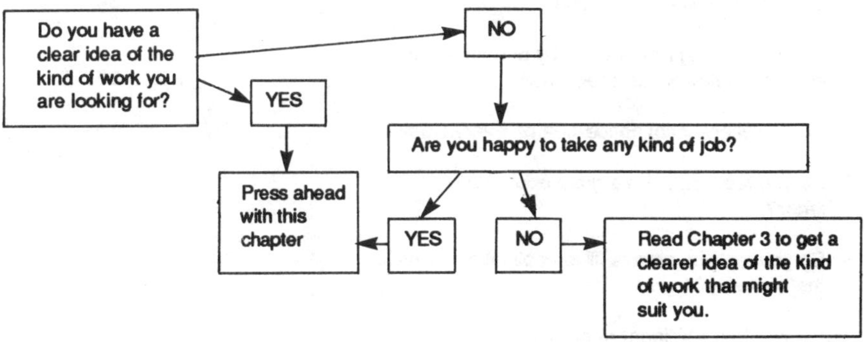

DO YOU NEED THIS CHAPTER?

Have a quick check through this exercise:	*Tick if 'Yes'*	See page
1. Have you written yourself a personal information chart or curriculum vitae?	.....	23-26
2. Are you pleased with it?	.....	
3. Have you had copies made of it?	.....	
4. Do you have a file where you can make lists and plans to keep your jobhunting organised?	.....	27
5. Are you calling at the Careers Office or Jobcentre regularly, or phoning if you cannot call?	.....	27/28

6.	Have you registered with employment agencies? How many?......	.....	29
7.	Do you keep a daily check on jobs in the daily papers?	.....	30
8.	Do you keep a weekly check on jobs in the weekly papers?	.....	30
9.	Do you keep a check on jobs in any relevant magazines, journals?	.....	31
10.	Are you writing letters 'on spec' to possible employers?	.....	32
11.	Are you making visits 'on spec' to possible employers on an organised basis?	.....	33
12.	Have you told your friends and neighbours that you are looking for work, so they can keep their eyes open for you?	.....	34
13.	Are you making new friends by becoming involved in new kinds of activity?	.....	35
14.	Do you check local notice-boards every week?	.....	35
15.	Do you feel you write a good application letter?	.....	36
16.	Do you feel you always fill in application forms in the best way?	.....	40
17.	Do you feel confident about your interview manner?	.....	
18.	Do you prepare carefully for an interview, by finding out about the job, thinking of questions to ask, etc?	.....	42
19.	Have you ever had any interview practice?	.....	42
20.	Do you feel confident about your manner on the telephone?	.....	44
21.	Have you applied to join one of the *jobclubs* run by the Jobcentre?	.....	45
	TOTAL	________	

Scoring:

- *15–21:* you are doing well in your jobhunting efforts. It might be useful to check the points you did not score on, just in case there is something useful for you there.
- *7–14:* you are doing quite well, and possibly as well as anyone else — but there is more you could do to help yourself. Read through the chapter, or at least the sections covering the points on which you did not score.
- *0–6:* you have good reason to feel hopeful, because there is room for a lot of improvement in your jobhunting which might bring you success. If you read through the whole chapter and develop a systematic approach to looking for work, your chances of getting a job will certainly improve.

If you want to be smart, and learn about jobhunting the quick way, go to the Jobcentre and ask to join a jobclub (see p. 45). If you want to do it on your own, then read on!

There are four stages of jobhunting to think about, each of which must be given proper attention:

1. Preparations

- Preparing a 'personal information chart' or 'curriculum vitae' to use with your application letters, when approaching employers directly and at interviews.
- *Keeping organised.* You will have a lot of information to keep track of, so a jobhunting file and a diary or notebook will be useful.

2. Finding out about jobs

Ten different sources are listed below, with advice and information on each.

3. The application letter

For every 100 letters that arrive after a job is advertised, 90 are thrown away the morning they arrive. Your own letter must survive.

4. The inteview

It is easy to waste a good opportunity by not preparing carefully enough.

STAGE 1: PREPARATIONS

The personal information chart

It is very important that an employer has a chance to find out about your good points, your skills and your experience. An application letter has to be short, and application forms never allow you to say very much about yourself.

If you prepare a special sheet of information about yourself to give to employers when you are applying for a job, writing letters or visiting 'on spec', and at interviews, you will give yourself a much better chance of getting the job. The employer will know everything about you that you want him or her to know.

A 'Personal Information Chart' ('PIC') allows you to write down details about yourself, covering your experience, work background, skills, abilities, qualifications, and anything else you want to say about yourself. Chapter 3 can help you to know what your natural skills and talents are.

Preparing a PIC

Take some scrap paper and give yourself at least two hours.

If you can arrange to do this with someone else who is also unemployed, so that you can help each other, so much the better. This is also something that a small group can very usefully do together. (See Chapter 5)

There are six headings which you can use on your PIC. Write it in rough first, before trying to write it out perfectly.

PERSONAL INFORMATION CHART

1. *Your name, address and telephone number*

   If you aren't on the telephone, do try to find a phone that you can give as a *contact number*. Ask friends and neighbours. (If they can't help, the local Social Services Department might put you in touch with someone who is housebound, who could take messages, and who would welcome regular visits.)

2. *'Experience', 'work experience' or 'employment history'*
   - Choose the heading you prefer.
   - Make a list of *all* the jobs (paid or voluntary) and activities you have done.
   - Choose the best 5 or 6 and write them in your PIC. (You can leave out anything you didn't enjoy.)

3. *Skills and abilities*
   - Check Chapter 3, and write in your skills from it.
   - Write in any practical skills (welding, typing, painting, child care, etc).
   - Give examples of when you've used each skill.
   - List all the equipment you can use (calculator, switchboard, sewing machine, etc. — at home, in a factory, in the garden, etc).
   - Choose the best of the skills, and write them in your PIC.

4. *Personal achievements*
   - Describe anything you have done that you feel particularly proud of. (Use Chapter 3 to help.)

5. *Education*
   - Give details of your schools, college, exams, qualifications, etc.
   - Mention any other education — evening classes, courses, projects, etc.

6. *Referees*
   - Give the names and addresses of two people who know you well and will write well of you — but not from your family.

Fig. 5: Personal Information Chart

Leave it for a day or two, in case you think of anything else, and get a friend to check it before you write it out. Make it as tidy and clean as you can. Get it typed, if you can, unless the advert asks for a handwritten application.

Making copies of your PIC

It usually costs between 6p and 10p a copy to use a photocopying machine commercially. You really need about 100 copies of your PIC, which might prove a bit expensive. Here are some suggestions:

- Print 10 at a time, and print more when you have used those.
- Ask a friendly estate agent, printer, building society, or a friend who works in an office, if they could do it for you at cost price.
- Ask the Careers Office, Jobcentre or Unemployed centre if they can print copies for you cheaply.

Making copies of your PIC

How should you use your PIC?

- Include a copy with application letters for jobs.
- Take copies when you go 'visiting' possible employers. (See below.)
- Take a copy to your interview.
- Ask your friends if they would take a few copies to give to anyone they know who might have a job going, or know about jobs going. (See below, 'The grapevine'.)

The curriculum vitae

This is for professional and managerial jobs. (Also sometimes known as 'Career History'.) The procedure is more formal. First work out what you want to write in rough, and show it to a friend for comments, before typing out the final version. It is important to make a first-class job of your c.v., since the impression it gives will be an impression of you.

The headings you should work with are:

- Name, address and telephone number.
- Your qualifications.
- A year-by-year run-through of the positions you have held, the work they involved, and the responsibilities you had.
- Other information — but avoid bringing in too many details of hobbies, etc., which are not relevant to applications for professional and managerial jobs. Only mention information which demonstrates your skills, abilities and responsibilities.

Use white A4 paper, type clearly, and space the information out on the page. Figure 6 gives a sample c.v.

CAREER HISTORY

PERSONAL DETAILS

Name:	John Joseph SMITH
Present address:	100, Main Close, Upton, Huntshire RO5 LMS
Telephone No:	(Home) Upton (0305) 777; (Day time) Selford (0753) 9922
Date of Birth:	7th April, 1940.
Marital Status:	Married, 2 children, 11 and 9 yrs

EDUCATION AND QUALIFICATIONS:

1952–58	King Edward VI School, Portchester GCE: 7 'O' levels; 4 'A' levels: French (Grade B), Physics (Grade B), Chemistry (Grade B), Botany (Grade C)
1958–61	Midlands University BSc 2 (i) Chemistry
Professional:	Member of the Institute of Sales Management

EXPERIENCE AND ACHIEVEMENTS

May 1974–to date	U.K. Paint Co. Ltd., White Lane, Selford (Specialist Paint and Varnish Manufacture) General Sales Manager responsible to the managing director for sales of paints and varnishes to the building, automotive and furniture industries, in the U.K. and parts of Europe. Staff of 75 representatives and 40 office staff. Also responsible for recruitment, training, sales and expense budgeting. Built up sales from £40M to over £85M in the past 5 years, set up and trained special teams to cover EEC markets.
June 69–March 74	Jordan and Brush (Paints) Ltd. Cover Way, Bramley. (Chemical and Paint Distributors). Sales Manager (paints) responsible to the general sales manager for sales in the UK to specialist retail outlets. Staff of 15 representatives and 8 office staff. Built up sales to £15m averaging a growth of over 20% a year; negotiated several contracts in excess of £1/4m and was responsible for setting up the company's new pricing structure.
Sept 63–June 69	Barneston-Meeds Ltd, Thornton (Synthetic Resins and Plastics). Technician/Assistant Laboratory Manager responsible to laboratory manager for quality of all incoming raw materials. Staff of 3.
62–63	Brampton Private School: Teacher (Chemistry, Physics, French)

OTHER INFORMATION:	1974: 8 week management course, Park Gate Management College Fluent French, both written and spoken; attend EEC conferences. I have written technical articles for journals and conference papers.

Fig. 6: An example Career History *(From Executive Post).*

A jobhunting file

A 'tried and tested' suggestion is to keep two lever arch files, one for pending applications and one for 'dead' ones. 'Every job application has a small plain sheet of paper, which has a number (numbered from 1 up) and a small description on it, and is followed by the original newspaper advertisement and any subsequent correspondence. At the front of this file is kept an index sheet, on which all applications are listed. When an application becomes dead, it is crossed off the index sheet, and the papers are transferred into the dead file. Any other matters not directly related to specific job applications can be kept at the front of the live file.' (Thanks to NJ Arnold of Leicester.)

A good diary/notebook

Being a successful 'dolebuster', that is living creatively and with style on the dole, requires good organisation. Most diaries are far too small to keep all the information you will need to collect. You can make a special personal notebook for yourself, using a Rymans 6" x 8" black-covered book and fixing an attractive postcard on to the front. This gives ample space for notes, lists and addresses. You will need to include:

- useful addresses and phone numbers
- lists of employers to write to or visit
- your jobhunting checklist (see below)
- your interview checklist (see below)
- weekly plans
- your list of long-term goals

STAGE 2: FINDING OUT ABOUT JOBS

There are many different ways of finding out about jobs. Most people ought to be able to use several of them. However high the level of unemployment, there are always new jobs coming up, simply because people constantly change their jobs, just as they change their houses. Only 23% of people looking for work find their jobs through the Jobcentre. The rest all find work through *other ways,* and if you ignore these other ways, you will have a much smaller chance of finding a job.

Here are the details of the various ways:

1. The Careers Service

The Careers Service is run by the local county or city council, and is completely independent of the Jobcentre.

The Careers Service works in two ways that are relevant here:

- It can offer help and advice to young people, and try to arrange interviews for jobs for them, when it has jobs available. Chapter 7 gives detailed advice for young people on how to get the best out of the Careers Service.

- It keeps an excellent library of careers information, which anyone is free to use. On the whole, and stupidly, Careers Offices are not able to give advice to adults, because they are overworked and underfunded.

  Don't just call in on spec, unless you want to browse through their literature and magazines. Phone first to make an appointment.

2. The Jobcentre

If you go to the Careers Service, you will get personal service. At the Jobcentre you will not get personal service unless you actually ask for it. The Jobcentres work on a 'self-service' basis which many people, in fact, prefer.

The basic details of all available jobs are typed on to cards displayed around the walls. If you see a job which interests you, ask about it at the counter, and you will be given the full details. You may be given an appointment then and there to go for an interview. There will be no need to write an application letter, but you may have to fill in an application form when you get there.

When you first register, you will be asked what your occupation is. You will then be put down in the files as looking for this kind of work, and if something comes up, you will be told about it. This sounds good, but it does also mean that if something *outside* your stated area of work comes up, you will not be told, so think carefully about how you want to be listed. You might want to put yourself on file as looking for two or three different types of work. Self-registration forms are in use in some offices. You fill in one of these yourself before the registration interview.

Jobcentres differ. Some are dull and bureaucratic, sticking narrowly to Department of Employment rules and only giving out information about government schemes. Others (such as Sunderland's) are beginning to see themselves as valuable community resources, willing to put up posters and give out information about community activities, and to play their part in community networks and initiatives (see Chapters 5 and 6). Maybe we are at last approaching the days when people will no longer set themselves up in isolated ivory castles, but will be willing to get stuck in along with the rest of us, as partners in a huge task — to overcome and eliminate unemployment. The resources which Jobcentres can offer are invaluable: any managers reading this — please take note!

Early visiting: details of new jobs arrive at the Jobcentre each morning, and are usually put up on the boards by 10.30 or so — so this is a good time to visit.

You could ask the Jobcentre staff if they know about any local work that is available, but not advertised, such as labouring.

What if you live some distance away from the Jobcentre, and cannot call in very often? You can still phone regularly. Ask when is the best time to do so. When you get to know them, you might be able to persuade them to phone *you* if any suitable jobs appear. If you have to phone from a call-box, ask them to call you back.

Sometimes Jobcentres put details of jobs in libraries, to help people who live some distance away. Always phone the Jobcentre about these jobs *before* getting in touch with the employer directly, since the cards are sometimes out of date.

- The staff at Jobcentres have learnt from experience that it is not worth their while to push anyone into a job against his or her will. The 'Claimant Advisers' appointed by the Government to 'encourage' people to get off the dole are employed by the DHSS, not by the Jobcentre.
- Keep in constant touch with the Jobcentre. If you assume they will look after you, nothing will happen.

Staff at Jobcentres will be able to inform you about the following:

- The **RESTART PROGRAMME** — special personal interviews and short courses if you have been out of work for 6 months or more. See p. 109
- The **JOBSTART ALLOWANCE** — If you are over 18, have been out of work for more than a year, and want to apply for a full-time job which offers gross earnings of less than £80 a week, you can be paid an additional £20 for six months, as an incentive to take the job.
- The **COMMUNITY PROGRAMME** — See below, p. 45
- The **NEW WORKERS' SCHEME** — for young people under 21. See p. 71
- **JOBCLUBS** — See below, p. 45
- **THE TRAVEL TO INTERVIEW SCHEME** — See p. 43
- **VOLUNTARY PROJECTS PROGRAMMES** — which may enable you to become involved in a variety of local community activities or classes.
- **HELP FOR DISABLED PEOPLE** — See Chapter 7
- The **JOB RELEASE SCHEME** — for older workers who want to retire early with an allowance. See p. 94
- The **JOB SPLITTING SCHEME** — which encourages employers to create new part-time jobs.
- The **JOB TRAINING SCHEME** — which offers a range of training courses to unemployed people. See p. 104
- **ACCESS TO INFORMATION TECHNOLOGY** — courses for beginners. See p. 107
- **CAREER DEVELOPMENT LOANS** — See p. 105
- The **ENTERPRISE ALLOWANCE SCHEME**, for unemployed people who want to become self-employed. See Chapter 11

3. Employment agencies

It is difficult to generalise about private employment agencies, since they vary a lot. Most are very good, and treat people well. Others unfortunately have a reputation for being a bit of a rip-off. The only way to find out is to visit them yourself, and ask your friends about them. If you do not use the agencies, you may be reducing your chances of finding work. Many people find that the way the agencies operate suits them excellently, offering them different kinds of work with regular variety. The agencies want to develop lists of good, reliable workers, and the people who are satisfied with the agencies are also the ones who are regularly kept in work. Agencies can also arrange permanent jobs, charging the employer a fee for doing so.

If you look up 'Employment Agencies' in the Yellow Pages, you will find the local and regional agencies listed. You will see that some specialise in secretarial or office work, etc., while others are all-purpose. The more agencies you are registered with the better, so ask every relevant agency to put you on their books. You will normally be sent a form to fill in, asking the kind of work you are willing to do.

Some agencies (e.g. 'Manpower') employ their staff directly and subcontract their workers to employers, while others live by the fees that the employers pay them.

A word of warning — you should be clear what the arrangements are about pay, sickness, dismissal, holidays, etc. Many people who live by work from agencies are not trade union members, so you cannot always depend on a union to get you out of a fix.

Private employment consultants

A number of private firms help people to find work (mostly professional and managerial people). A section in Chapter 7 (p. 96) covers jobhunting advice for these people. Certain groups of people can get help from specialist organisations such as the Armed Forces Resettlement Information Office and the Institute of Directors. The British Institute of Management runs its own advice and information service, and a counselling service for members who may be facing redundancy or a change in their career.

4. Advertisements in newspapers, magazines and journals

This is perhaps the chief method by which most employers advertise their vacancies. You will probably need to cover several local papers every week, if you are to see all the jobs coming up. If this is going to cost a lot, you may do better to make regular trips to the local library, where they will have the papers.

- Names of newspapers to check daily:

  (1). . . . .   (2). . . . .

  (3). . . . .   (4). . . . .

  (5). . . . .

- Names of newspapers to check weekly:

  (1). . . . .   (2). . . . .

  (3). . . . .   (4). . . . .

  (5). . . . .   (6). . . . .

If you think a job might go very quickly, reply at once, but you can afford to wait for a day or two for most jobs, so you have time to make sure your letter of application is just as you want it. Most employers wait for all the applications to come in before deciding who to call to an interview.

Phoning for more information

Newspaper advertisements are always very brief, because of the cost. Before you send off your letter of application, check that you have enough accurate information about the job. Use the list below to check which things you know, and phone up to ask about the things you don't know. Copy the list into your file, so that you can use it regularly.

- Where is the job?
- What type of work is it?
- Are there any age restrictions?
- Are any qualifications needed?
- Would training be given?
- What kind of a firm is it?
- What are the hours and the pay?
- How do you apply?

You may find yourself speaking to the employer when you phone, so be very polite and friendly, and be careful not to say anything which might write off your chances. The job might, for instance, require a special skill at riding camels. Don't say that you can't straight away — rush down to the local zoo and take lessons. When it comes to the interview, and the employer meets you face to face, she may decide it doesn't matter that you aren't very good at it yet, but if you had admitted you couldn't, you might have ruined your chances.

'The camels went this way ... no, that way!'

Magazines and journals

As well as the daily and weekly newspapers, magazines and journals carry advertisements. Some are local, some are specialist, such as:

- *The Lady* and *Nursery World*, for jobs with children.
- *New Society, Community Care* and the *Health and Social Service Journal*, for jobs in social service and youth work.
- *Accountants Weekly, Recruitment Accountant, Marketing Week, Marketing.*
- *Building, Computer Weekly, Construction News, Design, Electrical Times, Engineering, Heating and Ventilating Engineer, Municipal Journal, Nursing Mirror, Opportunities, Wireless World*, etc.
- Trade journals, for jobs in catering, grocery, hairdressing, etc.
- *The Times* and the *Guardian*, for occasional 'one-off' jobs, like working as a masseuse in the harem of the Sheikh of Arabi, or as a crew member on a Bahamas-cruising yacht.
- *Exchange and Mart* carries advertisements for books which offer to tell you everything about work on the North Sea oil rigs, at sea, or overseas.

There are *hundreds* of journals and magazines which carry job adverts. Ask for information in your local library. In Camden, for instance, the Employment Information Service publish a special free *Getting A Job* pack, which includes a listing of 200 journals and papers available in local libraries.

Remember: you can place advertisements in these papers yourself.

News items

It is worth keeping an eye open for news items which might tell you about possible jobs, such as 'Camels-for-children firm moving to town', which might have a job for you with your newly acquired skill in camel-riding, or £1/2 million granted for conservation work', which would definitely imply that someone is going to be offering work soon.

5. Writing letters 'on spec' (the direct approach)

You can write directly to employers, on the off chance that they might have a vacancy coming up. If they haven't, you can ask them to keep you in mind, if something comes up.

How can you find out the names of possible employers?

- Ask the Careers Service
- Use the Yellow Pages, and Thompson's local directories
- *The Job Book* (published by CRAC, Hobsons Press) gives the details of over 1,000 employers, training schemes, etc.
- *Which Company?* (published by the *Daily Telegraph*)
- *An A–Z of Careers and Jobs*, ed. Diane Burston (Kogan Page)
- *The Times* list of 1,000 Top British Companies
- *Jane's Major Companies of Europe*. (These last 4 will be in public libraries, and in Careers Service libraries.)

Using a page in your jobhunting file, make a list of all the firms you plan to write to, with a column where you can tick off when you wrote to them (noting the date), and what kind of response you receive.

Your letter

Your letter must be interesting. It must make an employer think you are genuinely interested in working for his or her firm, and that it is *not* simply one of 50 identical letters you have sent off to firms all over the place.

Address
Phone No.

November 10th 1988

Dear Sir or Madam,

I am writing to enquire whether you might have any vacancies.

I have worked with Extoll Ltd on the assembly line and in the cutting shop for the past 5 years, until they dismissed 300 workers this spring. I was satisfied with the work there and would be pleased to take similar work with your firm.

I am including a Personal Information Chart with this letter, which gives a wider picture of my abilities and experience.

If you do have any vacancies, either now or in the future, I would be grateful if you could bear me in mind when selecting new employees.

Yours faithfully,

(Signature) (NAME IN CAPITALS)

Fig. 7: A 'spec' letter

Your letter *must be* individually typed or hand-written. There are no two ways about this. If you think, 'How much quicker it would be to write one letter, and then get it photocopied', you are wasting your time. Such letters end up in the wastepaper bin.

The key to all the methods of application for a job is to put yourself in the employer's position, and imagine what you would think, if you received your letter, or form.

If you have written a PIC or c.v. (see above), you can write a short personal letter, and include a copy of the PIC/c.v., which no employer will expect to be individually written out.

6. Visiting

Some employers hardly ever advertise their vacancies, because they prefer to wait until people come to ask if there are any vacancies, believing this kind of person makes a more enthusiastic and reliable employee. Obviously, when using this method you may draw a lot of blanks; you'll be lucky to find an employer who has a job there and then. So *take copies of your PIC* with you; you can leave one with the employer and when a vacancy *does* come up he or she may contact you rather than advertising (which can be expensive).

If you make your visits with this idea in mind, then you need not feel depressed and gloomy if your hard day's work seems to bring you no joy. You have been out sowing seeds, and one of them might bear fruit later. It's like an investment in your own future.

Making plans

You can find out the addresses of possible employers by asking at the Jobcentre, at the Careers Office, and by using the Yellow Pages. Then sit down with a local map (and a bus timetable?) and plan your day carefully. You should remember the following points:

Making plans — take something to read.

- Dress as you would for an interview — smart (but not *too* smart);
- Take something to read, in case you have to wait a long time;
- Take enough copies of your PIC so that you can leave one with each employer you visit. Keep them in a folder, so they don't get dog-eared and scruffy;
- Take a sheet with your other personal details on it, in case you are asked to fill in

an application form — your NI number, details of previous employment (with addresses and dates), prepared reasons why you left the jobs (see below, 'Application Forms') and your qualifications, which you might not have put in your PIC;

- Ask to see the right person. The receptionist will tell you who is responsible for recruitment, and then you should ask if you can speak to him or her for a few minutes. They are sure to ask, 'Have you got an appointment?' Don't just answer, 'No' and then look blank. Say, 'No — but I don't mind waiting, and I'd be pleased if you could ask for me.'

So, now's the big minute. Play it right, and — who knows? — you might walk out the door with a job. Fluff it up, and it's another chance down the drain. Imagine you are the employer, busy at his day's work. As far as he is concerned, you are someone he has never met, who has come along unannounced and wants to take up his time. So if he begins to think you are a nuisance, your chances will soon evaporate. On the other hand, if he *does* happen to have an unfilled vacancy, or if there is something about you that he likes, he will be willing to sit and talk to you because he will wonder whether you would make a good employee.

When you get in to see him, shake his hand, and introduce yourself clearly. Explain that you don't want to take up his time unnecessarily, but that you *are* keen to find work with a good employer. Tell him a little about yourself. Hand him a copy of your PIC, saying, 'This will tell you something about me, if it's any help.' Once he has got that in his hand, most of the conversation should go to your advantage, since it will be about the things you chose to write on your PIC about yourself.

Soon after this stage, the conversation can go one of two ways — it can get more involved, which means there may be some possibility of a job for you. Or he might say, 'Well, this is very interesting, but I'm afraid we haven't got any vacancies.' Don't just give up, and wilt out of the door — keep the initiative, and say 'Well, that's quite all right, I knew that I would be very lucky if you did have a vacancy just like that. But could I leave this copy of the PIC with you, and if something does come up in the future, could you consider me then?' This way you are leaving your visiting card and your visit will not be a waste of time.

Leave with a smile and a handshake, and he might think, 'Well, she did seem to be a very pleasant and well-meaning person. I wonder if we *do* have anything coming up, where we could squeeze her in.' The impression you leave when you go will linger in the office for a while after you leave, and it is this that you will be remembered by.

There is a lot to be said for practice. Go over the things you might say with a friend (or with a support group — see Chapter 5). The shyest of people can learn to act as if they are confident. The more unconfident you are, the more important it is to practise.

In conclusion: you are bound to meet some employers who are completely negative to you. Well, never mind. Just forget about them. The world is full of hard people, worried people and people without the time to talk to you. Don't get depressed. The world is also full of well-meaning, caring people who might be willing to go to some effort on your behalf.

7. The grapevine

Once upon a time, this was the *only* way that anyone ever heard about jobs. It is still a very important way.

- Do all your *friends, neighbours and relatives* know that you are down on your luck and looking for work? Do they know what *kind* of job you are looking for? Once they know, the word will be passed around.

  Make a list of all the people you know who might be able to help. Take a page in your file for this. Some will be more help than others, and have many more contacts. You can go back to them, every so often, to keep in close touch.

- *Contacts.* By getting involved in new activities in your neighbourhood, you will meet new people. You go to an evening class, and learn how to weld; you become friendly with a man in the class; he's got a friend who runs this garage; he mentions you to his friend; and you end up with a job in his garage. That is the way it works.

8. Local notice-boards

Local notice-boards such as you see outside newspaper shops and post offices often carry small advertisments for local jobs. For some kinds of work you can place a card in the window yourself. They only cost about 10p a week, and if you can make the card attractive in some way, it will stand out and be noticed. This is especially good for any kind of 'jack-of-all-trades' work — gardening, odd jobs, cleaning, etc. If you are not much good at design, ask a friend to help.

Some factories keep notice-boards outside with details of vacancies, but the habit is slowly dying out.

9. Local radio stations

Local radio stations often carry regular weekly spots covering news of jobs. Find out if your own radio station does so, and tune in regularly.

10. Specialist Information Centres

Specialist *Information Centres* offer help and advice to people seeking work in their areas. See *Equal Opportunities: A Careers guide for Women and Men,* by Ruth Miller (Penguin Books) for addresses.

11. Jobsharing

This method of working is growing in popularity. Two people share one job. They decide between themselves and with the employer how they would like to divide the work (alternate weeks, $2^1/2$ days each a week, mornings and afternoons, etc.). Where employers have agreed to take on jobsharers, they generally like the arrangement, because although they have a little extra administrative work to do, they gain two people's ideas and energy for the price of one.

The advantages for the people sharing the job are that they have more time to themselves — time to take another part-time job, time to work as self-employed, or just free time. Jobsharing has been happening successfully for years in the USA and in Sweden, and it is becoming increasingly common in Britain.

To find a partner to share a job with, if you do not already know someone suitable, you could try advertising on local notice-boards or in the local papers. Perhaps in the future towns and cities may develop 'Jobsharing Banks', which could bring together people wanting to share similar kinds of work so they could make joint applications. If the idea interests you, get a leaflet called *Sharing a job?* by sending a stamped addressed envelope to 'New Ways to Work', 309 Upper Street, London N1 2TY.

A jobhunting checklist

Each week, tick off the things you have done, and tot up your 'score'. It is a very primitive method of scoring, so feel free to change it. All that really matters is that you use the same system of scoring each week, so that it gives you some idea how you are doing.

What if you find you are scoring less, week by week?

- You can tear the page out, so you no longer have any evidence that your efforts are slipping.
- You can ask yourself why you are slipping.
- You can take a full week or two's holiday from jobhunting, to give yourself a break, and then return to it with a fresh spirit.
- You might be chasing the wrong kind of work? Chapter 3 may help.
- You might simply have set a very high standard at the beginning, and it doesn't matter if you fall off a bit, as long as you don't give up altogether. Chapter 2 has ideas about survival when the going gets tough.

Week beginning:					
Visited/phoned the Careers Office	....	....	....	....	....
Visited/phoned the Jobcentre	....	....	....	....	....
Visited/phoned the employment agencies. How many?	....	....	....	....	....
Checked the papers/journals. How many?	....	....	....	....	....
Written letters 'on spec'. How many?	....	....	....	....	....
Went out visiting. How many employers?	....	....	....	....	....
Talked to friends or neighbours about jobhunting. How many?	....	....	....	....	....
Met any new people? How many?	....	....	....	....	....
Checked local notice-boards?	....	....	....	....	....
Listened to local radio jobhunting slot?	....	....	....	....	....
Sent off application letters? How many?	....	....	....	....	....
Had any replies. How many?	....	....	....	....	....
TOTAL SCORE:					

Fig. 8: Jobhunting Checklist

STAGE 3: APPLICATION LETTERS AND FORMS

Letters

Put yourself in the position of the employer. She (or he) has just advertised a vacancy, and the letters start pouring in. There may be 20 or 200 letters of application. Out of all of these, she has to pick just 5 or 10 to ask to an interview. What would *you* do? How would *you* pick out the small handful which 'win' this stage of the competition, and get invited to the grand finale at Company House? We will look at ways in which you can try to get your own letter among the winners.

1. *The first throw-out:* to begin with, she does not think about the good letters. Her first interest is in the *bad ones* — the ones she can throw straight into the bin. First, she will throw out letters that are dirty and badly written. Remember, she *wants* to find an excuse for throwing away all but a handful, so any excuse will be pounced on, and scrunch, toss, your hopes lie crumpled in the rubbish bin.

2. *The second throw-out:* she will then go through the letters again, and toss out a further batch, until she has left about twice the number she wants to interview. At this stage, she will only keep the letters which:

- are not too long;
- give relevant information about the applicant;
- avoid any attempt to show off;
- don't waffle, or give unnecessary information.

3. *The final choice:* finally, she will go through the pile a third time, looking for something positive, that certain 'something' that says, 'This person seems to be good. He (or she) seems to be the kind of person we ought to ask to an interview.'

Preparations

Check the advertisement carefully. Phone up for more information if you need to. (See above.) As well as the stated requirements there may also be 'hidden' requirements. Make two lists, one of the stated, and one of the hidden requirements, as in Figure 9.

MOTORCYCLE MESSENGER required

with knowledge of city

and clean licence

Stated requirements	*Hidden requirements*
Ability to ride motorcycle	reliability
knowledge of the city	responsibility
clean licence	

Fig.9: Sample ad.

Figure 10 shows you the points to remember and include when you write an application letter.

1. Follow this general layout. Your own address at the top, with a phone number. (If you are not on the phone, see p. 44)
2. The date.
3. The address of the firm.
4. If you know the name of the person you are writing to, this is best. You might phone the receptionist, to ask?
5. Clear indication of the post you are applying for.

'The Old Scrapyard',
Dungheap Lane,
Dirty Old Town, (1)
Mouldshire.

Tel: D.O.T. 3898

June 15th 1989 (2)

The Personnel Manager,
(3) Super Smart Ltd.,
Posh Street,
Snootyville.

(4) Dear Madam or Sir,

re: Position of General Cleaner (5)

(6) I would like to apply for the above post, as advertised in the Snootyville News on June 13th.

I have had several years' experience of general cleaning and maintenance work, which has most recently included a year with Everlasting Filth Ltd., where I held the position of Supervisor, responsible for 20 part-time sweepers and one mechanical sludge-eater. I enjoyed the ordinary work, as (7) (8) well as the tasks involved in supervision. I would be perfectly happy to accept an ordinary position as General Cleaner, as I find the work pleasurable, and enjoy doing a good job.

In a previous job with Awful Boilers Ltd., I trained as a specialist in cleaning uncleanable boilers, and also (7) (8) acquired a general skill at mending faulty taps, valves and pipes.

I hope to hear from you soon.

Yours faithfully,

Adam Edensweeper (10)

(ADAM EDENSWEEPER)

Fig. 10: Sample letter

6. Clear opening sentence.
7. Details of previous experience and employment.
8. Show that you can meet the stated and hidden requirements of the job. (Don't apologise for experience or qualifications you *haven't* got.)
9. Keep it short. If it's too long, employers might not read it at all. Avoid unnecessary details — hobbies, religion, previous salary, reasons for leaving the last job, etc. Only put in things that would interest *you* , if you were the employer. One side of paper is enough (if you are using large A4 paper). You can always include your PIC or c.v. to give extra information.
10. Print your name underneath your signature.

Make sure the whole letter is clean, clear and tidy, without any crossings out or mistakes. This is why it is always best to do a rough version first. Try to avoid any stale or over-used phrases.

Trying to write a good application letter

After you have written it.

- Now, the surprise — don't post it! Put it away for a day or two. When you come back to it with a fresh mind, you may be able to improve it. The employer won't fill the post all at once, so you'll lose nothing.
- Post it first class in a clean white envelope, clearly addressed. Keep a copy for yourself, so that you know what you said if you are asked to an interview.
- Then, wait. If you don't hear after ten days, telephone and ask, 'I wanted to check if my application letter for such-and-such a post had arrived.' This will put your mind at rest, and it won't reduce your chance (unless you say, 'Have I got the job?' or something equally pushy). Above all, it will stop you getting very angry with the firm, and — who knows? — you might well make a good impression!

Don't be thrown in the bin!!

Use this checklist each time you write a letter of application. Do not post your letter unless it has a tick by *every* point.

First hurdle	Clean sheet of paper, not lined.	......
	Straight margin, straight lines.	......
	Clean and tidy appearance, no crossings out.	......
	Correct spelling and grammar.	......
	Clean envelope, 1st class.	......
Second hurdle	Short and to the point. No waffle.	......
	Orderly presentation.	......
	Relevant details about your experience and qualifications.	......
	No additional personal details.	......
	No mention of previous salary.	......
	No mention of why you left last job.	......
	Something to suggest you have noticed and can meet the 'hidden requirements'.	......
Third hurdle	A calm and confident impression.	......
	Something to imply that you are hard-working, responsible, etc.	......
	Something to make the employer think, 'I must meet this person, to find out more.'	......
	Two days delay before posting.	......

Spelling hints:

personnel	advertisement	assistant
experience	responsible	opportunity
sincerely	appropriate	requirements
faithfully	relevant	*Dictionary (for the rest)!*

The application form

Nearly everyone who is looking for a job has to fill in an application form sooner or later. They are fairly straightforward things, but it is easy to make mistakes. Care and practice can help to make sure that yours does not bite the dust.

How can you practise?

The best way to practise is to get hold of a form. Phone any firm which is advertising vacancies in a type of work which might interest you, and ask if they would send you an application form. If you don't strike lucky first time, try again.

Here are a few guidelines, to help you fill it in:

- Fill it in in pencil first. Ask a friend to check it over, before you finally fill it in in ink. It *always* helps to have a second person look at your form, letter, PIC, c.v., etc.
- Follow the instructions very carefully. Keep your form neat and tidy. Don't overflow the spaces. If you *do* need to overflow, use any blank space that is provided, or the back, or an extra piece of blank paper.
- Under 'Previous employment', you might be asked to say why you left your last job. Be careful to write something that sounds good, such as, 'I wasn't satisfied with the work' or, 'There was no opportunity for training' or, if you were sacked, 'Unsatisfactory relationship with the employer'.
- Under 'Position and duties' describe what kind of work you did, and responsibilities you held.
- Under 'Hobbies and interests', concentrate on the ones that seem relevant to the

job, which might help you to get it. If you have no interests that you think worth writing down, it might be an idea to read through Chapter 8 and to take up some new interests, since they can help you in unexpected ways — e.g. getting experience, making new contacts, getting references, learning new skills.

- Under 'Any other information' you have a chance to mention anything else which you think might help you get the job. You might be able to bring in some of the 'achievements' from Chapter 3.
- Under 'Referees', give the names and addresses of two people who will speak well of you, and whom an employer would respect.

When you have completed your practice form, keep it somewhere safe. The next time you have to fill one in, you will find it much easier.

- When posting an application form, send a short covering letter with it. This makes it personal, and leaves a very good impression. Check that your letter is neat and tidy.
- If you haven't heard back within 10 days, phone to see what is happening.

STAGE 4: THE INTERVIEW

If you have got as far as having an interview, you are almost home, so it is worth putting a lot of care into preparations. Put yourself in the position of the interviewer. She has to choose from five or ten people. *What is she looking for?* She will have three kinds of question in mind when she meets you, and by thinking carefully about each one, you can prepare yourself.

1. She wants to satisfy herself that you are *basically polite, tidy and pleasant.* She wants to be sure that the person she chooses will fit into the firm, office, team, or whatever, and not be a constant source of difficulty.

2. She wants to find out either if you have got the *skills and experience* for the job, or if you seem likely to learn. It is not just qualifications that the interviewer is looking for; there are a lot of other, more ordinary, human qualities she will be pleased to see. If she is impressed by someone, and starts thinking, 'He would be a good person to have around', then she might not bother so much about the lack of the right paper qualifications.

   You should remember there are many ways of getting 'experience', apart from actually *doing* the work in question. Perhaps you are applying for a job in an accounts office, and have never done accounts work before. This need not matter — what about that job you held as an assistant in a library, when you had to keep the books in exact order? Isn't that the same kind of skill? You had to be tidy and accurate. You must think *around* the job. Try to work out what *general* kinds of ability are required, and then think back (Chapter 3 will help you there) to see whether anything you have done has shown this general kind of ability.

   When the discussion at the interview comes around to the matter of your experience, you can say, 'Well, I have never worked in an accounts office before, but I have thought about it, and it seems to me that a person working in an accounts office needs to be tidy and accurate. This is something I enjoy doing. I think my experience in the library, where I had to check the cataloguing and keep the books in order on the shelves, shows that I have this kind of ability. I hope I can pick up the details of accounts work quite quickly.'

   What if you haven't got the right exams or qualifications? Assuming this doesn't rule you out automatically, you could say that you would like to work for the necessary qualifications during the year, at evening class, if that would be all right. In other words — *don't assume defeat until you are actually defeated.* There is always more than just one way of doing something.

3. She will be looking for *sincerity*. She wants someone who is going to be serious about the job, someone who will be honest, and reliable. Then as well as these qualities, she will be *hoping* to find someone who shows this sincerity in a *positive spirit* towards the job, someone who has shown sufficient interest in the job to have done some homework on it before the interview.

Preparations for the interview

1. *Finding out about the firm, or job*

You could ask for copies of the firm's literature — leaflets, annual report, etc. If you phone the firm in advance, they might send you some stuff in the post. You could also ask around among your friends, and you could ask for information at the Careers Office and the Jobcentre.

2. *Thinking ahead about the job*

What does the job need? What are its stated and its hidden requirements? What kind of experience have you had, which you could talk about? Why do *you* think you could do the job well?

3. *Thinking ahead about questions and answers*
   - 'Why do you want this job?'
   - 'How much do you already know about the job?'
   - 'Do you think you would be able to manage the heavy demands of the job?'
   - Finally, 'Do you have any questions you want to ask?'.

Each question gives you an opportunity to talk. Don't just answer 'Yes' or 'No' to questions. Have courage, even if you haven't got much confidence!

- You should prepare for this last question. You might want to ask about training, or details of the job. Don't start asking about pay until you have asked the questions which show you are interested in the job. It is quite OK for you to take a notebook in with you, with a short list of questions you want to ask. It will help, because nerves very often make us forget everything we had planned to say. If you can't think of anything to ask, just pause, and then say, 'No, I don't think so, thank you.'

4. *Practice in interview technique*
   - If you have either joined or formed a support group, this is the kind of thing that is good to do together. You can do 'dummy' interviews, and practise what you might say with your friends. A local employer might come in to give you a hand, and add a touch of reality. (See Chapter 5)
   - If you are on your own, you can ask a friend to come and help, by giving you a 'dummy' interview, perhaps with a third person present, to make it seem real.
   - If you don't know anyone who could help, ask at the Careers Office if they would help you, or if they have any suggestions. They might be willing to get a small group together for a practice session. Another thing that helps is practice in 'public speaking'. Ask a friend if he or she would sit, listen and then comment, while you give a short one-minute (or three-minute) talk on any subject you like. After you have done this four or five times you should find your confidence improving.

5. *Practical preparations*
   - *Appearance:* It is worth putting an effort into your appearance for this one day so that you are well-dressed and tidy. Prepare the night before.
   - *Getting there:* Plan your journey, and work out how long it will take you to get there. Plan to get there about 15 minutes early. If you are travelling by bus, work out the bus times the day before — don't leave it until the morning to find out that they cancelled the 63 bus months ago. If you *are* going to be late, phone up to say so.
   - *What should you take with you?:* *Tick*
     — The details of the interview: time, place, name of the person seeing you, phone number. ....
     — 10p pieces for the phone, in case you are late. ....
     — Your PIC or c.v. ....
     — Details of your previous employment and NI number, in case you have to fill in an application form. ....
     — Pencil and rubber, for the application form (and a sheet of spare paper). ....
     — Any notes you have made for the interview, questions you want to ask, etc. ....
     — A 'memory card' (see end of this chapter). ....
     — A watch, a clean hanky, a smile. ....

Take a positive attitude with you. The interviewer will like it.

6. *The 'Travel to Interview' scheme*

There is a government scheme called *Travel to Interview*, which can pay for your travel expenses to an interview if these five conditions are met:

1. You must apply in advance, using form TS1 from the Jobcentre;
2. You must have been unemployed for four weeks or more;
3. Your interview must be confirmed by the employer (a phone-call to the Jobcentre by the employer is sufficient), and be 'beyond daily travelling distance';
4. The job must be expected to last at least a year, and be more than 21 hours a week;
5. The job should not be self-employed, an MSC programme or offering a salary over £12,000.

Overnight subsistence can be paid if necessary too.

The big day

Feeling nervous? Don't worry — it happens to everyone. Your body is creating adrenalin.Think of it as extra energy that you have got, which you can actually use in the interview.

The first few minutes: knock confidently, walk in confidently. If you've got a handshake like a wet fish, then for your own sake practise a good handshake beforehand. Don't smoke, unless invited to. Sit back comfortably in your chair; don't perch nervously on the edge.

The interview will probably be run along these lines:

1. Telling you something about the job and the firm (or organisation).

Feeling nervous?

2. Asking you questions designed to find out how well you would fit the job. (This is your chance to talk about experiences you have had which you think are relevant to the job).
3. Inviting you to ask any questions.

Should you use your PIC? If you think that it says useful things about you which you might not get a chance to talk about, then yes, show it to the interviewer. On the whole it is better if you can talk about yourself directly, and say why you think you can do the job. If you are less confident, your PIC might be a great help.

When you are talking, *stick to the point*. Don't gabble off on all sorts of things — that is another common mistake people make when they are nervous. When you are asked a question, *pause and think* before answering. There is no hurry.

If you don't succeed . . . just keep on trying. You can learn from your failures if you sit down and think about each interview after you have done it. Make some notes about the interview in your file as soon as you get home (before you even know the results), and note down any reminders for next time: e.g. 'I *must* think before answering questions.'

Unless you are very lucky, it *will* take you several interviews before you land a job. Treat the interviews as opportunities for practice — then you won't be so disappointed, or think they were just wasted time.

Professional and executive interviews

You may sometimes have to attend 2 or 3 interviews, perhaps a panel interview, and perhaps undergo a group exercise or test. The book *Getting the Job You Want* by Howard Dowding and Sheila Boyce (published by Ward Lock) has advice on this kind of interview.

Interview memory card

Copy these 9 points on to a postcard, and take it with you to interviews as a reminder:

	Remember before	Check after — did I?
1. Have I got everything I need to take with me?	.....	.....
2. Have I checked the travel times? (15 minutes early)	.....	.....
3. Clean and tidy?	.....	.....
4. Knock, enter, smile, shake hands confidently.	.....	.....
5. Pause, before answering.	.....	.....
6. Don't just answer 'Yes' or 'No'.	.....	.....
7. Stick to the point.	.....	.....
8. Have courage.	.....	.....
9. Make sure I get a chance to say the things I want to say.	.....	.....

TELEPHONE TECHNIQUE

If you are not very confident on the telephone, you ought to think about getting some practice. Ask someone you know if she would pretend to be an employer advertising a job, then phone to ask for information about it. Practise both from an ordinary phone, and from a call-box. When you are more confident, start getting 'real' practice by phoning up for real jobs advertised in the paper. Practice is the only way to build up confidence.

Here are some tips:

- Always start with 'Hello'. Then give your name.
- Explain clearly why you are telephoning, e.g. 'I am phoning for more information about the assistant's job you are advertising in the News' or, 'I am due in for an interview at 10.00 with Mr Miller, and I am phoning to say that I will be ten minutes late.'
- If someone says, 'Hold the line, I'll put you through' always start again from the beginning with the new person. It can sometimes take a while to get 'put through', so be patient.
- If you can find out the name of the manager or personnel manager from the receptionist before you speak to him, this will help, since you can then say, 'Mr Edwards?' or, 'Can I speak to Mr Edwards?'
- Always have a sheet of paper and a pen handy when you telephone, ready to take notes. A list to remind you what you want is also helpful.

Finally: if possible, arrange to make your call from an ordinary phone or a cardphone. If you have to use a coin-box, be sure to have plenty of 10p pieces with you.

JOBCLUBS

If you want help and support during the process of jobhunting, join a jobclub. These are small groups of 10–15 people who work on a group basis with a tutor for 4 half-days a week (or more), and put all their energy into jobhunting during that time.

The clubs are open to anyone who has been out of work for more than 6 months — just ask at the Jobcentre, and you will be able to sign up for one. There is no charge. Over a period of two weeks, you will receive continuous support, and be helped with your jobhunting techniques and interview skills. The use of a telephone, typewriter, stationery and photocopier are all provided free.

These groups are strongly recommended, since they yield good results — and even if you are still unable to find a job, you will have learnt a lot.

THE COMMUNITY PROGRAMME

The Community Programme is the government's scheme to provide unemployed people with full-time or part-time jobs for up to one year.

You can apply

- If you are aged between 18–24 and you have been out of work for 6 of the last 9 months (or 4 out of the last 9 months for disabled people).
- If you are aged 25 and over and you have been unemployed for 12 of the last 15 months (or 8 of the last 15 months for disabled people).

The schemes are organised by groups known as Community Programme Agencies. These are set up by churches, local authorities, voluntary and community groups and environmental groups.

People have many different views and experiences about Community Programme schemes. This is hardly surprising, since there are a huge number of different schemes, creating around 300,000 jobs in a large range of different areas:

- neighbourhood safety and crime prevention work
- sports projects

- building a 76ft steel-rigged ketch
- creating a new Pembrokeshire coastal path
- archaeological digs in Anglesey
- energy saving and home-insulation projects
- restoring old mills, wharves, canals and workshops
- creating nature conservation areas
- manufacturing window boxes, soft toys and equipment for playgroups

Some people see Community Programme schemes as being make-work projects which just dump you back on the dole a year later. Others appreciate the chance to get back into working life, build up skills and belong to a work-team again.

On some schemes, 60 per cent of people find full-time work or training on leaving; on others, only 30 per cent get jobs or a training place. The rest go back on the dole.

The wages on CP schemes are based upon the local rate for the job. The average weekly wage paid must not exceed a certain fixed level (£67 in1987), however, so for every person earning over £100 for a five-day week, there are others earning £40 for a two-day week. This basis of payment may change during 1988.

- If you have children, you can also apply for Family Income Supplement/Family Credit (through the Post Office)
- If you are paying rent, you can apply for Housing Benefit (through the Post Office/local Council)
- If you are working less than five days a week, you can take additional part-time work during the week, or work on a self-employed basis (see Chapter 11).

The Community Programme is developing all the time, and schemes are improving as their organisers gain experience. Additional training schemes, jobhunting support and (occasionally) life-planning support are becoming available on some schemes. In other words, keep an open mind.There may be an unexpected opportunity waiting for you! The details of vacancies are advertised through the Jobcentre, and you can apply for them in the normal way. (See the Stop Press on page 197, for latest information on CP schemes.)

Community Programme News is published free by the MSC, bringing updates, news and stories on CP and the Voluntary Projects Programme. You can receive it regularly by writing to MSC Distribution Unit, Room E825, Moorfoot, Sheffield S1 4PQ.

For other notes on MSC schemes, see chapter 5.

OBSTACLES TO JOBHUNTING

Racial discrimination — See p. 85, Chapter 7

Sex discrimination

An employer offering a job must not discriminate against you on the grounds of your sex, nor must he offer you a job on less favourable terms. (There are a few exceptions, such as work in single-sex establishments, or in private households.)

If you think you have been discriminated against, *do* have the confidence to do something about it. For advice and support, you should write to the Equal Opportunities Commission, Overseas House, Quay Street, Manchester M3 3HN (061–833 9244).

You are having special problems in getting a job because you have a criminal record

The 1975 'Rehabilitation of Offenders' Act sets out the periods of time after which certain types of conviction become 'spent'. This means you do not have to reveal the details of any such 'spent' convictions when you apply for a job, or fill in a form. You can get a leaflet from the Jobcentre/Employment Office called *Wiping the Slate Clean,* which gives all the details.

In general, you can go a long way towards wiping your own slate clean by the kinds of things you decide to do while you are unemployed. In an employer's eye, if you have a prison record but have been actively helping out in the neighbourhood with any kind of project or scheme, this will count in your favour whatever your past may be, and he may decide your present activities are more important than your past ones when considering you for the job.

If you have a record you should ask about Community Programme jobs at the Jobcentre. The organisers of these jobs are sometimes keen to help people with special employment problems.

Transport problems

It can be difficult to get to interviews, when you've got so little money. Some areas have special bus passes for unemployed people. (In Fife, unemployed people and single parents can all travel for half price.) In others, you have to get 'on yer bike'. What if you don't have a bike, or a moped? If you have a bank account, it is worth working out whether it would be sensible to ask for a loan to buy one (secondhand), with regular fortnightly repayments, as you might save enough on bus fares to pay off the loan. If you live out of town, and need to get in to sign on and look for work, advertise for a regular ride in the newsagents' window.

IN CONCLUSION

Some books tell you that if you are unemployed, jobhunting ought to be a full-time activity. I've even seen a book which says 'Don't let your wife (!) talk you into helping out around the house. You must treat your jobhunting as a full-time job.' These days, for most people, this kind of advice is crazy. No amount of job-hunting ever created a new job. For a few people, the advice might work — but for most, it is a recipe for guaranteed depression and despair. It *may* take you six months or longer until you strike lucky and get the job you want.

So the message is

DO KEEP ON TRYING, IF YOU WANT TO SUCCEED

but

DO ALSO USE YOUR TIME TO DO NEW THINGS IN YOUR LIFE.

The period of unemployment can be a blessing as well as being a pain, since it gives you the freedom to try out new things in your life. Use it well, and it will serve you well.

Booklist

This chapter has given some guidelines for successful jobhunting. The following books will give you additional ideas and advice, and can all be ordered through your local library:

- *What Color Is Your Parachute?: A Practical Manual for Jobhunters and Career-Changers*, by Richard Bolles (Ten Speed Press/Airlift, £4.95). This is the regular best seller from the USA, now available in Britain. Strongly recommended.
- *The Jobfinder's Book*, by Ruth Sandys and Alexa Stace (Kogan Page)
- *Pathways - A Holistic Guide to Jobhunting and Career Success*, by Guy Dauncey and Bernard Haldane (£5.95 from Lifeskills Associates, Clarendon Chambers, 51 Clarendon Road, Leeds LS2 9NZ, 1988). 'A guide to the process of finding the work which will bring you happiness, and enable you to be true to yourself.'
- *Changing Your Job After 35*, by Godfrey Golzen and Phillip Plumbley (Kogan Page)
- *Self-Marketing: A Guide to Creative Job Search*, by Chris Dunn and Barry Spence (Training and Development Publications, 1 Otho Court, Brentford Dock, Brentford, Middlesex)
- *Getting the Job You Want*, by Howard Dowding and Sheila Boyce (Ward Lock)
- *Great Answers to Tough Interview Questions*, by Martin John Yate (Kogan Page)
- *A User's Guide to the Manpower Services Commission*, by Alastair Thomson and Hilary Rosenberg (Kogan Page, £9.95). An independent guide, intended to help people using the MSC to reap the maximum benefit from it.

CHAPTER 5: WORKING TOGETHER, WE CAN HELP EACH OTHER

Joining a group – Getting organised: the tale of Katie McBlue – The first meeting – Six months later – Fundraising – Brainstorming – Earning money for group funds – How to set up your own Group Earning Scheme –'BUT IT'S NOT AS EASY AS THAT!' – RESOURCES – Books and Kits – Videos – Training

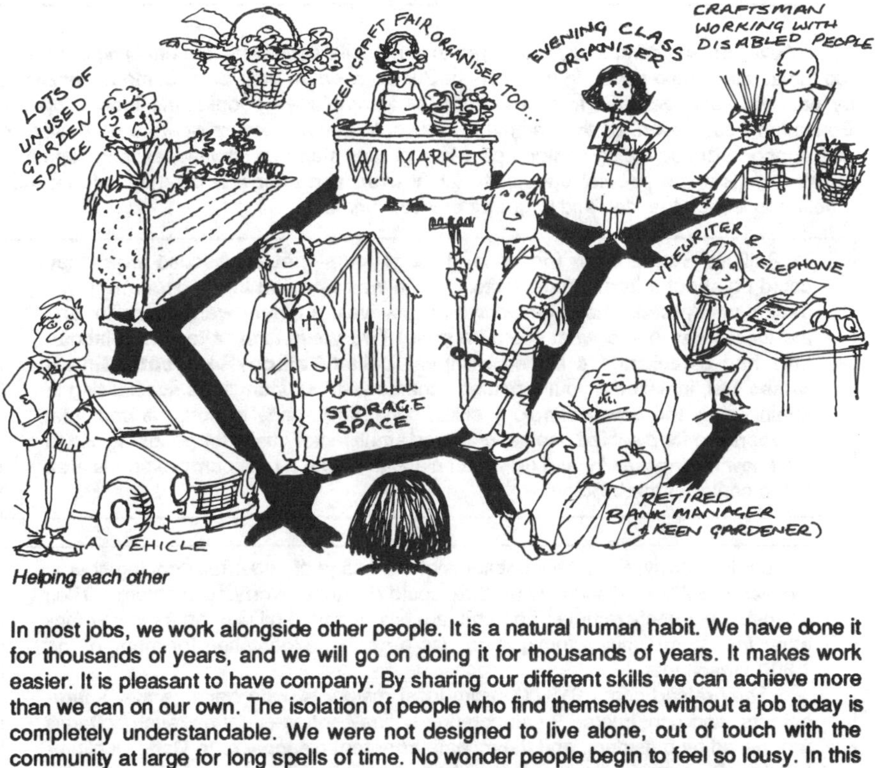

Helping each other

In most jobs, we work alongside other people. It is a natural human habit. We have done it for thousands of years, and we will go on doing it for thousands of years. It makes work easier. It is pleasant to have company. By sharing our different skills we can achieve more than we can on our own. The isolation of people who find themselves without a job today is completely understandable. We were not designed to live alone, out of touch with the community at large for long spells of time. No wonder people begin to feel so lousy. In this chapter, we look at ways in which people can work together to help each other.

Every week, from Monday to Friday, a group of people who are out of work and looking for a change meet together in a room borrowed from the Polytechnic of Central London. They help each other look for new opportunities and develop personal life-plans, set up new businesses, and learn how to approach job interviews (among other things). Access to the Polytechnic library is a valuable extra resource. They produce their own newsletter, arrange fund- raising and social events and generally enjoy each other's company. In 1985, when they ran a stand at the Wembley Job '85 Exhibition, they attracted over 1,000 enquiries. Past members keep in touch once they have moved on. The group is called the *Job Change Project*, and they have about 90 regular members at any one time.

In Penzance, a group of people calling themselves **Breadline,** mostly young and several of them unemployed, worked together for several years to open a centre for the town's young unemployed. They raised over £17,000: building their own inflatable to take to children's parties, fairs and festivals; doing parachute jumps; organising rock band contests; and working as volunteer marshalls at Elephant Fayre (a community festival). While doing all this, and enjoying each other's company, they have been linking up with other similar groups in the South-West through a network called CADURN (the Cornwall and Devon Unemployment Resource Network), which provides back-up, support and a stronger identity for its member groups.

All over Britain, community-based groups and self-help groups are enabling people to do things they could never, in a century of Sundays, do on their own. Some are assisted by paid workers, perhaps from a Centre for Unemployed people, the local Workers' Education Association, or the community or youth centre. Others operate on their own with support from agencies and groups. Many groups start in a similar way: someone has an idea, calls some people together to talk it over, and after a while they call a public meeting to launch the idea and to get wider involvement.

In Pallion, Sunderland, friends and neighbours met to discuss what they could do about a large empty factory which was worrying them, because it was getting vandalised. They elected two housewives, a former ward councillor and the local vicar to see what could be done. Two years later, after much labour, they had established a limited company called **Pallion Residents' Enterprises Ltd**, installed a youth training scheme with 30 youngsters specialising in engineering and new technology skills, converted space to house a computer co-operative for disabled people, prepared small factory units for people to use to start new businesses in, and drawn up plans to create a multipurpose sports area in the centre of the building.

In County Galway, Eire, the inhabitants of the village of Letterfrack got together in the early 1970s to discuss what they could do about worrying problems. Their village is extremely remote, the farms are tiny and the soil is poor; as in so many other Irish communities, emigration was a normal expectation for many of the 1,800 inhabitants.

They raised some £13,000 from local residents, who became the shareholders, and constructed 9 self-catering holiday cottages. Often, such cottages are owned by outsiders, and the income from rent disappears to Cork, Dublin or London. By keeping the rent themselves, they began to accumulate community capital. They formed a development company in 1971, called **Connemara West Ltd**, launched a cultural centre in 1977, and purchased a huge old disused reformatory in 1978, which they restored.

By 1985, they had established in the reformatory a co-operative agricultural store, a credit union (to enable them to do their own banking), a health centre, a sports centre, office space for Connemara West itself, crafts workshop space (being used for the production of ceramics, pewterware, quilts and patchwork, ironwork, pottery and woodturning), and a large youth craft training programme designed to foster enterprise development. All this, from almost nothing. It shows how much is possible when people start getting together.

Some groups have big ideas. Other groups have small ideas. It doesn't matter. Some groups start with a small idea, and then find that other ideas keep coming. It can be difficult to hold back. The process, when successful, is infectious.

Around Britain, unemployed and unwaged people are getting together and starting all sorts of activities to make life more enjoyable and rewarding:

- skills exchanges
- advice sessions on self-employment
- creative writing classes
- jobhunting groups
- holiday trips
- children's parties
- food co-operatives
- benefits advice
- permanent centres
- public meetings
- theatre groups
- football leagues
- concessions for unemployed people in local shops
- art festivals
- outings and excursions
- local magazines
- personal life-planning support
- crafts projects
- community businesses
- gardening projects
- worker co-operatives
- computer learning classes
- weightlifting groups
- marathon training groups
- driving lessons
- ecological action groups

Joining a group

To find out if there are any groups locally, ask people attached to these organisations (their addresses will be on p. vii if you have completed that page):

- Adult/Community Education
- Volunteer Bureau or Council for Voluntary Service
- Centre for Unemployed People
- Youth Service
- Community Relations Council
- local churches
- Workers' Education Association
- Citizens' Advice Bureau
- Social Services Department
- local council

If there are no groups which meet the needs of people who are out of work, you could start one yourself. The following story describes one way in which a group can be set up:

Getting organised: the tale of Katie McBlue

Katie McBlue, an unemployed housewife in Greentown, had a cup of coffee one morning with her friend, Jessie, and together they decided to see if they could start something. Their idea was to start a group with other people who wanted to develop new activities in their lives and have a good time doing it.

Their first step was to speak to the Greentown adult education organiser. She helped them talk through their ideas, and gave them a £30 grant to print a leaflet about the group. She also offered them a room to meet in once a week, and the use of a photocopier, telephone and typewriter if they needed them.

They invited a few friends round to discuss the idea further and drafted a simple leaflet with a cartoon on it, inviting people to come to the first meeting of the 'Greentown Initiatives Group'. They made a deliberate decision not to include the word 'unemployed' in the title, since they knew some people would be put off by it.

They chose a date two weeks ahead for their first meeting, and gave out leaflets at the library, evening classes, post offices, the Jobcentre, and in the dole queue. They phoned the local paper, and also phoned the local papers circulating in the West Indian and Indian communities, to make sure they knew about the meeting.

The first meeting

On the day of the meeting, they arrived an hour early, bringing some flowers to brighten up the room, and welcomed people as they came in. Katie and Jessie spoke about their ideas for the group, and suggested things they might do together. They asked people to introduce themselves, and had 15 minutes discussion, after which they broke up into groups of five people to get to know each other. They then did a group 'brainstorm' on possible ideas for activities (See over).

Each group came up with 30–40 ideas in a 20 minute period, which were written out on large posters. The groups then chose the five ideas which were most popular or interesting. Someone from each group read them out and a collective list was made. The posters were pinned up around the walls, and they stopped for coffee. They then spent half an hour discussing the ideas, chose five to proceed with, and set up working groups to start making plans. These covered Social activities, Jobhunting and career planning, Crafts enterprises, Computer skills, and Children's activities.

People also volunteered to sit on an overall steering committee to attend to such things as publicity, linking up with other groups in Greentown, and fundraising. They agreed to meet together as a whole every week for the groups to report on their activities, to make plans for the future, and for people to socialise.

BRAINSTORMING

Brainstorming is a valuable method which can help groups generate ideas, for fundraising and on other issues. The method can be used to think of 30 ways to raise money, 40 ways to improve the local DHSS offices, 50 ways to get to the Bahamas, etc. The rules of group brainstorming are as follows:

- Form small groups of 4–7 people. If your group is bigger, break it up into subgroups;
- Each group chooses someone to write down the ideas generated on large sheets of paper;
- Set a time limit; 3–5 minutes is often enough;
- Explain that the idea is for people to think of possible ideas as fast as they can, and write them down as soon as they are spoken;
- No ideas are criticised or questioned;
- Funny, crazy, illegal and immoral ideas are all encouraged the — laughter helps people relax and generate more ideas;
- Do a quick warm-up brainstorm first — e.g. 'Think of as many uses as you can for one old boot, in two minutes', followed by a brief feedback from the groups;
- Now do the brainstorm on the matter at hand;
- When the time is up, each group shares its ideas — or its best three ideas.

Six months later

The *social activities group* has arranged weekly cheap-rate sessions at the local swimming pool, organised a picnic outing into the hills which filled an entire coach, and is now planning a day at the seaside and a visit to a wildlife park at a special concessionary rate.

The *jobhunting and career planning group* made a visit to the Job Change Project in London to pick their brains, and have since set up a weekly group session, when people help each other to write out c.v.'s, do video interview practice sessions (borrowing the video equipment from the college), and look out for jobs for each other. Each person effectively jobhunts for 11 people as well as him or herself. They are currently holding discussions with the Adult Education department to see if they might pay someone to lead a second weekly group on personal life-planning.

The *crafts enterprise group* ran into problems when they planned to hold a regular market stall and put on a crafts exhibition, as their earnings would have infringed the DHSS earnings rules. However, the group had decided to subscribe to a number of newsletters and journals, and had learnt about a scheme called **STANDBY** which the DHSS had approved in Leicester and in the Medway Towns (1986). This allows unemployed people hoping to set up their own businesses to earn money while on benefit, and store it as individual 'cash credits', held in the group bank account of the Greentown Initiatives Group. (See p. 00). They negotiated with the DHSS Regional Office, and were given permission to launch their own scheme. This allowed the group to press ahead with their plans. Several members have begun to earn useful amounts of money, which is being stored in their name by the Initiative. If they stop receiving benefit, they will be able to receive the credits in cash, and simply pay tax on it.

The group has also joined the Greentown Enterprise Network, established to encourage new enterprise in the town. In conjunction with the Business Studies Department at the College, they have established a 'Support and Learning' group for people on the Enterprise Allowance Scheme, who were complaining of isolation once they joined the scheme. (See Chapter 11)

The *computer skills group* faced a problem in that no-one possessed a computer. They wrote a letter to the paper, and within a week had received several phone calls from people who had computers at home which were not used during the daytime. They also received an offer of free training sessions from an unemployed disabled man, and now hold a weekly training session, as well as having private keyboard time. Several of the group have joined the MSC's **'Access to Information Technology'** course. (See p. 107.)

The *children's activities group* arranged a babysitting rota and a day-time childcare rota, giving each member of the group at least one child-free day per week. They are in discussion with the Council for Voluntary Service to set up a regular childcare centre, using Community Programme workers to staff it. They wrote an open letter to the local newspaper asking for volunteer helpers to work with the children, and as a result have been able to establish a Saturday morning arts club, a football team and a bicycle skills and repairs club. They are now holding discussions with the Scouts and Guides movement to see whether children might join the Cubs and Brownies without having to buy the expensive new uniforms. They are also planning to form a Drugs Education Group in the town, which will work closely with schools, parents, social services and the police to educate young people to say 'No' and to control the spread of heroin in the area.

The GIG *Steering Committee* contacted 30 different groups in Greentown, and established a support list of 48 people, made up of individuals known to be sympathetic from groups such as the local college, the town council, the town band, the Workers' Education Association, the trades council, local businesses, local churches, the MSC, the youth service, the probation service, the community relations council, the women's centre, the careers service and the library, the DHSS and the Civil and Public Services Association.

As a result of these meetings, they discovered that most of the groups were fairly ignorant of what other groups were doing, and there was no co-ordination with regard to policies concerning unemployment. In fact, they discovered that there *was* no overall policy for assisting unemployed and unwaged people in Greentown. An exploratory meeting was held, and plans are now being made to launch a Greentown Unemployment Network. (See Chapter 6.)

Fundraising

As activities developed, the need for funds began to emerge. A *fundraising group* was established, which raised £1,250:

- Church Action with the Unemployed (see p. 70) gave a 'Launchpad Grant' of £200.
- Two local churches each gave £50, and the Rotary Club gave £25.
- The Adult Education department and Leisure Services department each gave £100. (Local government departments may give grants of up to £100 without much difficulty. Larger applications have to go before committees.)
- The Council gave a grant of £150.
- The Trades Council gave them £75, and an offer of help with printing.
- They raised £250 by running a raffle, a 'bring and buy' sale and a sponsored roller-skate run by their kids. Inspired by a sponsored hitch-hike to Rome by a member of the Hendon Young Peoples' Project, a 20 year-old member is now planning a sponsored hitch-hike to Athens.
- The Council's Economic Development Committee gave a £250 grant to the crafts group to help it buy tools and equipment.

- They discovered they could do paid work to earn money without their benefits being affected, following the precedent established by a group in Ipswich (see box below). Accordingly, they are discussing the possibility of setting up a gardening service, a tools restoration service and a house-cleaning service, to raise funds for the group. £4/5 a week out of the weekly earnings will go to individual workers, half of the rest will go to GIG, and the other half will be put into a bank account to buy tools and equipment.

In Scotland, they could also receive funds from the ***Unemployed Voluntary Action Fund*** *(Comely Park House, 80 New Row, Dunfermline, Fife KY12 7EJ), and from the* ***Carnegie Trust Action Fund,*** *(Artlink, 4 Forth Street, Edinburgh).*

Earning money for group funds

An informal precedent that allows unemployed people to earn funds for group activities was set in 1984–5 by a group of 20 unemployed people in Ipswich, who formed an odd jobs co-op. They took the £4 plus bus fares, which was allowed to them, and put the rest of their earnings into a kitty which they used to buy tools and pay for advertising, etc. The local DHSS at first approved, and then changed its mind. The group took the case to the local Social Security Tribunal and won. The DHSS appealed against the verdict, but were advised by the Chief Adjudicating Officer not to try to overrule it, which meant that the unemployed co-op could carry on what it was doing.

In Glastonbury, a group of unemployed people raised money in a similar way, pooling their earnings to buy tools and equipment, rain-gear and to pay for driving lessons for the group's members. The local DHSS knew about their activities, and did not interfere. In Bodmin, Cornwall, a group of unemployed people helped to equip an entire workshop ('The Attic workshop') in the same manner. This was approved by the local DHSS, on condition they kept proper accounts.

How to set up your own Group Earning Scheme:

1. Develop your ideas for earning income.
2. Open a bank account in your group's name, or ask a friendly voluntary organisation to open one for you.
3. Inform the DHSS of your intentions.
4. Start earning income, keeping clear accounts of all your expenditures and earnings.
5. Allow each person to keep £4/5 a week, and bank the rest, using it to purchase necessary tools and equipment, and to pay for training or tuition.

In April 1988, the DHSS earnings rule will change. Instead of being able to earn £4 a week plus expenses, you will be able to earn £5 a week, but not claim any expenses at all. People with a family who have been unemployed for over two years, people receiving the new disability premium and single parents will be able to earn £15 a week. Group Earning Schemes ought still to be possible, under the new rules.

If you want to start your own 'Standby' scheme to allow individual earnings, write to Marjorie Kingsland at the National Youth Bureau for advice (NYB, 17 Albion Street, Leicester LE1 6GD), sending 50p for a copy of 'Work Alternatives and Alternatives to Work' while you are at it.

Information on the development of 'Standby' schemes in Leicestershire can be obtained from Pam Chivers, Employment Unit, County Hall, Glenfield, Leicester LE3 8RA.

'BUT IT'S NOT AS EASY AS THAT!'

The account of the Greentown Initiatives Group is fictional. All over Britain there are real groups which are working towards similar goals. From such small acorns, great oak trees grow.

No groups experience their life as smooth, however. As with most things that are worth doing, there are problems along the way, both large and small. These can include:

- Lack of support from other unemployed people
- Lack of support from local councillors, business people and other people
- Difficulties when dealing with the local council or with the MSC when trying to arrange Community Programme or Voluntary Projects Programme schemes
- Lack of finance
- Lack of good group leadership
- A lack of 'style' and image
- A surplus of talking
- A deficit of action and fun
- Internal group arguments or power struggles
- Lack of contact, encouragement or support from other groups trying to achieve similar goals
- Lack of training in how to run meetings, good group management and goal planning
- An unwillingness to step out and seek help, advice, training or exposure to new possibilities

One answer to these problems is to raid the 'Resources' section below remorselessly, and ask for help from the people who are able to help. Many community self-help initiatives are started with an excess of enthusiasm and a shortage of practical experience. How could it be otherwise? We are stepping out into a new realm when we begin to work together to help each other. For centuries we have been taught to do otherwise.

The support which local self-help initiatives receive from the wider community is critically important to their success. The community business movement in Scotland, which in 1987 has around 100 member businesses of various kinds, manages to succeed in a very hostile economic climate because the people behind it have established strong support organisations, which provide advice, training and access to finance. This back-up support creates a friendly environment in which new initiatives can gain nourishment and strength while they grow.

The need for supportive back-up is given attention in the next chapter, on community networks. In ending this chapter, we want to acknowledge all the work being done by individual people in small groups, projects and initiatives 'out there'. It may sometimes seem that you are working away in a wilderness, or that it is a hopeless task. The first might indeed be true. The second is not. Stick to your beliefs. Your efforts are the making of a new and a better future.

RESOURCES

1. *Church Action with the Unemployed* (Norman Oliver, Director, CAWTU, Holywell Centre, 1 Phipp Street, London EC2A 4PS, Tel 01-729 1434) gives special encouragement to unemployed groups, including 'Launchpad' start-up grants to new groups to help them get going. You don't have to be a church group in order to apply.

2. *UNET* (c/o David Hopson, Holywell Centre, 1 Phipp Street, London EC2A 4PS, Tel 01-729 1434) is a computerised mailbox network serving community, church, voluntary and unemployed groups (see p. 00).
3. The *Open University MSC Community Programme* has set up a network of unemployed self-help learning projects around Britain. These are co-ordinated by workers on the Community Programme, who are given 'bare-foot' training in self-help group skills (Write for details to the National Agency Office, 3rd floor, Southfield House, 11 Liverpool Gardens, Worthing, West Sussex BN11 1SD,Tel 0903–201995).
4. The *Job Change Project at the Birmingham Settlement* (318 Summer Lane, Birmingham B19 3RL) has an outreach worker who is able to come and visit groups in England and Wales seeking help (Contact Dave Rothwell, Tel 021–359 6597).
5. The *Volunteer Centre* (29 Lower Kings Road, Berkhamsted, Herts HP4 2AB) has an Unemployment Unit, which publishes materials and runs training courses for groups (Contact Mark Rankin, Tel 04427–73311).
6. The *Scottish Community Education Council* (SCEC, Atholl House, 2 Canning Street, Edinburgh EH3 8EG, Tel 031–229 2433) can give direct help to groups in Scotland, and publishes a range of excellent material (see below) useful for people throughout Britain.
7. The *Job Change Project* (Room 217, Polytechnic of Central London, 35 Marylebone Road, London NW1 5LS) is open to visits and the sharing of experience (Contact Jill Austen, Tel 01–486 5811, Ext 209/210).
8. The *Trades Union Congress* (Services for the Unemployed, Congress House, Great Russell Street, London W1) employs one national and 12 regional organisers to assist the 200+ TUC Centres for the Unemployed. A regular newsletter is available which includes listings of the regional organisers. (Contact Ralph Don, Tel 01–636 4030, Ext 247).
9. *The National Council for Voluntary Organisations* (26 Bedford Square, London WC1B 3HU, Tel 01–636 4066) provides a home for the *National Self-Help Support Centre* which can give further help to groups. They also publish a range of useful materials (see below).

Books and Kits

- *Nice Work If You Can Get It — How to be Positive About Unemployment*, by Guy Dauncey. Includes chapters with further practical advice and ideas on forming local groups (£3.95 from NEC, 18 Brooklands Avenue, Cambridge CB2 2HN).
- *Adult Options — Three Million Opportunities,* eds Cann, Haughton and Melville. Includes a wide range of useful essays written about unemployment initiatives, groups and networks, including CADURN (see Chapter 6). (£3.95 from Educational Centres Association, c/o The Folk House, 40 Park Street, Bristol BS1 5JG)
- *The BURN Notes — Unemployed Self-Help in Action*, by Guy Dauncey, David Hopson and Andrew Howell. Includes articles reprinted from *The BURN Newsletter* between 1982–1984, concerning self-help initiatives. (£2.50 from CAWTU, Holywell Centre, 1 Phipp Street, London EC2A 4PS, Tel 01-729 1434)
- *A Start-Up Kit for Unwaged Groups*, by Kevin Dixon, Rhonda Lovell, Gary Magill, Guy Dauncey and others in CADURN. Includes information sheets on getting started, premises, making contacts, building support groups, group activities, funding, group development, women, young people, etc. (Free from Start-Up Kit, c/o Replan, 108c Stokes Croft, Bristol)

- The Scottish Community Education Council (Atholl House, 2 Canning Street, Edinburgh EH3 8EG) publish the following:
  — *SCAN,* a monthly magazine for community and youth educators which the authors find invaluable. (£5 per year).
  — *Unemployment: Communities Take Action,* ed Kate Vincent. An information pack bringing together over 60 stories showing what is being done in Scotland about unemployment; with a thorough information and organisations listing. (£3.50)
  — *Women and Unemployment* A compilation of papers written by Scottish women about their work with unemployed groups. (£1.00, cheques to the Scottish Adult Basic Education Unit [SABEU] at the SCEC address)
  — *Co-operative Learning With Unemployed People.* A practical guide giving ideas and initiatives for working with groups of unemployed people, and encouraging the use of their own resources. (£1.00 + 30p postage from SABEU, at the SCEC address)
  — *Getting Started — The Community Business Pack.* Covers deciding what to do, setting up, planning, resources, staffing and sample feasibility studies. (£9.00 from SABEU).
- *Community Organising? You've Never Really Tried It!* by James Pitt and Maurice Keane. Witty and concise, it contains case studies and practical advice on organising techniques. (£1.50 + 30p postage from LVSC, 68 Chalton Street, London NW1)
- *In and Out of Unemployment: Group Initiatives.* One of the practical kits produced by the OU's Unemployment Project. It contains valuable information and activities on self-help groups, housing initiatives and co-operatives. (£1.25 from Learning Materials Service, The Open University, PO Box 188, Milton Keynes MK7 6DH)
- *Community Start Up,* by Caroline Pinder, covers how to organise and run meetings, raise money, involve people, etc. (£4.95 from NEC, 18 Brooklands Avenue, Cambridge CB2 2HN)
- The *National Council for Voluntary Organisations (NCVO)* publishes a series of useful practical guides available by post (Harper & Row Distributors Ltd, Estover Road, Plymouth PL6 7PZ. Add 12 per cent of price for postage). Titles include:
  — *Finding and Running Premises* (£2.95)
  — *Government Grants — A Guide for Voluntary Organisations* (£3.95)
  — *Getting Organised — A Handbook for Non-statutory Organisations* (£4.95)
  — *Working with Self-Help Groups — A Guide for Local Professionals* (£2.50)
- *A Basic PR Guide for Charities,* by Dorothy and Alastair McIntosh
  Dealing with the press, developing campaigns, internal organisation, lobbying, etc. (£4.50 from Directory of Social Change, 9 Mansfield Place, London NW3)
- *Value for People.* A description of community initiatives in Wandsworth, South London, which contains useful experiences. (£2.50 from Popular Planning Project, Adult Education, 116 Battersea Park Road, London SW11 4BR)

Further organisations and books relating to women's issues, young people's initiatives, co-operatives and community businesses are listed at the ends of other chapters.

Videos

A directory of community self-help and local economic development videos, which can be used at public and group meetings is being compiled c/o the Planning Exchange (186 Bath Street, Glasgow G2 4HG. Contact Jim McNee.)

The following TV companies have produced good series covering community responses to unemployment: Thames TV ('Jobs Unlimited'); Yorkshire TV ('Nice Work If

You Can Get It'); HTV ('Working Alternatives'); Central TV ('Workout'); Tyne Tees ('Working for a Better Life'); STV ('Unemployment Matters'). A letter or phone call to the Community Education Officer might enable you to borrow videos.

Training

Many groups and centres have training budgets which unemployed volunteers and members of self-help groups can also make use of. You can obtain details of training courses (and enjoy a personal break away from home) from

- Volunteer Centre
- NCVO (address above)
- SCEC (address above)
- National Federation of Community Organisations (8/9 Upper Street, London N1 0PQ)
- 'Advance' (training for volunteer organisers and neighbourhood projects, 14 Bloomsbury Square, London WC1)
- Association of Community Workers, Grindon Lodge, Beech Grove Road, Newcastle-upon-Tyne NE4 2RS
- Federation of Community Work Training Groups (reduced prices for unemployed people, 356 Glossop Road, Sheffield S10 2HW)
- National Federation of Self-Help Organisations, 150 Townmead Road, London SW6.

CHAPTER 6: FORMING COMMUNITY NETWORKS

WHAT IS A COMMUNITY NETWORK? – Why are networks set up? – Who is involved? – How is a network formed? – What can a network do? – Positive support – Educating ourselves for change – REGIONAL NETWORKS – ELECTRONIC NETWORKS – RESOURCES

This chapter considers three types of network — the community network, the regional network and the electronic network. Each of these can be of great value to people who are involved in activities to do with unemployment.

WHAT IS A COMMUNITY NETWORK?

For many — if not all — unemployed people, life is a bit of a jungle. There may be dozens of people, groups, agencies and organisations, somewhere 'out there' wanting to help, but there are no paths cut to enable unemployed people to reach them, and vice-versa. There is an answer to this problem. It is known as a community network.

A network enables people working in a common field, or sharing a common interest, to meet together, learn from each other and develop new initiatives. The networks which concern us in this chapter are those that link people who share a need to do something positive about unemployment. Many others operate on a similar basis, such as the **Women in Community Enterprise Network** in Scotland (see Chapter 11) and the **Education for Enterprise Network** (see Chapter 11). A network creates pathways in the jungle of the unemployment business.

A successful network usually consists of:

- monthly, bi-monthly or quarterly meetings;
- a single person or a committee which agrees to hold it all together;
- smaller working groups;
- an annually updated directory which lists the members, with their addresses, skills, resources and interests;
- a newsletter, to keep people in touch.

Why are networks set up?

Networks are set up because it pays to know what everyone in the unemployment business is doing locally, and to get to know them face to face. Here are comments from a group of people in Kent when they were forming a network:

> To share thoughts with others/better communications/removing mistrust/closer liaison with job providers/better relationships with the DHSS and individual officers/ removing the feeling of trespass on other people's areas/sharing skills, retraining/ development of community leadership/mutual support/sharing of resources/better information about problems and projects.

Who is involved?

Individuals join networks from among the following groups:

Adult Education
Careers Service
'Unemployed Centre
local council
Jobcentre
Unemployment Benefit Office
Claimants Union
local library
Citizens Advice Bureau
sports groups
Probation Service
MSC
Community Programme schemes
Youth Training Schemes
business initiatives
Enterprise Agencies
leisure services
Women's Centre
local churches
youth Service
Information Technology Centre
Workers' Educational Association
DHSS
Council for Voluntary Service
Community Centre
Community Relations Council
local colleges
Community Programme Agencies
ethnic initiatives
voluntary projects
Chamber of Commerce
Co-operative Development Agencies
Police
Social Services
other unemployment initiatives

How is a network formed?

One agency usually assumes initial responsibility and plans an all-day conference, inviting people to come by written invitation and personally. A fee is charged to cover costs, and a special effort made to invite unemployed people, without charge. A decision is usually made at this stage about the intended geographical reach of the network. In Suffolk, for instance, the unemployment network embraces the whole county, and the founding meeting launched 6 separate regional networks on the same day.

At the conference, give everyone a typed list of all those present, with their contact addresses and telephone numbers, and name badges which state the group or agency they come from.

- Start off the day with a brief welcome, and do a round of introductions from everyone present — even if there are 50 people: it helps people get a sense of involvement.
- Next, have an invited speaker, or speakers, who can inspire people with a positive sense of what can be achieved.
- Before lunch, form into small groups with pre-arranged group leaders, and ask each person to write down (for instance):
  - — three ways in which they think they might benefit by being part of the network, and
  - — what they hope the network will achieve.

  Then ask people to share their ideas, with a volunteer to collect them on large sheets of paper.
- After lunch, each group's volunteer reports back to the group as a whole. This begins to build a sense of collective purpose.

The final part of the process needs someone with good group facilitation skills who can get democratic results by consensus in a short time. Choose someone who can be crisp, assertive and sensitive.

- Ask people to get into small groups of three or four and to brainstorm for a few minutes on the names of people who are not present, who ought to be involved in the network. Be sure to collect their lists.
- Finally, you need agreement on details:
  - How often will the network meet, and for how long?
  - What should the network's name be?
  - If you want to send out an initial newsletter, ask for volunteers.
  - Ask for volunteers to form a committee to pull together the day's results, and to plan the next meeting.

FORMING A NETWORK

9.30	Coffee
10.00	Welcome, and introductions.
10.30	Speakers
11.15	Questions and discussion
11.45	Small groups
12.45	Lunch
2.00	Groups report back
3.00	Setting up a Network Forming a committee
4.00	Tea
4.30	Close

What can a network do?

- Hold regular meetings for people to meet each other.
- Organise conferences and training events.
- Publish a local handbook for unemployed people (eg *Positive Action* produced in Falkirk).
- Draw unemployed people into local decision-making processes.
- Allow new staff in agencies to start effective work sooner.
- Help new initiatives get started.
- Help unemployed projects to get resources.
- Inform people about new schemes, courses and initiatives.
- Enable the provision of new courses relevant to the needs of unemployed people.
- Enable people to learn about initiatives in other parts of Britain.
- Create a clear voice in the community which can speak for the needs of unemployed people.
- Work for specific local and regional policy changes.
- Make sure the political representatives are properly informed about problems and issues.
- Begin to develop an integrated approach to tackle the problems of local unemployment.

Positive support

The philosophy behind community networks is the same as that behind community self-help initiatives — by working together, we can be more creative, less prone to depression and difficulty, and more willing to dream dreams and turn them into action.

In specific terms, community networks can help to produce solutions to some common problems:

- **The DHSS often operates in isolation from anything else that is going on in the community.** The 'Standby' scheme referred to on p. 53 was created because the group in question (Medway Youth Unemployed Project) believed in reaching out and setting up an effective (informal) network. The Regional DHSS staff themselves helped to work out the details of the scheme.
- **DHSS Claimant Advisers are often unaware of non-traditional possibilities for personal education and development that exist locally.** An Adviser who attended a network meeting in Kent was able to get information about local courses and community activities, so that she can now recommend them to people when she interviews them.
- **Some Community Programme Managing Agencies have not been able to develop good systems of personal support, life-planning and jobhunting encouragement, to maximise the benefit of the schemes to the people involved.** Contacts made with local colleges or the Workers' Educational Association could enable them to set up partnership arrangements to meet this need.
- **Some unemployed centres have been unable to develop a business start-up side to their activities.** After sharing this need in the network, the local enterprise agency might offer to come in and run a special course.
- **The police often find themselves in conflict with unemployed youngsters hanging around on the streets.** Awareness-raising sessions about unemployment, and about constructive attitudes and approaches, might be brought into police training courses as a result of personal relationships developed through the network. The police on the beat might be provided with handbooks listing local groups and projects, to guide them in their street contacts.
- **Community Health Visitors in some areas meet a lot of families where unemployment contributes to family stress, but are only trained to give dietary advice.** Through contact with network members, a special training course and self-help manual could be developed.
- **In some areas, people from ethnic minorities don't use local enterprise agencies as much as they might.** Having made contact, someone from the enterprise agency might come and run a business start-up course, for example, at a Bangladeshi cultural centre.
- **Jobcentres often don't carry information about local groups and projects which could help unemployed people.** A personal relationship between the Jobcentre manager and people from local groups could lead to a new policy over leaflets and posters.
- **Groups setting up schemes under the Community Programme often have difficulty getting MSC staff to bend beyond the formal guidelines laid down in their manuals.** The way around nearly all MSC-related problems lies through the development of a good personal link with staff working in the MSC. The Network can help this to happen.

- **People involved in community self-help initiatives often do not know how they can make use of Voluntary Projects Programme** or **'Opportunities for Volunteering' schemes.** The sharing of information about schemes, projects and initiatives in network meetings will help to increase awareness about these and other schemes.
- **Careers workers in many areas are not properly aware of local alternatives to unemployment for post-YTS young people.** A community directory published by the network, giving information about projects and initiatives, could provide them with the information they need.
- **College staff running 5-day *Restart* courses sometimes struggle to make their courses really effective.** Contact with the full range of opportunities that are available to unemployed people locally, through Network meetings and newsletters, and the Network directory, will help them to create a good course.

Take any two groups at random from the list on p. 62, and ask yourself:

> 'What three measures might assist these two groups to help each other improve their assistance to the unemployed community locally?'

and you will begin to realise the wealth of possibilities that lie untapped in most communities. The network simply brings people together in an organised way, enabling some of these possibilities to become realities.

Educating ourselves for change

If a community is to respond positively to the problems of unemployment, network members need to know about projects and initiatives going on elsewhere outside their own locality. There is a wealth of excellent work going on, and learning about it can be a source of ongoing inspiration:

- Take out subscriptions to magazines such as *Initiatives* and to the *LEDIS sheets* (see p. 68)
- Form study groups to learn about new ideas and initiatives in specific areas
- Make group visits to other projects.

Vision must always be nourished, and fed. In this way, we can continue to believe in what we know to be possible.

REGIONAL NETWORKS: CADURN

In the south-west, the Cornwall and Devon Unemployment Resource Network (CADURN) has been active since 1982. It is a grassroots network which links people in unemployment self-help initiatives in the west country, and provides a strong voice for unemployed people. Unemployed people must occupy at least half the seats on its committee, the other half generally being taken by people who are paid workers with unemployment initiatives.

CADURN has won its existence by a firm belief in the need for its own existence, and steady persistence in its goals, despite a constant lack of funds. It enables people from a wide area of the country to meet together on a regular basis and discuss matters of joint interest. So, what goes on in CADURN meetings?

A typical meeting in October 1986 saw members discussing the following:

- A new initiative by Devon County Council for young unemployed people ('Dayspace').
- The production of a Start-Up Kit for unemployed centres and groups.
- A television programme in which CADURN members took part.
- The success of a series of 28 Public Service Announcements which CADURN put out on television.
- The possibility of CADURN involvement in a new MSC initiative ('Training Access Points').
- Recent changes to the DHSS benefits rules concerning voluntary work (which the DHSS withdrew after protests).
- Liaison with South West Arts and the possibility of an SWA policy on arts and the unemployed.
- A residential weekend drama course for unemployed people.
- Marketing of the CADURN video.
- The Ballet Rambert's offer of concession-rate tuition for unemployed people.
- A welfare rights conference coming up in Torquay.
- The new Careers Service policy of co-operating with unemployed groups.
- CADURN's own funding, and 13 other matters about local projects, meetings and groups.

Information on all these items gets fed back to the projects which members are involved in. Case proven for the value of regional networks?

CADURN has produced a video about its work, and about regional networking, which is available for sale, price £20 to statutory groups, £17 to voluntary groups. A CADURN Strategy Paper for the south-west, *Unemployment — A Positive Future* is available price £1 + 50p postage (50p + 50p postage for unemployed) from CADURN, c/o Kevin Dixon, Community Education Office, Bridge House, Courtenay Street, Newton Abbot, Devon.

ELECTRONIC NETWORKING — UNET

A real need among people who are involved in unemployment nationally is for the easy transmission of information, experience, ideas, contacts, and 'how-to-do-it's. Everyone is searching around for solutions to the same massive problems in relative isolation.

Between 1981 and 1985, the British Unemployment Resource Network (BURN) began to meet this need, through conferences, a regular BURN Newsletter, and a national directory. BURN went into suspension in 1985, partly because it did not find the means to handle such a fast growing network of groups and initiatives.

UNET has grown directly out of BURN's experience. UNET is a computerised mailbox network. It enables community, church, voluntary and unemployed groups to improve the quality and flow of information, using electronic computer systems. It is supported by CAWTU (Church Action with the Unemployed).

The UNET Bulletin Board is putting practical information on-line concerning community development, local economic development, unemployment groups and initiatives, MSC schemes, and the how-to-do-it of good Community Programme schemes. Once you are on-line, you can access LEDIS (Local Economic Development Information Service), Green-Net, NACCPAS and other bulletin boards.

To grasp the possibilities that exist through UNET, you have to understand that you can put an open-ended request out into the network for help, answers to problems, sources of information, good contacts in special fields, etc, without having to know to whom you are addressing the request. For instance:

- A group of unemployed people wants to plan a group holiday together, and needs to know if other groups have experience of doing this, and if so, how they raised their funds. Through UNET, they put a general request for information out on the network. 48 hours later, three groups have sent back messages, and a direct contact has been made with one of them by phone.
- The funding which your project is receiving from the EEC has not come through. It is already 3 months late, and you need it urgently. You put a request out on UNET asking if anyone has found a way to speed up the bureaucracies. 6 hours later, the information comes back that a certain Euro MP knows how to work wonders in Brussels, and giving her phone number.
- The Community Programme Agency you work with has an idea for a particular kind of building project, but you feel that there may be union opposition to the scheme. It would help if you knew what the experience of other agencies was in this area before your committee meeting in two days' time. A request put out on UNET brings you the information you need in time for your meeting.
- An imminent change to the DHSS rules that was announced last night is going to create a huge amount of extra distress among the people you work with. You send out a 'What can we do?' request on the network, and a lively discussion develops over the next three days. By the end of the week, a co-ordinated strategy has been agreed to bring pressure to bear to overturn the ruling.

The possibilities inherent in electronic networking are enormous. It is not a substitute for the telephone, or the post: it is a form of communication which simply did not exist before. The potential advantages to people working in the unemployment field are very great.

UNET will also be offering a major easy-access information library on disc, covering unemployment, housing, community development and local economic development, available to IBM, Amstrad, Apricot and BBC users.

If you want to come on-line, you can get help from UNET with:

- advice about appropriate computers, modems and software
- discounts on hardware and software purchases
- support for development, and training in the use of mailbox systems.

The basic cost is £5 a month, plus your on-line usage costs. The greater the number of groups which join UNET, the more those groups will be able to take advantage of the opportunities which electronic networking and mailboxing allow.

UNET, David Hopson, CAWTU, Holywell Centre, 1 Phipp Street, London EC2A 4PS, Tel 01-729 1434.

RESOURCES

- *Initiatives* magazine, though expensive, is the best current source of news, information and stories about positive initiatives to tackle unemployment in Britain, and further afield too. Any group which has serious intentions about doing something in this field should subscribe, and then pass around their copy. Produced by the Centre for Employment Initiatives, London (see p. 188). (£17.50 per year from Longman Group, 4th Avenue, Harlow, Essex CM19 5AA).

- *The LEDIS Sheets* (Local Economic Development Information Service) is a monthly mailing consisting of detailed information sheets about local initiatives in Britain (and overseas). An invaluable (if expensive) source of hard facts and practical 'this is how they did it' details about successful projects. (£25 per year from the Planning Exchange, 186 Bath Street, Glasgow G2 4HG.) (See also p. 188)

- *Church Action With the Unemployed,* (CAWTU, Director Norman Oliver, Holywell Centre, 1 Phipp Street, London EC2A 4PS, Tel 01-729 1434) is a very effective organisation, which supports churches taking positive initiatives against unemployment. They have, among other things:
  — Set up the 'Launchpad' grants scheme to assist unemployed groups and individuals (see p. 56)
  — Launched and supported Local Action Groups and other initiatives in several places in Britain
  — Helped to establish UNET (see above)
  — Supported the development of local and regional networks
  — Helped to establish 'Unemployment Sunday', which happens each Spring (usually the last Sunday before Lent).

They can provide you with the names of local church contacts. Publications include:

- *Action with the Unemployed: 100 Projects with Unemployed People* (£2.95)
- *Unemployment Sunday,* a practical pack of leaflets for worship, study and action. (£1.00)
- *Church Action With The Unemployed — An Introduction,* a video on VHS and Beta (£12.75 including p&p and discussion materials)

CHAPTER 7: REDRESSING THE BALANCE

INTRODUCTION – YOUNG PEOPLE – WOMEN – ETHNIC MINORITIES – PEOPLE WITH DISABILITIES – EARLY RETIRED PEOPLE – REDUNDANT WORKERS – PROFESSIONAL AND EXECUTIVE WORKERS – MEN

INTRODUCTION

All human beings want, need and deserve the opportunity to use their energies creatively.

This chapter lists some of the important initiatives which are attempting to deal directly with the barriers of youth, sex, race, disability and age which currently affect many people's ability to get employment. It is not a chapter just for those directly affected by discrimination. A period of unemployment can provide a useful time for everyone to think through these key issues.

Do fear, mistrust and ignorance exist within me? Governments from time immemorial have used the technique of divide and rule. Do I fall into the trap of blaming my unemployment on another group — women, or black people? Have I read any factual information about these issues? Are any groups that I am involved in really open and welcoming to *everyone*? — The local Unemployment Centre, for example. Is it accessible to disabled people? Is it used by black people? Are its meetings generally dominated by white, able-bodied men? Are leaflets available in languages spoken by ethnic minority groups in the area?

We must work together to ensure that the energy, talents and perspectives of everyone are involved in shaping the future of our common world.

Good news!

(Well . . . it's a start!) Some inner city local authorities and a few major employers have finally been convinced by the evidence shown in employment statistics to take the issue of equal opportunities seriously.

The number of Equal Opportunities posts is increasing, and a small but growing number of local authorities are setting up units to promote equal treatment, and to monitor which people get interviews and jobs, to see if this reflects the overall population locally. The Department of Employment, CBI, TUC, the Institute of Personnel Management and other influential bodies are strongly urging employers to follow the new codes of practice recently introduced by the Commission for Racial Equality (1984) and the Equal Opportunities Commission. We intend an equal opportunities perspective to run right through this book (and welcome suggestions for improving this in the next edition).

Videos making lively use of music and humour to provoke discussion on racism, sexism, disablement, lesbian and gay issues, issues affecting young people (and also community action and housing) can be hired from Albany Video Distribution, The Albany, Douglas Way, London SE8 4AG, Tel 01–692 6322 (catalogue £1.00).

See also *Organising for Equality*, £1.00 from the Greater London Enterprise Board, 63 Newington Causeway, London SE1 6BD.

YOUNG PEOPLE

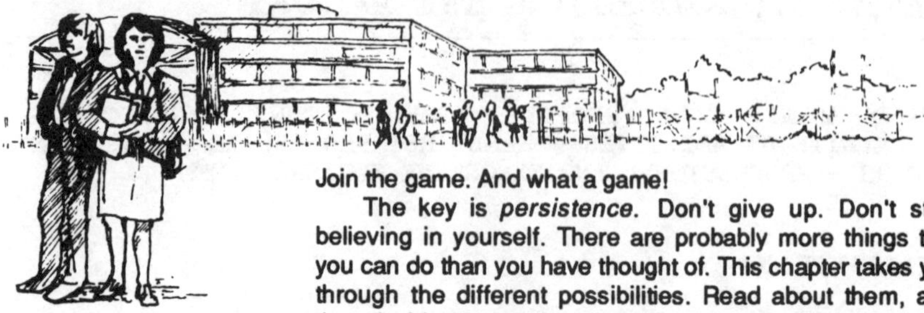

Join the game. And what a game!

The key is *persistence*. Don't give up. Don't stop believing in yourself. There are probably more things that you can do than you have thought of. This chapter takes you through the different possibilities. Read about them, and then decide what you are going to put your efforts into.

There are six basic paths which you can choose from:

1. Make an organised effort to get a **job**.
2. Get a place on the **Youth Training Scheme** or the **Community Programme**.
3. Get a place at **college**.
4. Apply for a place on the **Job Training Scheme**.
5. Follow a home-made, do-it-yourself **'Active Unemployment'** path — it can be an exciting journey!
6. Start **your own business**.

Before starting, you may find it helpful to know that:

- The Basic Skills Unit has produced a wide range of materials for young people without jobs, including:
  - help with reading, learning, maths, etc;
  - booklets written by other young people;
  - guides to working in shops, garages, etc.

  Write to BSU Ltd, Unit 43, Clifton Industrial Estate, Cambridge, for information.
- If you live in Scotland, for 50p you can get a copy of **'Young Scot'**, an invaluable survival guide. Send to SCEC, 2 Atholl House, Canning Street, Edinburgh EH3 8EG.
- The **Transport and General Workers' Union** is offering membership to all unemployed young people under 21, for only 10p a week. This will bring you full union rights, and the chance to attend and take part in meetings, and to learn how a large union works. To join, ask either through the nearest Centre for the Unemployed, or through the Trades Council.

1. Make an organised effort to get a job

Most of the stuff you need is in Chapter 4 so we will not reprint it here.The only things missing are notes about the Careers Service, and the New Workers Scheme:

The Careers Service

If you are under 19 you can choose to register for work with the Careers Office or the Jobcentre (see p. 27), and you can use both to find jobs. But you still have to sign on fortnightly at the Unemployment Benefit Office. The Careers Office is there to help you and has trained staff. Their address is on page vii.

To get the most out of the Careers Office, there are some useful guidelines to follow:

- Make an appointment by phone if you want to see a Careers Officer, to be sure of getting proper attention.
- When you call for your appointment, take some ideas in with you about the kind of work you'd like to do. It makes life much easier for the careers officers. Use Chapter 3 if you don't know what kind of work you want to do. This way, you can avoid ending up in a job you don't like.
- Keep in touch regularly to let them know you are still interested. When there are not many jobs to offer, it is only natural that the staff tend to offer interviews to the young people who show the most interest.
- If they send you for an interview for a job you find you don't want, don't give up on them. Go back, and tell them why you didn't want it.
- The Careers Office staff may also be able to give you helpful comments about your application letters, if you show them a copy of what you write. They *may* be able to arrange an interview practice session too, if you ask.
- Finally, remember they are there to help you, but this doesn't mean that you needn't do anything to help yourself. Make your own efforts too.

The New Workers Scheme is designed to help young people aged 18–20 to find work. Employers can receive a subsidy of £15 a week from the government as an incentive to give you a job, if your wages are £55 a week or less for 18–19 year olds, £65 a week or less for 20 year olds (1987 level).
Action: Ask the Careers Service or Jobcentre for details.

2. Get a place on the Youth Training Scheme or the Community Programme

The Youth Training Scheme is not to be written off without second thought. You could be wasting a huge opportunity if you do that. Many young people go on to get jobs after being a trainee on the scheme. If you are aged 16 or 17, check it out by a visit to the Careers Service. It does not pay much, but it can be a pathway to real skills and a good job. Some schemes are very high quality. Also ask about a scheme called *Community Industry* which runs in some cities.
Action: Phone the Careers Service to arrange to see them.

If you are over 18, the *Community Programme* will probably be able to offer you a job on either a full-time or a part-time basis. The jobs are different in every area, and some are very interesting. You will learn new skills, and probably make some good friends. See Chapter 4, p. 45, and the Stop Press on page 197 for further details and latest information.

3. Get a place at college

See Chapter 8 for the details. College is not like school — it is an adult place, where adults go to learn new skills. The more skill and learning you possess, the better the job you are likely to get.
Action: Read Chapter 8, and phone and arrange to speak with the college admissions tutor, to find out what courses are on offer.

4. Get a place on the Job Training Scheme.

There are *two* Job Training Schemes. The *new* Job Training Scheme offers you up to a year of personally designed training, with built-in work experience. You will receive the same money as you get on benefit, and all your travel expenses will be paid. Details on page 104.

The *old* Job Training Scheme offers you a range of courses in practical skills, lasting from a few weeks up to a year. The details are on page 104.

Take it from us - the better your skills, the better will be your chance of getting a job.
Action: Ask at the Jobcentre for details.

5. Active unemployment - do it yourself

> 'Five of us got together and joined a group called "Instant Muscle". We sell our labour, and earn money doing all sorts of jobs, some big, some small. We're off the dole now.' Rob, 18.

> 'I use the "21 hours a week rule" to go to college, where I'm taking two 'O' levels, and learning to weld.' Valerie, 17.

> 'I went away on a workcamp for three weeks in the summer. It was fantastic. We were up on Snowdon, in Wales, doing work to look after the place.' Pete, 20.

> 'We've formed our own motor-bike repair workshop; I've got this mate who really knows his stuff, and he comes and teaches us two nights a week.' Stu, Bill, Rich.

> 'We all go rock-climbing every weekend with the local club. We're thinking of entering the Duke of Edinburgh's award. It would be something to aim for.' Valerie, Rosie, Sonia.

> 'I go down to the Centre for the Unemployed about three times a week, where I have joined a karate class, and where I help out serving coffee and cleaning. We're a bunch of friends, really. I've also learnt how to produce a newsletter and learnt how to use the duplicator.' Kay, 24.

> 'I'm with a group that's making plans to start up a co-operative business making baby-carriers. We're getting lots of advice from people who know what they're talking about.' Carmen, 18.

> 'I've joined a youth action group, and we do things like go and clear old woodlands at weekends, and help handicapped children when they go swimming.' Sushila.

These show some of the possibilities: there are 100s more. The secret of these paths lies in getting out of your house and finding out what is happening where you live. You will meet new people, learn new skills, have some fun, and it will open up new doors for you. The details are all below.
Action: Read the notes below, and then either write off for details or go and visit your local Centre for Unemployed People or community centre.

Do-it-yourself: the details

- For information on *youth co-operatives groups* such as 'Instant Muscle', and the possibility of becoming self-employed, see Chapter 11.

- *Studying for 21 hours a week.* You can attend college and take part-time courses for up to 21 hours a week without your benefit being affected. See Chapter 8, p. 107.

- *Joining a workcamp.* On a workcamp a number of people, mostly young, work together for two to three weeks. They sometimes take place in cities, sometimes way out in the remote country. There's no pay, but all your costs are met while you are there.

  Workcamps offer many things, and can be great fun: not enough people know about them. You can make video films with younger children, restore old railways, do archaeological digs, work with handicapped people and 1,001 other activities. An unemployed youth group in Suffolk sends a group to a 'Tools for Self-Reliance' workcamp, which repairs tools to send out to farmers in Africa who really need them. You can go on receiving benefit while you are away, as long as you are 'available for work'. You collect your benefit when you return.

  For details of camps, write to: International Voluntary Service (53 Regent Street, Leicester LE1 6YL), or Friends Service Council (Euston Road, London NW1 2BJ). See also Chapter 13.

- *Other kinds of voluntary work.* There are many outlets for voluntary work, such as the Sue Ryder homes, which need volunteers to help care for disabled ex-service people, or the Edinburgh Cyrenians, who need volunteer workers for their city house and farm community.

  For details, send for a free copy of 'Sparetime Sharetime', NYB, 17 Albion Street, Leicester, LE1 6GD.

- *Motor-bike repair workshop.* If a small group of people wants such a workshop, you could go about getting help like this:
  - ask the adult education people (see p. 106) to put on an evening class for you;
  - try the police — they might release someone to work with you;
  - ask the local motor-bike shop if one of their mechanics would help you;
  - ask one of the youth club workers if he would help you get a group going.

  Allow time for all these suggestions — it might take a month or so to find a place and get it organised.

- *Earning money* Until April '88, anyone on Supplementary Benefit can earn up to £4 a week, after expenses, before their benefit is reduced. 'Expenses can cover anything from bus fares to tools and equipment.' After April '88, you can earn £5 a week, but with no allowance for expenses (see p. 150). If a group sets up a small 'agency', as young people in Ipswich did, you can earn more money, and use it to buy tools and equipment. See page 55, Chapter 5.

- *Summer jobs.* Ask your library to get copies of *Working Holidays* (£4.80 + 45p postage from CBEVE, 43 Dorset Street, London W1H 3EN), *Year On, Year Off* (£2.45 + 75p postage from CRAC, Bateman Street, Cambridge CB2 1LZ) and *Summer Jobs in Britain* (£4.95 from Vacation Work, 9 Park End Street, Oxford OX1 1HJ). These give details and addresses of paid work on farms, fruit-picking, in hotels, domestic work, workcamps, voluntary work openings, adventure courses and holidays, overseas work and workcamps, au pair work, etc. They will completely change your ideas about what is possible.

- *Community Service Volunteers.* CSV finds voluntary work positions for 2,000 people a year. Volunteers receive a small weekly allowance plus full board and lodging and travel expenses.They never turn away anyone who applies. You can choose what you want to do from a great variety of work. (CSV, 237 Pentonville Road, London N1 9NJ).

- *What about my signing on, if I go away on one of these things?* If you will be earning money, then you should sign off the dole and sign on again when you return. Explain what you are doing to the UBO and the DHSS.

  If you will not be earning any money (e.g. going on a workcamp) and you will be away for less than four weeks, ask the UBO for a *Holiday Form.* Fill it in, leaving an address where they can find you, in case a job turns up for you. (!) Then you can pick up your benefit when you get back. So long as you can show them that you are 'available for work' and able to return at once if need be, you should have no problems.

- *Travel. Hitch-hiker's Manual,* by Simon Calder (£3.95 from Vacation Work, 9 Park End Street, Oxford). Long distance coach; advertise for a lift on a local notice-board.

- *Daytime youth projects.* In most cities and some towns you will find good activities going on in Centres for the Unemployed and in Community Centres — photography, video-making, drama, crafts, canoe-making, radio-clubs, music bands, creative writing groups, etc. Enough to guarantee a good time.
  Action: Contact the adult/community education service, the youth service, the Centre for the Unemployed (addresses see p. vii) and the YMCA/YWCA to check out what's happening.

- *Duke of Edinburgh's Award groups.* These give you a chance to develop your skills.
  Action: Write for details to Duke of Edinburgh's Award, 5 Prince of Wales Terrace, London W8, or ask at the library for the local group.

- *Outward Bound courses* offer adventurous training courses both in the wild and in the city. There are sometimes schemes to cover fees for unemployed people.
  Action: Write to Outward Bound (City Challenge), Canal House, Drapers Field, Coventry CV1 4LG

- *The Drake Fellowship* offers a ten-day residential course in sailing for unemployed

people aged 16–24, including transport, for only £30, including five days out on expedition. Once you have completed the basic course, there are a variety of 'Follow on projects', including sailing on a Cornish shrimper (cost £1 per day).
Action: Write to The Drake Fellowship, 10 Trinity Square, London EC3P 3AX.

- *YMCA leadership courses* are open to young unemployed people aged 17–23 who have shown willingness and aptitude in working for the good of their community. Courses last 14 days and cost £20.
  Action: Write to Leadership Co-ordinator, YMCA National Centre, Ulverston, Cumbria LA12 8BD.

- *Action Sport:* In many cities there are now active sports projects and unemployed football leagues. In Wales, the Wales TUC organised a 'Dole Olympics' in 1985. In Leicester, there is a weekly programme of free sports activities all over the city.
  Action: Contact the youth service, Centre for the Unemployed or Council leisure services department (addresses p. vii).

- *Money:*
  1. If you want to do something active to help you develop your life, but you've got no money, the Prince's Trust may be able to help with a grant of up to £300.
     Action: Write to Prince's Trust, Royal Jubilee Trusts, 8 Bedford Row, London WC1R 4BU.
  2. You can also get financial help if you are involved in activities which help other people and the community from the Queen's Silver Jubilee Trust — same address.
  3. The King George's Jubilee Trust can help if you are involved in a 'voluntary youth project' — same address.
  4. If you are forming a new group with other young unemployed people, you can apply for a £200 'Launchpad' grant from **Church Action with the Unemployed, Holywell Centre, 1 Phipp Street, London EC2A 4PS**. They have also run successful projects in specific cities giving Personal Launch-pad Grants to unemployed people (see Chapter 14).
  5. Don't forget that you can also do odd jobs to raise money for a group activity — see Chapter 5, p. 55.

6. Starting your own business

With the right kind of support, young people are managing to set up their own small businesses successfully. The details are in Chapter 11.

Other kinds of work

- *Building sites* take on labourers at 8.00 am in the morning. *Hotels and cafés* take on extra staff in the summer. *Farms* take on extra labour at harvest time: potato-picking in Dyfed, Cornwall and on the east coast in early June, elsewhere inland later; soft fruit picking, early July; plums and apples later in Worcestershire. This kind of work is all piece-work, so it takes a week or two before you are quick enough to earn any big money.

- *Residential jobs. The Lady* carries small ads for living-in jobs as maids, au-pairs, home-helps, etc. Social Service Departments can give you lists of private homes for old people and children where there might be work. *Horse and Hound* has small ads for living-in jobs with horses and other outdoor work. You could advertise in either of these magazines yourself e.g.:

> **Strong lad/healthy lass**
> **seeks work**
>
> **Will consider anything legal.**
>
> Box300

Notes for youth workers

The **National Youth Bureau** publishes excellent directories and information packs. Particularly recommended are:

- *Beyond The Drop-In Centre* (free)
- *Work Alternatives and Alternatives to Work* (£1.75)
- *Anti-Racist Youth Work* (0.95p)
- *Working with Girls* (£2.95)
- *Rural Youth Work* (£1.00)
- *Sparetime Sharetime* (free)

Send 50p postage when ordering free materials, and ask for their publications list. (National Youth Bureau (Sales), 17 Albion Street, Leicester LE1 6GD)

Training, Unemployment and the Meaning of Life, by Guy Dauncey, is especially written for young people to encourage them to adopt a positive approach to being unemployed. It builds a lot of group exercises into the text. Price £3.95 from CRAC, Bateman Street, Cambridge CB2 2HN.

Also highly recommended is *A Sense of Direction: Exploring New Prospects with Unemployed Young People*, which explains the need for detailed personal encouragement work, alongside well organised group activities. £3.00 from Community Projects Foundation, 60 Highbury Grove, London N5 2AG.

WOMEN

Introduction

As unemployment rises, so do the little voices that say 'The women should go back home, and leave the jobs for the men'. In a number of places, women are the first to be told they are no longer needed, and you can almost *hear* the employer saying to himself 'The job isn't so important to them, so we'll throw them out first.'

If some men feel so strongly that children need a parent at home, they are at liberty to stay at home themselves. It is very important that the unemployment crisis is not used to erode women's rights, and their freedom to choose what they do with their lives.

Although women's unemployment is rising faster than men's, 'the unemployed' are often taken to mean men, single women, and young people only. Much is talked about equality, but when it comes down to it, women so often still end up in traditional women's jobs such as clerks, cashiers, secretaries, maids, cleaners, shop assistants, nurses and factory hands. Only 1 per cent of bank managers, electrical engineers and surgeons are women. 92 per cent of nurses, 91 per cent of office cleaners, and 99 per cent of secretaries/typists are women. Why not consider working in a traditionally male job? Whatever you want to do, aim high!

The microprocessor revolution is going to cut quite sharply into one particular area that has traditionally been women's — typing — which could lose up to 40 per cent of its workforce to the word processor. Much of the low-paid routine factory work is also in line for takeover by automation and robots.

Adequate child-care, training and school holiday provision are needed, and above all a shift in values and attitudes by men. It is not 'unmanly' to take joint responsibility for child-care and housework. Men who are unemployed with families have a wonderful opportunity to develop the caring, nurturing side of their personality by undertaking these tasks, but all too often stick to outdated sex-roles.

The good news is that women's projects and initiatives are expanding and there is a supportive network of women's centres and self-help groups around the country, as well as a growing number of useful books and publications.

Survival strategies

In a realistic survival strategy for the 1980s, these might be the choices:

1. Plan on getting a *full-time job,* in competition with men. This means being sharper, brighter and better than men. If women give up their assaults on men's jobs then woe betide us all, because those jobs *need* women to prise apart the self-satisfied male 'we-know-it-all' attitudes that still prevail. When our organisations and enterprises begin to be a real partnership between men and women, then we'll be getting somewhere. Chapter 4 has advice on practical job-hunting. See also below.

2. Aim to get decent *part-time work.* If this isn't going to mean the normal choice of dead-end jobs, it will have to mean that *jobsharing* becomes more a part of everyday life, so that two people can share a good job together, and work out the hours or weeks as they find best (see Chapter 4, p. 35).

   You can also use your own initiative to combine part-time work with training (see Chapter 8).

   There is also *home-work*, which has traditionally been one of the most exploited areas of women's work (See Resource Q).

3. Become *self-employed,* setting up a new *co-operative*, as 'Little Women' did, or converting an existing way of working into a co-operative, as the Kennington Office Cleaners Co-operative did (See Chapter 11).

4. *Involvement in local neighbourhood action and activities*. If there is no paid work going, life need not return to being a trap. Many women are involved in local activities, tenants' associations, and setting up community enterprises (see Chapter 5).

5. *Involvement in women's groups.* These help women build up their self-confidence, find their voices, and discover their strength. In a male-dominated society, these groups are vital for developing local strategies for action and activity, and giving support and encouragement to women.

   There are women's groups in most cities and towns, and in the larger cities there are often women's centres.

   Write to the **Spare Rib Collective**, enclosing a stamped addressed envelope and asking for details of the nearest group, or contact **A Woman's Place** or the Information Unit at EOC. Information about black women's centres and networks for lesbians, women with disabilities, and for young and older women can also be obtained from these sources. If all else fails, advertise (in *Spare Rib* or your local paper), and set up your own group, using advice and support from existing groups (See A, B, R below).

6. *Study, education, training.* The MSC's 'Wider Opportunities for Women' courses, and 'Return to Work' or 'Return to Study' courses are particularly useful for women who have had a break to have children. Approach your local adult education centre or WEA and check out what women's courses they run. Contact Sue Waddington, NIACE, 47 New Walk, Leicester LE1 6TE to find out about 'Replan' adult education initiatives for unemployed women (see p. 107). It is also worth investigating women's training workshops. There are ways of studying at home too — e.g. the Open University and local self-help study circle (see Chapter 8). (See A, B, C, L, M, N, O, P, Q, S below).

Child care. Don't struggle with this on your own. It is important to raise the question of child-care if you plan to do a training course, as more adult education providers are beginning to recognise child-care needs and offer assistance. Others may need to be pushed. Likewise some community organisations offer crèches or play-schemes. If you live with a man, encourage him to take more responsibility (a women's group/assertiveness training may provide useful support for this!). There are useful organisations and publications available for women who have sole responsibility for child-care. See below (A,B,X)

Resources listing

A. The **Equal Opportunities Commission (EOC)** has produced a *free* booklet called *Fresh Start*, which covers most things to do with training and education for women returning to work, or thinking about a change of work. They produce a bi-monthly newsletter called *EOC Update*. Available from Jobcentres, or the Equal Opportunities Commission. They also provide:

- a comprehensive information service on women's organisations, women's courses, and women's rights, plus reading lists on a variety of topics including jobsharing and part-time work, new technology, black women.
- legal advice on the application of Sex Discrimination and Equal Pay Acts. Do you know, for example, that interviewers are not allowed to ask women what arrangements they have made for childcare, or whether they are planning to have children, as this is discriminatory?
- research reports on subjects like jobsharing and day care for children. They also give grants to voluntary organisations and individuals for research projects or conferences, which ought to be useful if you want to organise an event.

Write to: EOC, Overseas House, Manchester M3 3HN, Tel 061–833 9244

B. A Woman's Place, Hungerford House, Victoria Embankment, London WC2, Tel 01–836 6081 is a useful contact point for information about women's networks, courses and training.

C. The base for a number of women's organisations which can give national as well as local information is **Tindle Manor**, 52-54 Featherstone Street, London EC1 8RT. It is also the postal address for Sisters Against Disablement. Useful telephone numbers are:

Women and Manual Trades	01–251 9192
Rights of Women	01–251 6577
Feminist Audio Books (for partially sighted and blind women)	01–251 2908
Lesbian Line	01–251 6911

D. The **Women's National Commission**. Government Offices, Great George Street, London SW1P 3AQ, Tel 01–233 4208 attached to the Cabinet Office, has a free list of the more formal women's organisations in Great Britain and produces a leaflet *Second Chances for Women.*

E. The **National Council for Civil Liberties**, 21 Tabard Street, London SE1 4LA, Tel 01–403 3888. The Women's Rights Unit can answer questions about legal rights and produces useful 'women's rights' sheets.

F. Useful sources of information on choosing a career are

- *Equal Opportunities: A Careers Guide for Women and Men*, by Ruth Miller (Penguin, revised regularly).
- *What Else Can a Housewife Do?,* published by Careers and Occupational Information Centre (COIC), MSC, Sheffield. Available from the Careers Services (see p. vii) in larger towns, or MSC. The COIC also publish *What Else Can a Nurse/Teacher/Secretary Do?*, and many other useful leaflets.

G. Careers advice. See Chapter 8 regarding free education and careers advice services. Women in London with a little cash to spare can seek careers advice from the *National Advisory Centre on Careers for Women,* Drayton House, 30 Garden Street, London WC1H 0AY, Tel 01–799 2129. This is a long-established charity which offers good professional advice and also publishes a useful directory of professions with notes on openings for mature entrants and part-timers called *Returners.*

H. Useful books designed to help women at work move up the ladder, but also useful for women getting back into employment are:

- *The Working Women's Guide*, by Liz Hodkinson (Thorson, 1985)
- *Strategies for Women at Work*, by Janice Larouche/Regina Ryan (Unwin, 1985)

I. Women's employment projects and training workshops. There are a growing number of women's employment projects and women's only workshops, generally financed jointly by EEC funding, local authorities and Urban Programme. The EOC can provide a full list. e.g.:

- *Lewisham Women and Employment Project,* 74 Deptford High Street, London SE8. This well-established group provides information and advice about training, employment and co-operative working opportunities for local women, and is involved in campaigning and project development with groups of women, including developing plans for a women's training centre, helping a mobile crèche, and assisting a group of women to establish Urdu classes. They have published some interesting research studies including *Lewisham's Wageless Women, The Invisible Unemployed,* and *Women's Work in Deptford, the Double Shift.*

- *Women and Employment in Merseyside* is an umbrella group for a number of women's employment groups. It has produced reports on women and employment in Merseyside. Women's Employment Project Group, 14 Colquitt Street, Liverpool L14.
- *Milton Keynes Women and Work,* The Bake House, 6 Church Street, Wolverton, Milton Keynes MK13 5JM, Tel 0908-310372. This group organises return to work courses; gives information on, e.g. child-care; produces pamphlets, and gives talks on equal opportunities in schools.

J. Women's training workshops offer training, confidence-building and support in learning traditionally 'masculine' skills such as woodwork, plumbing, bricklaying and electronics. They exist in a number of areas including Lambeth, Harringay, Charlton, Southwark and Notting Hill in London, and Bristol, Bath, South Glamorgan, Leeds and Sheffield. Child-care is usually available. A full list of addresses can be obtained from the EOC or Women and Manual Trades Groups (see K below).

K. Women and Manual Trades Groups (WAMT). There are currently some thirteen branches which aim to create and support a network of tradeswomen and produce a directory and newsletter. They also operate a job vacancy and training information system, campaign against discrimination and visit schools to encourage young women. The London group will give contacts around the country. (Resource C above.)

L. Women and new technology. Women in Information Technology (WIT) is a network of women involved in technology. Contact: WIT, c/o Microsyster. (Resource N above.)

Some recent books offer useful information about the effects of new technology on women's jobs. These include:

- *Your job in the 1980s: A Women's Guide to New Technology* (Pluto, 1982);
- *Machinery of Dominance: Women, Men and Technical Know How,* by Cynthia Cockburn (Pluto, 1986).

The EOC have a list of science and technology courses aimed particularly at women; e.g. The Merseyside Women's Technology Scheme, and the Strathclyde Practical Training and Refresher Course for Women.

The Open University now runs a Women and Technology Returner course (OU, Walton Hall, Milton Keynes).

M. Women Into Science and Engineering (WISE). The EOC and Engineering Council launched the WISE Campaign in 1984 to encourage girls and women to study science and consider the opportunities in engineering. Much useful information, posters and videos were produced and can be obtained from the EOC. The Engineering Council currently offers scholarships to encourage women who have had a break to have children to undertake further training or research in engineering. Contact EOC (Resource A).

N. Women and computing. Computing doesn't have to be violent Space Invader games and mystifying!

- *Microsyster* help groups of women use computers and are a focus of information about women's computer training and useful 'women friendly' publications about computing. Microsyster, Wesley House, 4 Wild Court, off Kingsway London WC2B 5AU, Tel 01–430 0655.

- *Teaching Computing to Women* by Mary Jennings and Robyn Smits. A women's computer course teaching pack which provides material for discussion relating to computer-based technology, and also outlines for introductory courses. Available from National Extension College, 18 Brooklands Avenue, Cambridge CB2 2HN, price £9.95).

O. Professional networks. If you're out of work but trained in a particular career and wanting to get back to it, check if there are any women's networks.

Examples of such networks include: Women in the Media, Women in Banking, Women in Personnel Management, Women in Technology, (information from resources A, B and D). The National Organisation for Women's Management Education (NOWME), 29 Burkes Road, Beaconsfield, Bucks have a newsletter and may provide useful information and contacts for women seeking to enter or return to this field. See *Your Brilliant Career* by Audrey Slaughter (Optium), which gives addresses of several networks.

P. Women Returners. Useful publications are:

- *Simple Steps for Returners,* by Pamela Anderson, from 9 Poland Street, London W1V 3DG. This helps women explore paid and unpaid options, and is full of useful case studies.
- *Women Returning to Work,* by Sherce Smith, is the report of 6 consultation days to discuss the issues held by the Job-Change Project, 318 Summer Lane, Newtown, Birmingham, in 1985.
- *Equality for Some* is a tape study pack to help women returning to work or study. (National Extension College, 18 Brooklands Avenue, Cambridge CB2 2HN.)

Q. Part-time work, Jobsharing and Working at Home.

- *Part-time Work,* by Judith Humphries, 1986 (Kogan Page), includes interviews with over thirty women and opportunities in six broad occupational groups from shop work to the professions.
- *Jobsharing information* can be obtained from New Ways to Work, 309 Upper Street, London N1 2TY, Tel 01–226 4026, and from the EOC.
- *The Home-Workers Association* (9 Poland Street, London W1V 3DG) exists to support people who do piece-work at home (often at very low rates). They publish a newsletter, called *Home News.* The group is campaigning for higher wages and for better organisation among home-workers. In order to be an organisation with any influence, it needs home-workers to get in touch and help the campaign.
- *Earning Money at Home* lists many useful ideas. (£5.95, Consumers Association 14 Buckingham Street, London WC2)

R. Women's groups and magazines.

- *Getting Started* is a collection of ideas and information of practical use to groups of women. (WEA, 9 Upper Berkeley Street, London W1H 8BY.)
- *Raising Money for Women: A Survivor's Guide*, by Marion Bourman and Michael Norton (NCVO/ Bedford Press, 1986). Could help get funds for projects.
- The magazine *Spare Rib* contains a lot of material of interest to women, including features on employment and women's projects, and regular listings of meetings, events, groups' addresses, practical advice, etc. It is available monthly from news-agents, price 70p, or from 27 Clerkenwell Close, London EC1R 0AT.

Other useful magazines which contain adverts for jobs in women's projects:

- *Everywoman* — a monthly magazine bridging the gap between conventional women's magazines and *Spare Rib*.
- *Outwrite* — a women's newspaper. 30p from newsagents, £4 per year (unwaged) from Oxford House, Derbyshire Street, London E2. Strong, fighting spirit, runs regular features on unemployment, women's rights, etc.
- *Black Feminist Newsletter* — unwaged £1.50 for 6 copies, from A Woman's Place (see Resource B).

Women's Centres often have back copies of these magazines available to look at free. It can be inspiring to read of other women's struggles and successes, and to feel connected with the women's movement.

- *Women's counselling networks*. There is an inspiring and empowering *Re-evaluation, Counselling Women's Newsletter,* available from Rosie Brennan, High Street, Stratford-on-Avon (90p + postage).

S. Inspiration from books and other people's stories. Take a trip to the library and be inspired by reading some of the recent books published by women's presses such as Virago, Sheba and Pandora Press, e.g.

- *Through the Break: Women and Personal Crisis,* Pearlie McNeil, *et al* (eds), Sheba,1985, which explores personal crisis. Women from many backgrounds write of their experiences and how they coped (often gaining great strength from self-help groups).
- *A Wealth of Experience: The Lives of Older Women,* Pandora Press, 1985. Chapters by different women, including 'Staying Power', 'Making a Home Away from Home' (A Jamaican woman's experience in England) and 'Finding the Strong Inner Core'.
- *The Things that Divide Us,* Faith Conlan, *et al* (eds), Seal Press, 1985, is a collection of fictional stories exploring in a thought-provoking way issues such as racism, sexism and fear of homosexuality (homophobia) which can divide women.

T. Videos. Looking at a video can provoke valuable discussion about women's issues in a women's group or mixed Unemployment Action Group/Drop In Centre. *Circles* — Women's Film and Video Distribution, 113 Roman Road, London E2 0HU, Tel 01–981 6828, and *Cinema of Women* (COW films), Unit 13, 31 Clerkenwell Close, London EC1R 0AT, Tel 01–251 4978. You may be able to get involved in a women's video project such as WIMPS (Women in Moving Pictures) in Bristol and learn film-making skills yourself.

U. Wider Opportunities for Women courses (WOW) are part of the wider opportunities training programme run by the Manpower Services Commission (MSC) to help adults return to work. In some areas they are called 'New Opportunities for Women', or something similar. If you can get a full-time place on one of these courses, you will be paid an allowance.

The courses are both full- and part-time. They give you a chance to try your hand at a wide range of different kinds of work — welding, car maintenance, TV repair, hairdressing, typing, office work, catering, work in a design office, carpentry, gardening, hotel work, etc. You will be offered relevant information about jobs, training, education, etc., and you will be able to visit factories, offices, day nurseries, etc. You will also get advice concerning children, tax, application forms and interviews, effective speaking, etc.

You can apply for a WOW course if:

- you have not worked full-time for at least two years;
- you are available for work;

- you are at least 18 years old and you can tot up a total of two years that you have been away from full-time education;
- you are not sure what sort of work you'd like to do.

'Open Forum' groups: all the women on a course are given the chance to join in an 'Open Forum' group, where they get together to talk things over, and to share their feelings, ideas, problems, etc. (e.g. how to cope with picking the children up from school). The groups are very helpful for discovering that you are not alone in feeling guilty, inadequate or nervous about returning to work.

How to find out more: ask at the Jobcentre.

> Valerie, who now runs a domestic valeting company, attended a 'women only' course: 'I would have thought twice about attending the course if it hadn't been just women. What was really good was that it fitted in with school hours, and for women with children under school age child-minding was organised.'

V. 'Return to Work' and 'Return to Study' courses. There is a vast variety of courses for people who left school some years ago, perhaps with no or only a few 'O' levels, or who have a rusty 'A' level or two, and who now want to train for a new career and/or go on to higher education, or just keep their brains in trim.

'Courses vary enormously in content and organisation, but they all have one thing in common: they act as confidence restorers.' (From *Second Chance Education,* by Ruth Miller. See Chapter 8.)

The courses are not always well advertised, so you should ask at your local college.

Study at Home

If you would like to return to study but are unable to get to a college easily, you may be able to study at home. The Open University and the National Extension College produce useful courses. See the 'study at home' section of Chapter 8, p. 108.

Other sources of information in this area are:

- *Women Returners Network,* Park Square, Luton, Bedfordshire, Tel 0582-34111, who produce a national directory of courses and contacts for women who wish to return to education or training;
- *It's Never Too Late,* by Joan Perkins, published by Harrap. A practical guide for continuing education for women of all ages.
- *Fresh Start,* by the EOC, see Resource A.

Assertiveness courses for women are now widespread. Check with your local adult education department, and see Chapter 10.

W. WEA produce a *Women's Studies Publications List* with some useful publications including *Women at the Crossroads: Ten Years of New Opportunities for Women, courses in the Northern District,* a case study describing NOW courses. This costs 75p. They also produce a *Women's Studies Newsletter* — a twice-yearly journal for supporters of and participants in women's education. Annual subscription £2.50, both from WEA (9 Upper Berkeley Street, London W1)

X. Child-care. There is great need for the provision of good, flexible crèches, nurseries, child minders, play groups after school and holiday play schemes. Much has been done in some areas by groups of women getting together and campaigning for facilities. Some groups have put together useful local directories of facilities. These include:

- *The Working Mothers Handbook*, (Working Mothers Association, 23 Webbs Road, London SW11 6RO, £2.00)
- *The Titch Hikers Guide to Bristol,* by the NCT Bristol branch, third edition 1985, (PO Box 296, Bristol BS99 71R, £1.50)

The National Childbirth Trust, 9 Queensborough Terrace, London W2 3TB, produces a number of useful leaflets.

The *National Childminding Association* is a rapidly growing organisation. Its publications include booklets on organising childminding: NCMA 204/206 High Street, Bromley, Kent.

Classes with Childcare, a WEA pamphlet, is designed to win greater support for childcare provision in adult education, and offers practical support in its planning and organisation. (Resource W)

Single Parents. Gingerbread run a large number of groups. (35 Wellington Street, London WC2 7BN, Tel 01–240 0953.)

On Your Own, by Jean Shapiro, Pandora Press, 1985. A book for women on their own, including single parents. It includes a wide range of helpful information, and lists a wide range of organisations. It should be obtainable from libraries.

Women x Two: How to Cope with a Double Life, by Mary Kenny, Hamlyn, is useful reading for women seeking to combine work with children.

Y. Campaigning on women's issues.

- *Women and policy-making.* Do you know how many women MPs there are? In 1987 the figures stand at 41 women to 609 male MPs. Women represent the majority of the population (52 per cent), and yet 'women's issues' are relegated to the margins of political concerns. Women are also very under- represented in local government. The new women's committees being set up in some of the most progressive local authorities urgently need support and backing from women in the community.
- Women's energy is needed to transform our male-dominated political structures. Try reading *'52% Getting Women's Power Into Politics,'* by Barbara Rogers, The Women's Press, 1983.
- Another idea might be joining a women's peace group or women and social security group (information from EOC — Resources A).
- Finally, finding out about the struggles of women world-wide can be inspiring. For example, try reading a United Nations Report *Nairobi: Forward Looking Strategies for the Advancement of Women to the Year 2000.* This report was drawn up following the UN Women's Conference in Nairobi, Kenya, in 1985. The conference was attended by nearly 2,000 women from 160 countries. The report lays out strategies to be taken at national, regional and international levels to improve women's status and increase women's participation in planning and implementation of all policies. This report is available from the Women's National Commission. (Resource D).

  A leaflet from the EOC, *Forward with Nairobi,* highlights sections which women's groups can use to support campaigns for more resources and political action by Government.

  A book with a wonderful title, *Sisterhood is Global,* by Robin Morgan, Penguin, 1985, contains original articles by leading women from 70 countries.

Z. **Women and unemployed centres.** In many unemployed centres, women feel unwelcome. There are ways to overcome this:
- best of all, encourage women to apply for the positions running the centre, especially manager;
- set aside a women's day, when the men are not present;
- set up a joint men/women discussion group, to find ways to encourage more women to come in.

> In Ashington, a woman became Centre Manager and obtained special grant aid to develop women's activities. They set up special women's courses with a crèche. They ran a Women's Fair, and have gone on to establish the Wansbeck Craft Group, a new children's clothes shop, two all-women co-operatives (a day nursery and a secretarial service), a regular DIY Women's Workshop running every week, and a Women's Health Advice Centre. Whoever said that Centres for the Unemployed didn't work? (For information about Centres for the Unemployed, see Chapter 8, p. 107.)

ETHNIC MINORITIES

Racism and effective 'whites only' discrimination add considerably to the difficulties that unemployed black people experience. The unemployment rate for people in ethnic minorities is consistently higher than for similar white people.

Figures from the 1985 Labour Force Survey show that unemployment in the UK is shared out among different racial groups as follows:

Whites: 10%
Indians: 17%
West Indians: 21%
Pakistani/Bangladeshi: 31%

On your own, there is very little that you can do. You can take a case of discrimination to an industrial tribunal, if you have good evidence that an employer is discriminating against you because of your race, colour or nationality, or if you have evidence that you have been offered a job on less favourable terms than others. But without help from others, you'll find it difficult to get far.

With help from others who share your colour, race or nationality, everything changes.

Group support

- In Camden, The Bengali Workers Action Group provides personal, emotional and moral support to Bengali people who are unemployed. They will intervene, if they think that there has been discrimination, and will take individual cases to the Commission for Racial Equality. (1 Robert Street, London NW1)
- Also in Camden, the Chinese centre, the Afro-Caribbean Organisation, Camden Black Sisters (and other groups) do likewise. When someone meets with trouble, the weight of the group is there to fight, support, campaign and do whatever needs doing.

- The Camden Black Workers Group, with several hundred members, helps unite these different ethnic initiatives. They will intervene and support black workers who need support — legal, emotional or practical. Funded jointly by NALGO and Camden Council. (c/o Camden Town Hall, Euston Road, London NW1)
- In Stepney, the Bangladesh Youth League has established a special Employment Development Project to assist their unemployed members. They encourage young people to start their own businesses, run an advice centre for young people, and run their own training schemes for restaurant workers, in tailoring and in how to operate computers. They also offer counselling, mother-tongue classes, provide confidence-building and interview technique sessions, and run a youth club. (41a Brick Lane, London E1)
- In Wandsworth, a number of different black people's organisations have joined forces, to set up a pioneering Black People's Development Agency, to promote racially just, viable economic development in Wandsworth. The Agency will cover all aspects of black economic development in the borough, including business creation and funding, employment, education and training. (c/o Donald McTernan, Popular Planning Project, Old Chesterton Centre, 116 Battersea Park Road, London SW11 4LY)

Whether or not you want specific help with a problem, such as discrimination, the process of mutual support has a thousand things to recommend it. In most of Britain's major cities, there are similar groups, many of which are developing support systems for unemployed people. To get in touch with a group locally, contact your local Council for Community Relations (ask the Citizens Advice Bureau).

Legal help

If there are no such groups locally, and you want help to take action against an employer for discrimination, you will be able to get help from a youth or community worker, a Neighbourhood Law Centre or the Citizens Advice Bureau. You can get free legal advice under the 'Green Form' scheme. Ask at the Citizens Advice Bureau to find out which local solicitors have a reputation for doing good work in this area, and then ask for an appointment.

For further advice and support, write to the Commission for Racial Equality, Elliot House, 10/12 Allington Street, London SW1E 5EH, Tel 01–828 7022, explaining your case, and also asking for a copy of *Employment — Your Rights to Equal Treatment under the Race Relations Act, 1976.*

Equal opportunities – theory and practice

A second essential part of anti-racist employment work concerns 'equal opportunities' policy and practice. A small but growing number of companies are adopting equal opportunities policies, and adorning their advertisements with big print telling the world; but between policy and practice is quite a gap. In Camden, one of the boroughs in the forefront of anti-racist intentions, only 5 per cent of 'equal opportunities' employers are reckoned by the Community Relations Council to really follow through on their commitment.

An important aspect of community race relations work, therefore, concerns getting employers to implement their commitment:

- by adopting a clear policy statement in favour of equal opportunities;
- by helping people in ethnic minorities to upgrade their skills and apply for promotion, with the help of specific training courses;
- by collecting a thorough database, giving information about the numbers and positions of black people;
- by monitoring recruitment and internal promotion;
- by looking critically at their recruitment practices — never filling positions via the grapevine, which usually keeps jobs in the (white) family, advertising in the ethnic newspapers, and carrying out special recruitment drives in community organisations and training schemes attended by people from minority groups;
- by developing a proper action plan to implement equal opportunities policies, involving assignment of responsibilities, targeting, proper resourcing and timetabling.

Language training

The MSC runs special English language training courses for members of ethnic minorities, including job-related aspects of the language. The courses run in the Wider Opportunities Training Programme include *Skills-linked and Preparatory English as a Second Language* modules (see p. 109).

Ashram community service project

Something else to set your mind thinking! In Sparkbrook, Birmingham, a group of people have created a neighbourhood employment project in which they are attempting to generate meaningful work, based on the traditional handicraft and rural skills of the local Pakistani Muslim community. In Ashram Acres, another aspect of the project, a series of gardens have been rescued from dereliction and are now being cultivated organically with Asian vegetables. Goats, rabbits, chickens, ducks and bees are kept there and solar panels help provide energy. And in Ashram House, a third aspect, a group of people are living collectively, committed to developing a new lifestyle, 'sharing commitments and obligations to our neighbours, money, time, energy, meals, laughs and anxieties'.

For more information, write to Ashram Community Service Project, 23/25 Grantham Road, Sparkbrook, Birmingham B11 1LU.

Resources

Resources On and Against Racism (£2.25, National Youth Bureau, 17 Albion Street, Leicester LE1 6GD) is a detailed information pack covering books, pamphlets, videos, posters, organisations etc.

PEOPLE WITH DISABILITIES

Special help

Needless to say, circumstances are always that much harder for people with a disability than for those without.

There are various ways in which disabled people can get special help in finding suitable employment:

1. The Employment Services Division employs *Disablement Resettlement Officers* (DROs) whose job it is to assess, advise and help any person who is disabled. They can be found through the Jobcentre. The ESD also runs Employment Rehabilitation Centres which put on special residential and non-residential training courses for disabled people. 'Disablement' can cover such things as recurring depression or nervousness, as well as physical disability. If a person has a problem which effectively prevents him or her from settling into steady employment, help from the DRO may be possible.

   Rehabilitation, Retraining, Resettlement, published by the MSC, gives vital information and advice on training and employment. Ask at Jobcentres. MSC also publishes leaflets on *Employing Disabled People* (EPL 61 — mention it to an employer), *Into Work* (EPL 41) as well as *Aids and Adaptations* (EPL 71).

2. If a person who is disabled carries a *Green Disablement Card* which certifies that the disability is officially recognised, employers can then claim the person as one of their required quota of disabled people. Also, if a disability is obvious, an employer may want to see the green card, and without it the person may not get the job. However, people with minor, invisible disabilities holding green cards do not have to show them if they choose not to, and can also ask to have them withdrawn.

3. Disabled people over 16 can join any MSC Adult Training Scheme course without waiting until they are 18. The other rules may also be suspended — you can take longer over a course and receive extra help with housing and transport problems, for instance. See the leaflets *Training Opportunities for Disabled People*, *Residential Training for Disabled People* and *The Open Tech Programme*, available at Jobcentres.

4. The leaflet HB1 *Help for Handicapped people* (from post offices) gives details of what is available through the DHSS by way of extra benefits and services. The Social Services Department will probably be able to help too. See also the leaflet HB2 *Aids for the Disabled.*

5. *Job Introduction for Disabled Workers* is a scheme that encourages employers to take

disabled people on trial, in the hope that this might lead to permanent employment. The employer receives £45 a week for a trial period. Details from Job Centres.

6. Under certain circumstances a registered disabled person who is unable to use public transport can get *help with travel costs* to and from work. See leaflet DPL 13, from Jobcentres.

7. *Employers can receive a wide range of aids* from the Manpower Services Commission to help a disabled person more easily — special fittings for tools and typewriters, special machine modifications, etc. Many employers may not know this, and may therefore think it would be very difficult to take on a disabled person. If you carry leaflet EPL 71 (from Jobcentres) with you when you go jobhunting, this might help. Get advice from the DROs, too. Adaptations to buildings necessary for the disabled employee may also be carried out by MSC. See also *Employing Disabled People,* EPL 147. For certain visually handicapped people a part-time sighted reader may be employed with financial help from MSC.

8. *Sheltered employment.* DROs can give information about the availability of sheltered employment for severely disabled people in special workshops or in sheltered placement schemes where participants work in ordinary companies. Special workshops are run by Remploy, local authorities, and voluntary bodies. See leaflets DPL 1, *Employment in Sheltered Workshops*, and EPL 99, *Sheltered Employment and You.*

9. The MSC publishes a free newspaper called *New Outlook*, which gives news and stories on its various disability schemes. You can receive free copies by writing to MSC, Distribution Unit (NO), Room E825, Moorfoot, Sheffield S1 4PQ.

Sources of advice and information

1. *The Disabled Living Foundation,* 346 Kensington High Street, London W14 8NS offers an information service covering almost every subject with guides and information sheets, including one on *Further Adult and Higher Education — Assessment and Training for the Physically Handicapped* which is **essential reading**. Members of the general public may use the service free of charge.

   See also *Coping with Disability*, 1984, a practical handbook, and *Employment for Handicapped People: Bibliography* (£7.00).

2. *Organisations/campaign groups run by disabled people who have first-hand experience of the difficulties.* Such groups are now active in many large cities, although often struggling for funds.

   One very successful example is the *Derbyshire Coalition of Disabled People* (DCDP) at 117 High Street, Clay Cross, Derbyshire, Tel Chesterfield 865305/566362. This was started following the 1981 'International Year of the Disabled' and is supported by Derbyshire City Council. 'Traditionally disabled people have been spoken for by others speaking on their behalf. DCDP gives all disabled people in Derbyshire a voice of their own.' Their motto is 'Full participation and equality'. As well as offering practical help and supportive counselling, they campaign to 'actively involve people on all advisory and consultative committees in the council', and to 'promote and create opportunities for employment for disabled people'.

   For instance, the *Inter-help Co-op* (c/o Clay Cross address above) is a co-operative run by disabled and able-bodied people working together to provide practical personal help to any disabled person in need, in their own home. Clients generally use their State Attendance Allowance to pay for the help.

DIAL (UK) is a national organisation also based at 117 High Street, Clay Cross, linking together over eighty Disability Information Advice Lines around the country which as a matter of policy generally aim to employ disabled workers. Tel Chesterfield 864498.

The British Council of Organisations of Disabled People (BCODP), Yeoman House, 76 St James Lane, London N10 3DF, is made up of new and long-standing organisations of disabled people, controlled by disabled people. It has standing committees including 'housing and personal support' and 'education', but as yet none specifically on employment. The Secretary can give details of member organisations, including Union of the Physically Impaired against Segregation, DIAL UK, Association of Disabled Professionals, DCDP, and the Nottinghamshire Coalition of Disabled People.

Survivors Speak Out is a network of people who have been in psychiatric hospitals or who have used psychiatric services and want their voice to be heard in the planning of services. It has members around the country, including Bristol and Glasgow, but the contact address is again in Chesterfield! Details from Ivy Buckland, Tontine Road Centre, Chesterfield.

The *Disability Rights Handbook,* published every year in July, is obtainable from Disability Alliance, 25 Denmark Street, London WC2M 8NJ. The 1986 edition costs £2.60. It is reliable, accurate and thorough. *Disability Rights Bulletins* are published to update the handbook (price £1.50, or £5.00 for the *Handbook* and 2 *Bulletins*). The Alliance also publishes *Check Your Rights* guides and *A Right to Work — Disability and Employment.*

3. *RADAR* (Royal Association for Disability and Rehabilitation), 25 Mortimer Street, London W1W 8AB, Tel 01–637 5400, works to remove barriers for disabled people in the areas of education, access and mobility, housing, welfare, holiday and employment. They operate an Education and Training Bureau which can provide home tuition for disabled people, or can enrol them with a correspondence college. Their marvellously comprehensive publications include the following:
   - *Into Work — A Guide For Disabled People,* an attractively produced loose-leaf pack with advice and details on all matters connected with seeking employment. You can obtain this simply by sending an SAE — and it's well worth it.
   - *Employability — Are You Using Your Assets?* Advice to employers on the engagement and retention of individuals who become disabled (1985, 17p).
   - *Get Yourself Going — An Action Handbook For The Handicapped Office Worker.* Useful for disabled people wanting to work in an office or run a business from home.
   - *Opportunities in Micro Electronics for Disabled People* (1982, SAE only).
   - An annual guide published in December, *Holidays for Disabled People,* and a series of *Holiday Factsheets.*
   - *All Write Now* — journalism for disabled people — gives guidelines on writing about disability in local papers or magazines.
   - Monthly newsletter *Radar* (£4.50 annual subscription) and quarterly magazine *Contact* (£3.50 annual subscription).
   - RADAR's publications list includes a full list of relevant MSC leaflets and DHSS leaflets.

4. *Outset,* Drake House, 18 Creekside, Deptford, London SE8 3DZ, Tel 01–692 7141,

is a national charity dedicated to pioneering research and innovative action on issues of concern to people with disabilities. The central employment unit supports employment initiatives in London including Outset Office Services and Outset ITEC.

They have a 'development' package for people interested in setting up similar initiatives, and are particularly keen to develop opportunities and training for disabled people in the expanding area of information technology.

5. *For Students*
   (a) *National Bureau for Handicapped Students,* 40 Brunswick Square, London WC1, Tel 01–278 3459/3450, gives educational advice, organises conferences, and produces a newsletter and useful publications including:
   - *Directory of Residential Colleges for Students with Disabilities;*
   - *Financial Assistance for Students with Disabilities* (revised annually)
   - *After 16 What Next? A Comprehensive Guide For The Disabled School Leaver,* which examines the options of work, education and training.

   (b) *The Open University* can provide considerable assistance for disabled students taking their courses. Contact The Advisor for Disabled Students, The Open University, Walton Hall, Milton Keynes MK7 6AA, Tel 0908-74066.
   (c) *Directory of Opportunities for School Leavers with Disabilities* from Queen Elizabeth Foundation for the Disabled, Leatherhead, Surrey KT22 0BN is another useful guide.

6. *Employment Agencies. Opportunities for the Disabled* provides an employment service which helps with the recruitment, rehabilitation or career development of disabled employees. Its senior staff are on secondment from industry or commerce. There are six regional offices — in London, Birmingham, Leicestershire, Kent, Sussex and Manchester. London office — 1 Bank Buildings, Princes Street, London EC2R 8EV, Tel 01–726 4963, or for other addresses see MSC leaflet EPL 147.

7. *Home working.* See p. 81 and contact Home Opportunities for Professional Employment, 96 Greencraft Gardens, London NW6 3PH.

   Modern technology makes it possible for people with a variety of disabilities to work from home in a wide range of jobs, although it can be lonely. Local authorities and Remploy Ltd also run home working schemes for severely disabled people. You should apply for these through the Jobcentre.

8. *Books*
   (a) *The Directory for Disabled People,* by Ann Darnbrough and Derek Kinrade, (4th Edition, 1985, published by Woodhead/Faulkner with RADAR). This is expensive, but is an extremely comprehensive handbook of information and opportunities for disabled people so it would be worth borrowing from the library.
   (b) *Co-ops With A Difference,* by Maggie Sikking (£4.50, ICOM Co-Publications, 7 Bradbury Street, London N16 8JN) tells the tale of two co-operatives which employ people with a range of special needs.
   (c) *Able to Work,* by Bernadette Fallen, provides a straightforward explanation of the services set up to help disabled people in the fields of education and training. It is obtainable from the Spinal Injuries Association, Yeomans House, 76 St James Lane, Muswell Hill, London N10. (£3 including postage.)
   (d) *With The Power of Each Breath, A Disabled Women's Anthology,* published by Cleis Press, 1986. This is a personal, inspiring and moving book which documents through their own stories the lives of women with different disabilities and 'breaks the silence that exists between themselves and non-disabled women'.

9. *Community Service Volunteers,* 237 Pentonville Road, London N1 9NJ, is a national volunteer agency which involves people of all ages and abilities in community service. It is active in breaking down barriers for disabled people.
   - *The Independent Living Scheme* links long-term (usually one-year full-time) volunteers with severely physically or mentally handicapped individuals to enable them to live in their own home. In some instances volunteers have enabled severely disabled students to complete courses, or have supported people working at home. This scheme is expanding.
   - The *Able to Help Scheme* involves severely disabled young people as full-time volunteers using their abilities to help others.
   - The CSV Advisory Service produces a number of valuable training packs including:

     In Our Own Right (1986 cost £9.50), which looks at issues facing disabled people and encourages the integration of projects for able-bodied and disabled people. Unemployment Centres are not mentioned but might well be. The pack suggests six projects for able-bodied and disabled people, including designing individual aids and clearing country walks together.

     Design with Disabled People (£6.00, 1982) is a guide to involving young people in designing and making aids with and for disabled people. This is an area where there is a great need and considerable scope for job creation.

10. *Help for Specific Disabilities.* There are a large number of specialist organisations which can give specific help. The larger ones, such as the Spastics Society, the Royal National Institute for the Blind (RNIB), and the Royal National Institute for the Deaf (RNID), can provide considerable advice and information on seeking employment or training for people with these handicaps.

    Leaflet EPC 147 from the MSC lists eighteen of these larger specialist organisations, including those mentioned.

    These addresses, and those of other organisations for less common disabilities, can also be obtained from RADAR.

11. *Mental Handicap and Mental Illness.* People suffering from these two disabilities are frequently the victims of considerable prejudice which prevents them from obtaining appropriate employment.

    The Pathway Employment Service, 169a City Road, Cardiff, Tel 0222-482072 (MENCAP) seeks to help mentally handicapped people find employment. They can arrange for a grant to be paid to employers to enable mentally handicapped workers to have a job trial or training.

    A number of other organisations, such as the Home Farm Trust and the Camphill Villages provide opportunities for mentally handicapped people in special communities.

    MIND, The National Association for Mental Health, 22 Harley Street, London W1N 2ED, provides advice and information for people suffering from a period of severe mental illness, such as schizophrenia, and also supports people suffering from the exceedingly common problems of stress, anxiety, depression or agoraphobia. They have a register of creative employment projects, some of which (e.g. the Daily Bread Wholefood co-op in Northampton) mix people recovering from mental breakdowns with other workers in a caring setting, making the most of everyone's abilities.

Inspiring examples

Southwark Enterprise for Disabled Persons is run by a group of disabled people, with six staff, and promotes opportunities for disabled people in both the public and private sectors. It also helps those who wish to work at home find work.

Pallion Business Services in Sunderland is a co-operative of disabled people set up using the Enterprise Allowance Scheme which successfully makes use of computers to provide office and business services for local companies.

Share Community, Alexandra House, 140 Battersea Park Road, London SW11 4NB, Tel 01–622 6885, undertakes action research on training disabled people for open employment. Disabled workers at Share gather and publish information on self help.

EARLY RETIRED PEOPLE

Sources of advice and information

Retirement is a strange idea. It never existed until very recent times. Why should people suddenly stop working, just because they have passed a certain age? Why should they or anyone else without a normal paid 'job' be made to feel they are outside normal society?

The pressures for early retirement are likely to increase, so here are details of a few schemes which offer alternatives:

- *Retired Executives Action Clearing House (REACH)* links retired professionals with charities, voluntary organisations and community groups which need their skills, but cannot afford to pay for them. Many early-retired people work for such organisations for expenses only. (REACH, 89 Southwark Street, London SE1, Tel 01–928 0452)
- *Age Concern* has a number of enterprising self-help schemes to enable the early-retired and the retired to use their skills and abilities actively in the community. (Age Concern, Bernard Sunley House, 60 Pitcairn Road, Mitcham, Surrey.)
- *Success After Sixty* is a special agency for jobs for the retired and the early-retired. (Success after Sixty, 40/41 Old Bond Street, London W1X 3AF.)
- *Trades Skills Register:* the Estate Department at Dartington Hall in Totnes, South Devon has established a service for people living on pensions who can't afford the cost of hiring tradesmen to carry out repair work on their homes. It consists of a register of retired people who are willing to put their skills at the service of other retired people. How much they choose to charge is up to them.

  Anyone with initiative could launch a similar scheme: all it requires is publicity, some leafleting and door-knocking, and keeping a register in a place where people can see it — or duplicating copies, so that every member of the scheme can have one. If members are still drawing Unemployment Benefit or Supplementary Benefit/Income Support, they will need to keep any earnings within the legal limits (see Chapter 12), unless and until that system is changed.
- *Rebuilding supports:* if you have little prospect of finding another job at all before you reach retirement age, the advice in Chapter 2 becomes very important. The transition from work to non-work can be extremely destructive if the supports are not rebuilt. If a positive attitude is taken this crisis can be turned into an opportunity, and the transition to a new pattern of living and working can be achieved successfully.
- *Branching Out: A Workbook for Early Retirement*, by Maggie Smith. This is a very thorough book, written from long experience in running early retirement workshops, and including 25 exercises to help you 'branch out'. Recommended. It is

produced by the same people who publish *Build Your Own Rainbow* — see Chapter 10. (£8.95 or library), Lifeskills Associates, Clarendon Chambers, 51 Clarendon Road, Leeds LS2 9NZ.

- The *Retired Senior Volunteers Project,* run by CSV in Avon and Newcastle, recruits older volunteers to use their skills helping single parent families or linking with schools, teaching for example photography. The *Sesame Project* links retired business people to advise young people setting up in business. (CSV, 237 Pentonville Road, London N1 9JN.)
- *Cross-Over* gives people approaching retirement the chance to sample community work on day release from their jobs. (c/o the Volunteer Centre, 29 Lower Kings Road, Berkhamstead, Herts HP4 2AB.)
- The *Pre-Retirement Association* produces a list of local groups and courses, and publishes *Choice*, and other publications such as *Your Money and Retirement.* (PRA, 19 Undine Street, London SW17 8PP.)
- The *University of the Third Age* organises groups who learn and study together in an informal way. (U3A, 6 Parkside Gardens, London SW19 5EY.)
- The *Open University* encourages older students — see Chapter 8.
- The *Forum on the Rights of the Elderly to Education* (FREE) encourages educational establishments to welcome older people. They produce a newsletter and a Directory of Education Initiatives involving older adults. (Contact Diane Norton, Age Concern, address above.)
- *Become a speaker or an adult education tutor.* If you have skills, whether cactus growing, astronomy or icing cakes, there will be people interested in learning from you, and you can receive a small income too. Approach your local adult education centre (see p. vii). Clubs for old age pensioners or physically handicapped people are also always looking out for people with skills to offer, and for speakers or musicians.
- *New Horizons* (12 Bedford Row, London WC1R 4PU), is a charitable organisation which gives grants to projects involving elderly people, such as the Cheltenham Network, where a group of retired craftspeople teach skills at workshops for able-bodied and physically handicapped unemployed people.
- The *Job Release Scheme*, run by the MSC, lets older workers retire early with an allowance, provided their employer agrees and replaces them with an unemployed person. Contact the Jobcentre for details.

REDUNDANT WORKERS

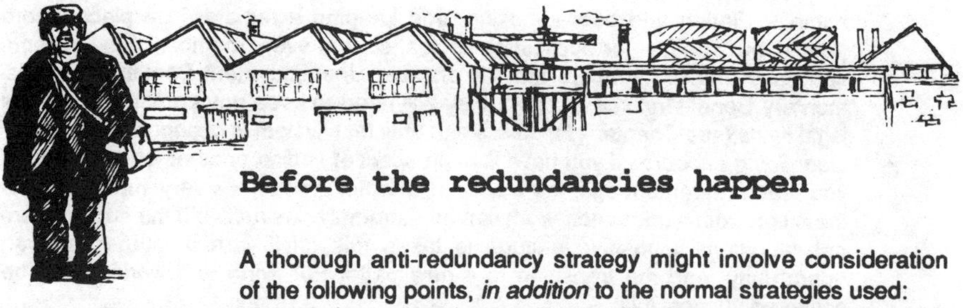

Before the redundancies happen

A thorough anti-redundancy strategy might involve consideration of the following points, *in addition* to the normal strategies used:

- The trade union branch (or a workers/staff council) must try to get access to all the facts, in order to develop appropriate policies. If you don't have information, you will be powerless. A trade union research department may be able to advise.

Is the firm really in severe difficulties? Are the difficulties being caused by internal mismanagement? Is one branch being run down?

- The entire workforce ought to be consulted about ways in which efficiency can be improved, new ideas brought in, or how the firm could diversify into new, more profitable areas. Workers on the shop-floor often have good ideas for change which never get through to management, for various reasons. When the shop stewards combined committee at Lucas Aerospace were facing redundancies several years ago, they circulated the entire workforce for their ideas about socially useful products the firm could make, and received suggestions back that enabled them to put together an alternative 'Corporate Plan', consisting of 200 possible products. If the overall problem is presented as a *collective* problem, the stage is open for the development of collective solutions.
- Once the problem is being looked at collectively, an option such as the entire workforce taking a 10% cut in wages, instead of a 10% cut in numbers, can be considered. One textile firm in Yorkshire has done just this, since the workers were all so keen to keep the firm going.
- Similarly, some workers might be interested in jobsharing, by which two workers agree to share one job between them. It is often the case that some workers would prefer this way of working, since it would leave them half the week (or every other week) for other kinds of work, or for self-employment, etc. (See Chapter 4.)
- *All* firms (especially the larger ones) ought to be working out ideas and plans *now* for future cut-backs in order to widen their range of options when difficulties arise. Trade unions could be pressing for firms to come up with positive and creative approaches. Some firms, for instance, have started encouraging employees to think about ways in which the company might foster new small enterprises under a protective family umbrella which could later become autonomous. ICI are doing some creative work along these lines.
- When redundancies are inevitable, trade unions should widen the normal basis of redundancy negotiations, and ask the firm to include two 'Social Clauses':
  (a) Personal career and jobhunting counselling, as well as money for redundant workers. Professionally-led workshops can help people approach redundancy positively, instead of with despair. Some of the methods in this Handbook can be adapted quite easily to workshop use.
  (b) Funds for the development of new community-based initiatives, to help the community develop its own local economic strength. Chapter 14 mentions some of the work already proceeding in this field; it urgently needs a more secure funding basis.

Information

- *Focus on Redundancy* (Kogan Page)
- The Consumers' Association publish a small book called *Dismissal, Redundancy and Job Hunting* which explains legal aspects concerning redundancy and dismissal that this Handbook does not go into. (Available through libraries, bookshops, or the Consumers' Association, Caxton Hill, Hertford SG13 7LZ.)
- The Department of Employment publishes a series of booklets about the Employment Protection (Consolidation) Act, 1978, which you can obtain free from the Jobcentre. In particular:
  No. 2: *Procedure For Handling Redundancies.*
  No. 6: *Facing Redundancy? Time off for jobhunting or to arrange training.*

The Redundancy Payments Scheme (complete details + basis of payments).
Dismissal — Employees' Rights (complete details).

- *Redundancy: How to Cope with the Psychological and Practical Problems*, by Theresa Crowley. This contains a list of vocational guidance agencies, careers councils and information on the mechanics of redundancy, redeployment, unfair selection for redundancy, short-time working and lay-off problems in obtaining compensation, severance packages, pension rights and other useful information. (Turnstone Press.)
- *The Redundancy File*, by Cooper, Walsh and Blackburn. Practical, lively and humorous, written by people who know what it is like to be out of work. (Edward Arnold, 41 Bedford Square, London WC1B 3QD)
- *Redundant Women* uses research and interviews with Yorkshire factory workers, now redundant, to convey some of the issues. (Womens Press)

Redundancy payments

The minimum qualifying period of employment for redundancy payment is two years — 104 weeks continuous service. Part-time workers must have worked for 16 hours a week or more (or eight hours per week for five years or more).

If an employer offers suitable alternative employment, which is unreasonably refused, payment cannot be claimed. Employees have a four-week statutory trial period in which to find out if the job fulfils its promise or not. If it does not, you may leave and still claim redundancy payment.

There are various ways of interpreting these and other provisions. If you are in any doubt, consult one of the booklets mentioned above.

Tax and benefits

Any redundancy payment which you receive is free of tax.

If you are entitled to redundancy payment, you are also entitled to receive Unemployment Benefit.

You are entitled to claim Housing Benefit while on Unemployment Benefit.

You are also allowed to work part-time while on Unemployment Benefit, if you forego benefit for the days on which you work. (You will need to calculate whether the pay from your part-time job will come to less or more than one-sixth of the weekly benefit.) (Part time work on the Community Programme is excluded.)

For full details of benefits see Chapter 12.

PROFESSIONAL AND EXECUTIVE WORKERS

Introduction

Being unemployed is just as hard for a manager whose firm has gone to the wall, or who has been dismissed, as it is for the redundant steel worker. Many professional people who lose their jobs find that one of the hardest things is the feeling of isolation. The contrast between then and now is acute. All the perks, the status, have gone, and the outlook for finding a new job can sometimes seem pretty bleak.

The underlying philosophy of this Handbook applies just as much, however. Focus on the negative, and you will feel negative, and you will actually lose energy. Focus on the positive, seek the ways in which being unemployed brings you opportunities, and you will find things are not so bad, and that you have the personal resources to pull through.

Professional and executive recruitment

PER is a branch of the Employment Services Division of the MSC which offers a specialist job-finding service to professional and executive people.Anyone who is registered with PER benefits from a lot of help that is simply not available to other unemployed people:

1. PER's free introductory *folder of information,* which includes a copy of a *Guide to Successful Jobhunting.*

2. A free weekly jobs magazine that you receive through the post, called *Executive Post,* which details all the jobs on PER's lists in either (a) sales, marketing, purchasing and distribution, or (b) managerial, executive, professional, technical and scientific occupations. It also carries articles on jobhunting, etc. *Executive Post* can be obtained from Ray Ward, PER, FREEPOST, Runcorn, Cheshire.

   Previous articles including profiles on different careers and articles on jobhunting, redundancy, retirement, and working abroad, etc., can be obtained from *Executive Post* (Previous articles), Fitzwilliam House, 2-4 Fitzwilliam Gate, Sheffield S1 4JH, if you send a large SAE.

3. Free half-day 'Job Hunting Seminars', which include an opportunity to get help in preparing a plan of action for your own job search.

4. Three-day 'Self Presentation Courses', available to candidates who are unemployed or facing redundancy and who have a clear idea of what job they want, but who need to improve their jobhunting skills.

5. Special courses, lasting two weeks, called 'Career Development Courses', suitable for people who feel they need to change their jobs in mid-career, or who are in need of counselling. These courses enlarge on the self presentation courses, with additional opportunity to review one's career so far and one's abilities, with a view to taking new directions. Generous allowances are payable, and the courses are sometimes residential.

The value of these courses should not be under-estimated. Apart from the practical skills you can learn, the opportunity to tackle your own problems in companionship with others is valuable. In some areas of the country these courses are often under-subscribed.

PER's services are available to anyone seeking a job who has 'A' levels or above, or the equivalent. Interviews with PER consultants can be arranged by appointment. You can contact PER through the Jobcentre, or through the phone-book.

PER also offers the 'Bridge Programme', which is available for four months. Unemployed managers are offered the chance to talk over their experiences, and to attend workshops on self-presentation. They can use PER premises as an operating base with reference books, telephones and secretarial help available. You must be over 21 and eligible to register with PER.

Other information

- *Job Training Scheme.* You can obtain a list of MSC-funded higher level courses either through PER or through the Jobcentre. Examples of the kind of higher level course available are management studies, computer programming, higher certificate in electronics, small business management. See Chapter 8 for full details.
- *Career consultancy firms.* There are a number of private firms specialising in career counselling, all of which have something of value to offer, at varying costs, and some of which are excellent. It is *always* worth phoning or writing to get initial information about their service and their costs. The Centre for Professional and Executive Career Development and Counselling, for example, offers employers and individual men and women a range of services to assist them in career development and in a career or employment crisis. It is concerned with career reviews, mid-life changes, career planning and redundancy (CEPEC, Sundridge Park, Bromley, Kent BR1 3JW).

  The Vocational Guidance Association (7 Harley House, Upper Harley Sreet, London NW1) and Career Analysts (Career House, 90 Gloucester Place, London W1H), will take you through psychological tests and draw up personality, interest and aptitude charts, on the basis of which they will suggest suitable lines of work.

  In most larger urban areas you will find details of Career Consultancies in the Yellow Pages under 'Careers Advice'. Find out exactly what a firm is offering before committing your money.
- *Executive Stand-by* is a specialist organisation which deals primarily (though not exclusively) with experienced executives and directors. People aged 50 and over. Short contract employment.

  The role of Executive Stand-by is to bring together employers in need of short-term, temporary or long-term contracts, and people with the experience and skills to meet the needs. They also include voluntary organisations on their books, as well as firms from industry and commerce. Information: Executive Stand-by (310 Chester Road, Hartford, Northwich, Cheshire CW8 2AB, Tel 0606–883 849). They also have offices in Birmingham, Durham and London.
- *Voluntary Services Overseas* places skilled people over 21 in voluntary positions in developing countries outside Europe. Fares and a living allowance are paid. They are keen to take volunteers with skills in education, health services, agriculture, engineering, crafts and trades, and social or business development. Details from VSO, 19 Belgrave Square, London SW1X 8PW.
- You could also write to *International Voluntary Service* for their current vacancy list for skilled volunteer posts overseas. They seek people who:
  - — have a vision of a world-wide community based on justice, equality and co-operation;
  - — genuinely want to assist those disadvantaged by international competitive and exploitative structures;
  - — have useful skills, training and experience to use and pass on.

  Write to Section OS54 IVS (HB), 53 Regent Road, Leicester LE1 6YL.
- *Colleges and universities.* Most colleges and universities have their own careers appointment services. If you are a graduate, or have a college degree of any kind, you can use the careers service of your nearest college or university.
- The MSC offers an opportunity for unemployed managers to be seconded to firms in need of help through the *Management Extension Programme.* Details through the Jobcentre.
- *The Job Change Project* in London offers a free friendly welcome, operating on a self-help basis — see Chapter 5.

Books

- *Guidelines For The Redundant Manager,* by Sue Webb (British Institute of Management [BIM], Management House, Cottingham Road, Corby, Northants). BIM also provide an information and advisory service, Tel 05363–4222.
- *Redundancy Counselling for Managers* (Institute of Personnel Management, 35 Camp Road, London SW19) outlines the services offered by 16 private redundancy counselling services.

MEN

The traditional divisions, which see men as rational, invulnerable and aggressive, and women as emotional, dependent, vulnerable and caring, put us in strait-jackets. Both sexes have the potential for far richer lives than this division permits.

Unemployment can provide a time to think over these issues and create new self-definitions with support from other men who want to escape from the traditional limiting image of masculinity.

Some helpful publications and organisations are:

- *Men's Antisexist Newsletter (MAN),* from 60 Rhymney Street, Cathays, Cardiff, (80p, or £4 for 5 issues).

  Typical articles include 'Personal experiences of trying to live up to a real man image', 'Families', 'Fatherhood', and 'Male friendship'.

  The magazine acts as a contact point for men wishing to join or form a men's group. There are men's support groups in over sixty areas in the United Kingdom. It also lists specific groups — e.g. mental health and men, disabled men's group, and has links with similar organisations in other countries.

- *Men Overcoming Violence (MOVE),* 90 Hampstead Road, Brislington, Bristol, Tel 0272–710767. Set up in 1984 to support and counsel men wishing to change patterns of violent behaviour. It runs group meetings and counselling sessions in Bristol, and workshops around the country on subjects such as 'Dealing with violence and aggression'. It has links with Women's Aid and Incest Survivors projects, and with men in other cities developing similar 'projects of hope', which explore how the conditioning of many boys can lead men to respond to stress (unemployment, relationship difficulties, etc.) with violence. Such projects offer help in changing these destructive patterns.

- *Creche Group Network.* Mark Long, 60 Blantyre Road, Liverpool 15, links groups of men involved in running crèches, and has an excellent newsletter.

Books

- *About Men,* from Broadcasting Support Services, P.O. Box 4000, London W3 6XJ. Published to accompany an excellent series of three films shown on Channel 4 in 1983. The three films, 'About Men & Women', 'About Men and Children' and 'About Men and Men', can be hired from Concord Films Council, 201 Felixstowe Road, Nacton, Ipswich, Suffolk.

- *The Limits of Masculinity,* by Andrew Tolston (Tavistock, 1977). Published some time ago, but still very relevant and thought provoking.
- *Men and Friendship,* by Stuart Miller (Gateway Books). Looks at why men tend to confide in women and are often frightened of deep friendship with other men. It was written after the author experienced deep loneliness following his divorce. It is based on interviews with men in England and the USA.
- *Father Journal — 5 years of awakening to fatherhood,* by David Steinberg (Times Change Press), available from Compendium, 234 Camden High Street, London WC1 and other progressive bookshops. A personal, unglorified account of the role conflicts of a man seeking a close relationship with his new-born son.
- *The Changing Role of Fathers* (Open University Press, 1983). Written in a more academic style, but includes interesting research on patterns of participation by fathers in childcare, and a useful chapter on adopting a shared care-giving lifestyle.
- *Fathers at Home,* by Jan Harper (Penguin, 1980). Again, written in a rather academic style. It looks at the experiences of couples where the mother worked outside the home and the father cared for the children. Based on Australian research at a time before the full impact of unemployment, and therefore tends to look at role swapping as a choice rather than enforced. Nevertheless, it contains useful personal accounts of the rewards and problems of 'challenging traditional roles'.

CHAPTER 8: EDUCATION AND TRAINING

INTRODUCTION – Help with the basics – A training in a skill – Full-time study for a diploma or degree – Residential adult education colleges – Part-time courses – Do a course from home at your own speed – Do a course to widen your horizons and consider new options – Share your skills and knowledge with others – A story of success – Finding out more and getting advice – A few words of frustration – A general word of advice

INTRODUCTION

'After being stuck without work for four months, I was just beginning to rot away in my own boredom. I thought, "Right, this is no good. I'm going to find out everything I can about courses, and studying, I've had enough of going silly at home." I didn't know much about it all to begin with. I called in at the Technical College, and asked to speak to someone about courses.

'Well, by the end of that week I had joined an evening class in home wine-making, and had started thinking about doing a couple of 'O' level courses, to get my rusty brain back into gear. What really shook me, and changed my life, you could say, was when I learnt that as an adult, or "mature student", I could apply for a place at a university or polytechnic, for a degree. A degree! I ask you. I'd never dreamt that I might be able to do that kind of thing. I didn't have any 'A' levels — but I was told it didn't matter.

'I had an interview at Hull University last month — quite a long one — and I had to write a paper for them, and they accepted me! I'm starting a three-year degree course in geography in October, and I'll be getting a full grant to support myself and my family. It's going to make a big difference to my life.'

(Driver, aged 29.)

Did you know that:

You can be paid to learn or train? (through MSC-funded courses and various grants) ......

You can go to university without 'O' or 'A' levels (or GCSEs)? (there are many special entry schemes and access courses for mature students) ......

You can do a degree without going to a university? ......

You can spend up to 21 hours a week studying at college, without your right to benefit being affected? ......

Most evening classes are either half-price or free for unemployed people? ......

You can get a part-time course started specially for you, if there are several of you? ......

There are eight residential colleges just for adults, where you can study on a grant for one or two years? ......

You can get help to improve your reading, writing and maths, usually for free? ......

You can study at home by a correspondence course, radio or TV programme? ......

Although cuts are being made, there is still a huge variety of different kinds of course available? ......

There are people whose job it is to help you find out what is available? ......

There is a move taking place from formal 'chalk and talk' courses towards 'open learning' courses, which are flexible and based around your personal needs and interests? ......

What kind of thing do you think you might want?

Tick if interested

.... 1.	Help with the basics — improving reading, writing and numbers skills	Adult literacy and numeracy schemes, and linked skill courses.
.... 2.	A training in a skill (Full-time).	Job Training Scheme courses and vocational courses at colleges.
.... 3.	To study full-time for a diploma or degree.	Full-time study on a grant at a university, polytechnic or college of higher education.
.... 4.	To spend one or two years at a residential adult education college.	There are eight such colleges in the country.
.... 5.	To study and train on a part-time basis.	There are classes available in everything from car-maintenance to bee-keeping, or 'O' and 'A' levels.
.... 6.	To do a course from home, learning at your own speed.	There are correspondence courses and FlexiStudy courses you can do.
.... 7.	To do a course to widen your horizons and consider new options.	There are Wider Opportunities courses, and Restart courses.
.... 8.	To share your knowledge and skills with others.	Set up a self-help group or a learning network, to swap skills.

Why bother?

- It will keep me occupied, and give me something to do. . . . .
- When I apply for a job, or go for an interview, it will *show* that I've been keeping occupied, which will be to my advantage. . . . .

- It will bring me new ideas and stimulation, and perhaps lead me in new, unexpected directions. . . . .
- I will meet new people and find myself in new situations. It is possible that one of these people will indirectly lead me to a job. . . . .
- I could gain a new skill or a qualification. . . . .
- It *might* help me to get a job at the end (but it *can't* guarantee me a job). . . . .

Total score . . . . (Max = 30)

Give yourself a score for each of the reasons above, where:

5	=	a very good reason.	4	=	a good reason.
3	=	quite a good reason.	2	=	maybe a good reason.
1	=	not much of a reason.	0	=	not a good reason.

What do you think about your total score? Do you think it shows that there are probably enough good reasons for you to read on, to find out more? Yes ...... No ......

1. Help with the basics

'I was rather embarrassed about my problems over reading and writing, and didn't like to talk to anyone about them. Then I saw the television programme Write Away and got in touch with the phone number they gave out. I'm getting regular help now at an evening class. The tutor's been doing things like application letters and forms too. It's good to know I'm not alone.'

(Unemployed storeman, aged 39.)

In almost every area, there are courses that give help with reading, writing and numbers skills; and 'linked skills' courses where improving basics is linked to learning a skill such as car maintenance, photography, Caribbean cookery. The Adult Education Department (see p. 00) will have details.

The Adult Literacy and Basic Skills Unit co-ordinates information about the range of different courses and learning resources available in England and Wales (ALBSU, Kingsbourne House, 229 High Holborn, London WC1V 7DA.) In Scotland, contact the Scottish Community Education Council, Atholl House, 2 Canning Street, Edinburgh EH3 8EG. In Northern Ireland contact the Library Boards, or Dorothy Eagleson, Educational Guidance Service, Room 208, Bryson House, 28 Bedford Street, Belfast BT2 7FE.

The MSC's 'Wider Opportunities Training Scheme' offers (among other things) a programme in basics, geared to help in finding work, and a programme of language training for people who are learning English. Contact the Jobcentre.

Many local colleges offer special help, too.

2. A training in a skill

There are *two* **Job Training Schemes**, both run by the MSC.

The *new* Job Training Scheme offers you up to a year of training and experience, personally designed to fit your skills. The details of this are given first. The *old* Job Training Scheme offers a range of set courses in practical skills. The details of these are given second.

The new Job Training Scheme

If you are aged 18 or over, and have been unemployed and registered for employment for over 6 months, you can join the government's new Job Training Scheme for anything from 3 to 12 months.

The purpose of the scheme is to give you new skills, to update your existing skills and to assist your chances of getting a full-time job.

- If you decide to join the Job Training Scheme, you will be offered training and work experience for at least 30 hours a week, often with employers;
- You will receive exactly the same *money* that you received in Supplementary Benefit/Income Support, or in Unemployment Benefit, but these will now be called 'training supplement' or 'training allowance';
- All your travel expenses will be repaid;
- Your scheme will start with a one week assessment, during which you will draw up an 'Action Plan' with the supervisor, covering the new skills you want to learn, and the existing skills, which you need to update;
- During your time on the scheme you will also receive training and information concerning new technologies, and self-employment;
- The training you receive will give you access to a recognised qualification, or credits towards one;
- The training will take place in colleges, at training centres, or on employers' premises;
- The skills that can be offered will vary from place to place, depending on the Managing Agent running the scheme;
- If you were receiving Unemployment Benefit before joining the scheme, you will be able to earn extra income through part-time work at evenings and weekends without your training allowance being affected;
- If you were receiving Supplementary Benefit/Income Support before joining the scheme, you will probably only be able to earn £4 a week of additional income (£5 from April 1988) before your training supplement will be affected;
- The scheme is voluntary. At the time of writing (1987), if you are invited to join a JTS scheme through (for example) a Restart interview, there may be penalties if you refuse. Who knows - the world may get better, or the world may get worse!

You can get full details of schemes from the Jobcentre.

The old Job Training Scheme

The old JTS covers a wide range of training courses run by colleges, Skillcentres and private agencies. These are both full-time and part-time, though there is a clear move in the direction of courses lasting less than 21 hours a week.

There will probably soon be a new title to cover these courses, as 'the old JTS' doesn't really sound very good. At the time of writing, however, this was still its name.

If you get a place on a full-time course, you will receive a weekly allowance, and a travel and lodgings allowance if you have to live away from home. You are encouraged to find out what courses are available locally.

Anyone can apply to go on an MSC-funded course, if these conditions are all met:

- You are aged 18 or over, and have been away from full-time education for a total of two years. Yes ...... No ......
- You intend to take up employment using the skill for which training will be given. Yes ...... No ......
- You have not been on a government training course for a fifty-week total in the last three years (some exceptions). Yes ...... No ......

Examples of courses: engineering, construction skills, electrical skills, office skills, automative skills, management skills, hotels and catering, HGV licence, higher level courses, various different computer courses, stock-keeping, hairdressing, keyboard skills, word processing, office skills/new technology, plumbing, tailoring, etc.

How to find out full details
Ask at the Jobcentre about possible courses that might suit you. Useful leaflets are:

- *Adult Training and Jobs* (ATL 55) — explains the main courses under the old Job Training Programme.
- While at the Jobcentre, ask for a copy of *Action for Jobs*, which gives a complete listing of MSC schemes and programmes.

If you live or intend to train in Aberdeen, Bristol/Bath, Greater Manchester or Reading/Slough, there is a new Career Development Loan scheme available, to help people pay for private vocational training courses. Details from Jobcentres in those areas.

How to get on to a Job Training Scheme course
You can apply through the Jobcentre or directly through colleges at any time, bearing in mind that there is sometimes a waiting list (perhaps several months long). For some courses you may be able to start straight away. For Job Training courses you may be asked to do short aptitude tests, or maths or English courses, and possibly meet an interview panel to find out how serious you are about training. The courses often have attendance hours from 8.00 to 4.45.

If you are accepted, and have time to wait, use Chapters 2, 9 and 10 to help you plan your next few months so that you make the best use of your time.

3. Full-time study for a diploma or degree

There is a huge range of courses available. If you left school thinking 'Thank God for that', you might be surprised to learn that even if you left with no exams, you can still think about studying for a degree or diploma. There are full-time courses at colleges, polytechnics and universities, agricultural colleges, nursery nursing colleges, etc.

An Adult can apply to join a course as a 'mature student'. There are also an increasing number of taster courses called 'Access' or 'Return to Study'. These are one-year courses which offer a very broad introduction to humanities and social sciences courses. After the year is up, you can transfer to the course of your choice. A directory of Access courses is available from CNAA, 344–5 Grays Inn Road, London WC1X 8BP — ask in the library. (See also Chapter 7, Women.) 'Open Colleges' (e.g. in south London, the North-West and Manchester) are bringing together different colleges, in order to provide many more such courses for mature students, unemployed and disadvantaged people.

The range of full-time courses available is too large for this Handbook to attempt to describe. The book *Second Chances for Adults* (details below) gives a complete description of what is available.

As for grants, if you are accepted on to a degree course (and some other higher educational qualifications) you will automatically get a grant, so long as you've not had one before. For other qualifications, the grants are only 'discretionary' and your local authority can decide whether it wants to give you one or not. Policy varies a lot from one county to another. *The Grants Handbook* (see below) will help.

Useful publications:

- *Second Chances — an annual guide to adult education and training opportunities*, by Andrew Pates and Martin Good, (18 Brooklands Avenue, Cambridge CB2 2HN).
- *The Grants Handbook* (NUS, 3 Endsleigh Street, London WC1)
- *Educational Charities* (NUS)
- *Directory of Further Education* (Hobsons Press)
- *Handbook of Polytechnic Courses* (Lund Humphries)
- *Handbook of Degree and Advanced Courses in Education* (Lund Humphries)
- *Year Book of Technical Education and Training* (A & C Black)

4. Residential adult education colleges

There are eight of these colleges in the country. They are all for adults who want to take a one or two-year education (not training) course, mostly in the humanities, social sciences, industrial relations and trade union studies. Acceptance is by interview, not by qualifications, and if you are accepted there is a standard procedure for getting a full grant. Their standards of academic education are of a very high quality.

To find out more, write for information to:

- The Registrar, Coleg Harlech, Harlech, Gwynedd LL46 2PU.
- Director of Studies, Co-operative College, Stanford Hall, Loughborough, Leics.
- The Bursar, Fircroft College, Selly Oak, Birmingham B29 6LH.
- The Secretary (AE), Hillcroft College, South Bank, Surbiton, Surrey KT6 6DF.
- The College Secretary, Newbattle Abbey Adult College, Dalkeith, Midlothian.
- The Registrar, Northern College, Wentworth Castle, Stainborough, Barnsley, South Yorks S75 3ET.
- The College Secretary, Plater College, Pullens Lane, Oxford OX3 0DT.
- The General Secretary, Ruskin College, Oxford OX1 2HE.

5. Part-time courses

Many unemployed people who do not want to do a full-time course are joining part-time courses, and thoroughly enjoying themselves. They are studying everything from creative writing to car maintenance, from counselling skills to cookery, from pottery to portrait painting, and from 'O' level computer studies to karate! They are also doing part-time diploma or degree courses in, for example, law, engineering or business studies. In some places, there are as many as 500 different courses on offer. Increasingly, Job Training Scheme courses are going to be part-time (and not full-time) — see above for details.

Courses are offered by seven different types of organisation:

1. The MSC, through colleges and Skill Centres (Job Training Scheme)
2. local colleges of further education
3. adult and community education departments
4. centres for unemployed people
5. independent educational centres
6. the Workers Educational Association
7. university extra-mural departments.

You will be able to find details of nearly all these courses by asking both at the library and at the jobcentre. Many courses will be either free or half-price to unemployed people.

A rule issued by the DHSS states that if you receive benefit you may not study part-time for more than 21 hours a week in total, or 15 hours a week if you have been receiving benefit for less than 3 months. This sounds as if it has been designed to ensure that unemployed people's braincells do not burn out through overstress; in reality it arises because once you become a full-time student you are not eligible to receive supplementary benefit. Some colleges are now designing special 3-days-a-week courses for unemployed people, to fit the rule.

Access to Information Technology courses are provided, free of charge to unemployed people, to give a general introduction to different aspects of computers, word processors, robots, CNC machines, and much more. The courses are open to anyone over 17 and under 65, and not in full-time education. They take place in the evenings and at weekends. For details — contact the Jobcentre.

Useful addresses and contacts:

- *Workers' Educational Association* (WEA), 9 Upper Berkeley Street, London W1H 8BY (newsletter, details of work with unemployed people).
- *Educational Centres Association* (ECA), Chequer Centre, Chequer Street, Burnhill Row, London EC1 8PL (directory).
- *TUC Centres for the Unemployed,* Congress House, Gt Russell Street, London WC1B 3CS (newsletter).
- *'Replan'* — a government initiative to encourage better educational opportunities for unemployed people. Bill Boaden, NIACE, 19b De Montford Street, Leicester LE1 7GE.
- *Adult Options — Three Million Opportunities,* a book produced by the ECA describing inspiring examples of courses and projects around the country involving unemployed people. For example: Shillington Unemployed Young Women's Project, the Vietnamese Co-operative initiative in Lewisham, and CADURN, in the west country. (£4.95, Weavers Press, Tregeraint House, Kerrowe, Zennor, St. Ives, Cornwall)

Centres for the Unemployed

There are now well over 200 special centres for the unemployed in Britain, run by churches, voluntary groups, educational centres and the TUC. They are all different, and each one offers its own range of activities. These include computer classes, welfare rights advice, canoe-making, producing a magazine for unemployed people, literacy classes, supporting local charities, local voluntary work, creative writing groups, campaigning, badminton, aerobics, or business advice.

Some centres are run by workers on the Community Programme, others by volunteers, and some by full-time salaried staff. In Liverpool, the trade unions collectively fund the unemployed centres through 'One Fund For All', into which union members pay something out of their pay packets every week.

Every centre welcomes offers of help. Most centres have users' committees, through which you can make your voice heard and suggest new courses and activities or changes of policy. The TUC produces a regular newsletter for its centres — see above.

Creative writing

There is a thriving network of unemployed writers and worker-writers groups, who encourage each other and publish booklets written by members — life-stories and collections of poetry and prose. Write to the *Federation of Worker Writers and Community Publishers,* The Consortium, 16 Cliffsend House, Cowley Estate, London SW9 for their booklist and details of groups.

Learning English as a second language
The local adult education centre will have details of courses for people whose native language is not English. It may also be possible to receive individual tuition.

6. Doing a course from home, at your own speed

Doing a course from home

Some people prefer to work at courses at home, at their own speed, either as well as or instead of joining a class. The National Extension College offers over 90 courses at different levels, including basic Fresh Start and study skills courses, 'O' and 'A' levels, Open University preparatory courses, business and professional courses, and leisure courses, such as bird-watching and playwriting. Write for their Home Learning Catalogue and Degree and Professional booklet. (NEC, 18 Brooklands Avenue, Cambridge CB2 2HN).

For details of other correspondence courses, write to the Council for the Accreditation of Correspondence Courses, 27 Marylebone Road, London NW1 5JS.

The Open University (Walton Hall, Milton Keynes MK7 6AX) offers both degree courses (which require around 20 hours work a week) and short courses, for which detailed brochures are available. You do not need to have 'O' or 'A' levels.

The Department of Education and Science has a special sponsorship scheme for unemployed people and people on Supplementary Benefit, which allows individuals or groups to obtain a number of the Open University's excellent courses and discussion packs for only £5. Included are: 'Work Choices', 'Health Choices', 'Healthy Eating', 'Family Relationships', 'Pregnancy and Birth', 'Women and Young Children', 'The Pre-School Child', 'Childhood 5–10', 'Parents and Teenagers', 'Governing Schools', 'Planning Retirement', and 'Caring for Elderly People'. (Yes, unemployed people CAN and SHOULD become school governors.) Write for details to Learning Materials Service, Open University, PO Box 188, Milton Keynes MK7 6DH, **making sure you ask for form LM86**, which you will need to get the discount.

There are Open University regional centres in East Grinstead, London, Cambridge, Leeds, Manchester, Newcastle, Cardiff, Edinburgh and Belfast, where you can receive information and view some course materials.

Many colleges now operate 'distance learning' and 'flexi-study' correspondence schemes, and 'open learning' schemes, through which they offer you help to draw up your own learning programme, using OU and NEC materials, and videos and computer-based learning methods, supported by a tutor.

BBC2 and Channel 4 both have many excellent educational programmes, with written back-up materials to help you learn more about the programmes. Radio 4 runs regular educational programmes, especially on Sundays and late at night. Write for Channel 4's *See 4* magazine, PO Box 4000, London W3 6XJ. **Starting in September 1987, the new Open College will be running courses on all 4 TV channels, especially geared to unemployed people.**

7. Do a course to widen your horizons and consider new options

- The *Wider Opportunities Training Programme*, run by the MSC, offers a variety of full-time and part-time courses which have been designed to help you decide what kind of work you really want to do, and to give you a chance to try your hand out at a range of different skills.

  The purpose of the Wider Opportunities courses is not to give you actual skills (for which you can join a Job Training Scheme course), but to allow you to try out different kinds of work and activities.

  If you join a full-time course, which lasts 6–8 weeks, you will get an allowance in place of your benefit. Increasingly, however, courses are on a part-time basis, so your benefit will not be affected (though you may get help with bus fares in some areas).

  The part-time courses are run on a modular basis, which means that you can choose whether you want to explore manual crafts, new technology, cookery or hairdressing, office skills, etc. All courses also offer you a personal development module, which includes confidence building, assertiveness training and jobhunting skills. There are also special modules covering literacy, numeracy, and language training for people whose native language is not English.

  For the full details of all these courses, ask at the Jobcentre.

- *Restart courses.* These courses have been specially designed to help you if you have been out of work for more than 6 months, to overcome uncertainty, and begin to plan for personal goals, whether it is to join a training course, to join a Jobclub and look for work in an organised manner, or to enroll at an evening class.

  The courses last five days and are run at local colleges, and other centres. Once you have completed the course, you can follow it up with a personal advice session to help you sort out your personal goals and to start acting on them. You can also get help in drafting a good c.v., and can call in for help from the tutors at any time. For details, contact the Jobcentre.

8. Share your knowledge and skills with others

The Learning Network (Prince of Wales Hospital, London N15 4AW), for example, is a free network which enables all sorts of people, from schoolchildren to grandparents to share their skills with other local people. Over 200 skills and interests are on offer, ranging from Dogs, Drumming, Form-Filling and Turkish History, to Sitar and Rock Group Production.

The National Extension College has developed a lot of experience with self-help learning groups, which are organised, but friendly. They have published two guides: *Learning Together* and *Studying Together*, both containing useful case studies. (From NEC, 18 Brooklands Avenue, Cambridge CB2 2HN.)

The spread of computers offers us many new possibilities. It will not be long (hopefully) before all the available courses are listed on computer locally, and you will be able to register to learn a course or to teach a course by keying in. In this way, community learning might really begin to take off.

A story of success

Another approach to community learning is being developed on the Gibshill housing estate in Greenock, near Glasgow. The local community education worker, Cathie Cox, invited local people to join an advisory committee to develop educational courses in the area. Twelve local unemployed people got involved, and since then the number of people attending courses has increased three times; and the number of people taking Open University short courses (see above) has increased five times. The committee has also set up an unemployed club and a thriving food co-op. Classes are now going on in 20 different venues in the area, and the region has doubled the local adult education budget and financed the conversion of two classrooms into permanent adult education bases. Local people have started leading classes in health and fitness. 'Sometimes we seem to have meetings every day, but I wouldn't miss it. It's a lot more interesting than staying in the house. It keeps me going!' (Jeanette Watt, committee member)

(Thanks to SCAN Magazine, see p. 58)

Finding out more, and getting advice

The great variety of further education and training possibilities can make it seem very complicated. So here is the basic advice if you want to find out more:

Get in touch with your *local college*, and ask for a meeting to talk to someone about further education in general. He or she will probably be able to tell you many things you didn't know. Phone first, and make an appointment; you'll get much better advice that way.

In many areas there are specialist *educational advice services*. The local Citizens Advice Bureau ought to know if there is one locally, so phone and ask. You can also write or phone direct to the Educational Counselling and Credit Transfer Information Service (ECCTIS), for information on your local advice service. They also publish an annual Directory of Educational Guidance Services for Adults. (ECCTIS, Po Box 88, Walton Hall, Milton Keynes, MK7 6DB, Tel 0908–368924)

Second Chances for Adults by Andrew Pates and Martin Good (NEC) is an invaluable and comprehensive guide to the opportunities available. It is updated every year, the new edition coming out in September. If your library hasn't a copy, ask them to get one. This will answer most of your questions, and point you in the direction you need for more detailed information.

Ask at the Jobcentre about *Training Access Points (TAP)*. These provide computerised information on training and educational opportunities.

A few words of frustration

It would not be right to let this chapter pass without some comment on the cut-backs taking place in education. It's crazy — a time of high unemployment and rapid social change has to be a time for big *expansion* of all education and training facilities, in preparation for the future. Even evening classes are being cut back in many areas. The lack of any well-supported educational response to the unemployment crisis, in the form of new courses, new learning arrangements and extra finance for grants and courses is very depressing. It's one extra thing to fight for.

A general word of advice

If someone says to you, 'It isn't possible', 'There aren't any places left' or, 'She's too busy to see you', *persist*. Don't just walk away. The variety of courses available is large, and it is quite common to find that people at one end of a college don't know what's happening at the other end of the same college. Also, it's just life that some people seem to enjoy telling people it *can't* be done, whereas others enjoy trying to bend every rule so that it *can* be done. Go on till you find one of the second kind. Remember, too, the higher up you go, the more power people have to make exceptions to their own rules. So — *persist!*

CHAPTER 9 — LIFE-PLANNING

QUIZ — Why life-planning? Transcending the 'employee culture' — HOW TO GET YOUR ACT TOGETHER IN SEVEN 'EASY' (?) STAGES — Foundations — Goals — Needs — Obstacles — Emergencies — Values — Letting go of stress and renewing your spiritual resources.

This chapter contains several activities and practical tasks, each of which takes time to do. Don't try to rush these, or you may feel overloaded. You may only want to do one a week, to give each one time to sink in.

QUIZ

1. Do you feel you watch too much TV?
   (a) Often (b) Sometimes (c) Not very often

2. Do you have periods of inertia, when you don't really do anything at all?
   (a) Often (b) Sometimes (c) Not very often

3. Do you have a clear idea of your goals for the next 6 months or so?
   (a) No (b) Sort of (c) Yes

4. Do you have a weekly plan or goal list?
   (a) No (b) Sometimes (c) Yes

5. Do you keep a diary and/or notebook?
   (a) No (b) Small diary, no notebook (c) Yes to both

6. Do you ever run out of money before your new giro arrives?
   (a) Frequently (b) Sometimes (c) No, never

7. A red electricity bill has just arrived, and you have not got the cash to pay it. Do you
   (a) Either burn it or write a cheque you know will bounce?
   (b) Phone a friend to ask for advice?
   (c) Phone the Electricity Board to discuss new methods of payment?

8. Do you keep a number of different files, to store papers in?
   (a) No (b) Piles, but not files, (c) Yes

9. Do you fulfil one part of your life (eg your body or your feelings), but neglect another (e.g. your mind, your intuitions or your creativity)?
   (a) Yes (Which part do you neglect? ....)
   (b) Some parts of my life don't do as well as they might (Which parts? ....)
   (c) No — all parts of my life are fulfilled.

10. Do you consider you are working towards doing what you want to do in life?
    (a) Not at all (b) Yes, partly (c) Yes

11. Do you have a way of relaxing and letting go of the stresses of life?
    (a) Not really (b) Yes, but I don't often use them (c) Yes

12. Do you have a way of developing your own inner self and renewing your spiritual resources?
(a) I've never thought about it (b) That sounds like a good idea (c) Yes

Scoring: (a) = 0 (b) = 1 (c) = 2

0–6	You are not really very organised, are you? This chapter might give you the means you need to begin to get control over your life.
7–14	You mean well, but it doesn't always work — right? Use this chapter to get a tighter rein on things, so that your own life does not sabotage you.
15–20	You enjoy organising your life — so you will probably appreciate a few extra ideas.
20–24	What are you doing reading this book? You must be the Superbrat of the dole queue!

Why life-planning? Transcending the 'employee culture'

During the industrial age, many people were compelled by necessity to live under someone else's banner, not their own. Their lives belonged to their employer, not to themselves. The alternative was starvation. Out of this 'Age of Necessity', we developed what is now being called an 'employee culture', in which people grew dependent upon someone else to organise their lives, to tell them when to work, when to take a holiday and when to retire.

This is all very well if there is someone out there to employ you. If there is not, the habits and attitudes of the culture become self-destructive. Waiting at home for someone to produce a job or provide some answers is very foolish if there is no-one out there any more.

The alternative to the 'employee culture' is a 'self-empowered' or an 'own-work' culture, encouraging independence of mind and action, and self-reliance, both individually and in our communities. Life-planning is the process by which as individuals we can overcome the employee culture, and become more self-empowered and self-reliant. Community planning is the process by which communities can overcome the same dependent culture, and become more self-empowered and self-reliant.

An excellent book on life-planning is *Build Your Own Rainbow: A Workbook for Career and Life Management* contains 41 exercises which can be used either personally or in groups. (£10.95 + £1.20 p&p from Lifeskills Associates, Clarendon Chambers, 51 Clarendon Road, Leeds LS2 9NZ). Available to unemployed people for £5 through the DES/Open University, as the *Work Choices* Course (see p. 108). Also through libraries (ISBN 0 907042 03).

HOW TO GET YOUR ACT TOGETHER IN SEVEN EASY (?) STAGES

A. Foundations

To begin to create order in your life, it will be useful to set up a few basic systems to help you cope with practical matters.

1. Create a proper personal working space for yourself
You need an area you can call your own, where you can sit and create order in your mind. It doesn't have to be a whole office, but it should be somewhere where you can spread your papers and make your plans. Rearrange the furniture if need be, and put up your favourite postcards and photos to make the space feel good. You'll need some shelves and storage space for files.

2. Keep a personal notebook, and a diary
It is worth investing in a good-sized notebook to use for your lists, budgets, etc., as well as keeping a diary for addresses, and appointments.

3. Set up a filing system
A simple filing system allows you to create some order in your mind. You might find the following headings useful:

Finances needing attention
Finances — finished
Children
Job applications — 'to do'
Job applications — dead
Personal letters — 'to do'
Personal letters — finished
Local activities, classes, groups
Special interest files — several

If we don't keep files, we keep piles — it seems to be a law of life. It is worth investing time in setting up a good system that will work for you.

If we don't keep files, we keep piles

4. Keep lists
Lists are to the muddled mind what massage is to the tense body.

Keep your lists in a notebook with clear headings, giving each list a separate page, not on tiny scraps of paper, which soon look tatty.

You will find it helpful to keep three different types of list:

- long-range — covering your goals for the next six months;
- medium-range — 'things to do', eg:
  - things to do — family and household
  - things to do — jobhunting
  - things to do — personal fulfilment, activities
  - things to do — special projects
  - letters to write
- short-range — for 'today' and 'this week'. Some people find it useful to sit down every Sunday evening and draw up a list of the things they would like to achieve during the week ahead.

5. Make your household run itself

Spend some time in each room that you have; think about the activities that go on there, and work out how you could create greater order. You might want some new cupboards or shelves. It is remarkable what you can pick up for little or no price at bargain secondhand furniture stores. Social Services departments and Councils for Voluntary Service (see p.vii) often run secondhand furniture depots for people on low incomes. A spot of creative carpentry will produce some extra shelves — wood can be found in city skips, and tools borrowed from a friend.

6. Avoid red-bill disease

Life on a low income leaves very little room for manoeuvre, and a lot of room for anger. An outbreak of nasty 'red-bill disease' on the doormat is dangerous and to be avoided at all costs. The disease lies dormant for about ten days, and then produces fairly instant paralysis. Go through Chapter 12 and work out a list of your financial strategies — drawing up a budget sheet, eliminating expensive HP payments, selling some items of equipment, earning the £4/£5/£15 (see p. 150) per week that is permissible, forming a group to help meet expenses such as holidays (see Chapter 13), etc. Add the things you have to do to your weekly goal lists. Belonging to a group will help get you through financial crises — a good laugh lessens the size of life's problems!

B. Goals

Your goals determine where you are going. The employee culture expects you to follow a ready-made path through life — until the redundancy notices are given out and the path no longer exists. By setting your own goals, you create your own personal path, designed to take you where YOU want to go.

Chapter 2 includes an exercise on goals (p. 5/6) which you should work through now if you have not already done so. Then set aside two hours with a cup of tea, and develop your goals list using specific headings, such as:

- Household
- Work — career — jobhunting
- A learning strategy (use Chapter 8)
- Personal activities, interests and growth
- Community activities
- Physical activity and exercise
- Special projects
- Crazy ideas!

Some people do this type of exercise better with a friend; others work best alone.

I once met a group of people at 6.00am on top of Dartmoor, while sleeping out overnight. They belonged to a 'Crazy Club' which existed in order to do crazy things together. They had set off at 4.30am from Torquay in a 1930 Austin 7 and a pre-war Triumph motorbike to see the sun rise from the top of Haytor! Spend an evening with some friends over some home-brew and make a list of crazy things you could do together. A crazy activity a month will keep you sane, young and laughing!

C. Needs

The degree to which your needs are met will determine how comfortable your life-journey is. If your needs are met, you will feel good and enjoy the ride. If they are not, it might be dull and lonely. The exercise below will help you recognise your own needs, and take steps to meet them.

Step one: below are listed 17 commonly experienced human needs, with room for you to add more. Fill in Column 1, asking yourself how much you need each of these, on a scale from 0 to 10.

Step two: fill in Column 2, asking yourself how much these needs are being satisfied at the moment, using the same scale. Put a star by needs which fall 4 or more points short of being met, and two stars by needs which fall 6 or more points short.

	Column 1 How much do I NEED this in my life? (0-10)	*Column 2* How much do I RECEIVE this in my life? (0-10)
Friendship	....	....
Affection (non-sexual)	....	....
Expression of deep feeling	....	....
Sexual affection	....	....
Movement, exercise, dance	....	....
Laughter	....	....
Mental stimulation	....	....
Silence, stillness	....	....
Beauty	....	....
Shared beliefs and ideals	....	....
Spiritual understanding	....	....
Use of my hands, crafts	....	....
Open mountains, heaths, lakes, seas	....	....
Music	....	....
Speed, excitement	....	....
Adventure	....	....
Contact with children	....	....
....	....	....
....	....	....

Step three: spend ten minutes with ONE of your starred needs, doing a drawing to express what you feel when you think of this need, and then writing down everything that comes into your mind concerning it. After ten minutes, see if you can make a list of things you could do to increase your satisfaction of this need. Pick the ideas which seem reasonable, and add them to your 'Goals' lists.

• *Personal support* is an important need. Some people find it helps to set up a regular arrangement with a friend. You meet every two weeks and spend 45 minutes each reviewing the highs and lows since you last saw each other. This method (and other support structures) is described in *Guidelines to Finding Your Own Support* by Warren Redman (£0.60 from NAYC, 30 Peacock Lane, Leicester).

The practices of Co-counselling is praised by many people for teaching the skills necessary to help us help each other. See *How to Change Yourself and Your World: A Manual of Co-counselling Theory and Practice* by Rose Evison and Richard Horobin (1983), available from Co-counselling Phoenix, 5 Victoria Road, Sheffield S10 2DJ (£2.50), which also contains contact addresses.

Many people are finding that attending assertiveness and confidence-building classes helps them build up their self-esteem, and enables them to ask for what they want and to say no to things they don't want, without becoming angry or tongue-tied. Courses are run in many adult education centres and women's centres (see p. 106). See *A Woman in Your Own Right* by Anne Dickson (Quartet Books).

D. Obstacles

'There have to be some snags!' I can hear you thinking (e.g. 'I hate lists'). These are some of the common obstacles that stand in the way of us realising our goals:

people — parents, partners
self-doubts
over-stress
isolation
lack of clear personal direction
high local unemployment
lack of money
prejudice, racism, sexism
children
housing situations
depressing neighbourhoods
....

Step one: choose one obstacle that gets in your way and spent ten minutes writing down everything that comes into your head about it, or doing a drawing of the obstacle.

Step two: with a friend, in a support group or on your own, spend some time thinking of things you could do which might make a difference.

Step three: when you come across a good idea, make a written note of it, and fit it onto a list somewhere, so that it has a chance of being turned into reality.

E. Emergencies

It happens to the best of us, even when we are following all the rules of life-planning — we still end up in a mess. The best of plans threaten to fall to pieces, thanks to the following:

- the breakdown of a relationship with a partner or parent
- the death of someone close
- trouble with the law
- a housing emergency
- a money emergency
- a children emergency
- falling into a 'black hole'
- nothing seems to be going right
- .... (add your own!)

There are five basic remedies which are useful in these situations:

1. Find someone to talk to who will listen to you with full attention, or a close friend who will come and see you through.
2. Self-forgiveness — remind yourself insistently that it's OK to have a crisis, they happen to all of us. Don't make it worse by punishing yourself as well.
3. Take the opportunity to try asking for help, going to a church, a temple or a quiet place and using prayer or meditation, or words spoken silently to the hills or the earth. If you don't believe in this kind of thing, try it as an experiment: it is more likely that we are connected to the universe as a whole than that we are not. 'We all need a love resurrection, just a little divine intervention' — Alison Moyet.
4. Find someone practical who will help you to work out a rescue plan.
5. Pick yourself up, laugh at the muddles we get ourselves into, and stand ready to meet the next day!

F. Values

Why do we live?

That's a big question, but one we all face sooner or later. In general, people who live in accordance with their inner values enjoy greater fulfilment and meaning than people who do not know why they are doing anything.

We all have values, whether we know it or not. There is an activity you can do — alone, or with a friend — to help you to be clearer about what your own values are, and to consider how you could live in greater accord with the things you believe in:

Step one: take half an hour, and make a list of some of the things you really care about, however large or small, focusing in turn on personal and family life, society in general, the planet as a whole, and spiritual, religious or humanistic things. Start each sentence with the words 'I really care about . . .'

Step two: choose three or four of the sentences you have written down, and continue them by writing down three reasons why you care about them, starting with the word 'because . . .': this will help you to focus more clearly on your values. *For example:* 'I really care about the way we are destroying our countryside and nature — because the countryside lets me feel whole, and hopeful; because there is a peaceful- ness there, which I can't find in the cities; and because I like to feel close to trees, flowers and wildlife.'

Step three: for each of the sentences in turn, spend time considering what practical things you could do to express that value more in your life, and write them down. E.g. *Actions:* (1) make more visits to the countryside; (2) join a nature and wildlife conservation society and offer to help.

A second example: 'I really care about children being honest', and the reasons 'because that way, they will grow up as better children; because it will save them from getting into trouble; because I find it hard to feel loving towards dishonest people'. *Actions:* (1) maybe I should consider how honest I am myself, (2) we could have a weekly family meeting, when we begin to share honestly what we feel, and what is happening in our lives.

Step four: when practical suggestions emerge, add them onto a list, so that they can be turned into reality.

G. Letting go of stress and renewing your spiritual resources

Living isn't easy: it never was, except perhaps in special 'interludes' and special places. Yet there are bodies of wisdom to be found which can help us towards an easier and more tranquil life. They are not announced on the news but they still exist. In this final section, we offer you three of these wisdoms.

(i) Learning to relax

The pressures of unemployment, low income, personal uncertainty and loss of confidence can be very stressful. If stress is allowed to build up over time, it can become dangerous to our health. Our bodies respond in different ways to stress — some people get migraines, others back-ache, stomach problems, skin complaints, asthma, depression or heart problems. We may also find ourselves short-tempered or unable to sleep well at night.

A treatment commonly prescribed for stress and worry is a tranquilliser drug such as valium. These don't do anything to heal the stress itself — they simply suppress it, and bring risks of addiction. By learning to relax, you can begin to bring that same tranquillity into your life by natural means.

A Relaxation Activity

Taking this book with you, go to the sofa and lie down, having first turned off the radio, TV and any other noise-making device. Stretch out and get comfortable, without your arms or your feet crossed. Close your eyes, and breathe in and out deeply three times, consciously slowing up your whole being, letting yourself relax. Now work through your whole body, from your toes upwards, clenching and then unclenching every joint and limb — feet, calf muscles, thighs, pelvis, stomach, fists, forearms, shoulders and upper arms, shoulders and neck, jaw and teeth, eyes and forehead. After every unclench, take a deep breath, and enjoy the feeling.

When you have worked through your whole body, continue to lie still with your eyes closed, breathing deeply. Picture yourself lying somewhere really peaceful: e.g. in a summer meadow, on a seashore, by a river or under a tree, and allow yourself to breathe in all the fragrance and calm of the atmosphere. Stay here as long as you feel comfortable, and then slowly open your eyes and return to yourself. If you can practice doing this once a day for ten minutes, so that it becomes a habit, you will begin to enjoy it.

There are also some useful books and cassettes to help you learn to relax :

- *Stress and Relaxation*, by Jane Madders (Martin Dunitz 1984);
- *Relaxation*, by Laura Mitchell (John Murray, 1979).

Cassettes, leaflets, and details of relaxation courses in Britain are obtainable from:

- *Relaxation for Living,* 29 Burwood Park Road, Walton on Thames, Surrey (Tel 0932–227826). Many local adult education departments (see p.vii) also offer relaxation courses.

The important wisdom within these relaxation exercises is that your internal 'weather' can lie within your own control, instead of being like the weather outside, which is beyond your control. By choosing to do a relaxation exercise you can learn how to ease away your inner tensions, just as if you were blowing away nasty weather and bringing in the calm.

(ii) Learning to meditate

Meditation goes a step further than relaxation. Behind nearly every meditational tradition lies the second body of wisdom, which consists of the understanding that we are part of a huge universe, both inwardly and outwardly; that if we learn how to calm the mind and the heart, we can begin to experience this connection personally; and that when we make this connection, we discover the universe we are connecting with is an incredibly peaceful and harmonious place. We begin to experience this peace within our own lives.

Learning how to meditate is not difficult: it takes a willingness to sit down every day for about 20 minutes and to use a meditational technique to calm the wandering mind. A useful little book is *How to Meditate,* by Lawrence Leshan (Prism). In many towns and cities you will find meditation classes, and the British Meditation Society (PO Box 38, Braintree, Essex) can provide a list of meditation teachers. You may also find Buddhist and Christian centres which run meditation or contemplation groups. Joining a yoga class is also a good way to begin learning inner stillness. Many yoga teachers know where to direct you if you want to join a meditation group. A good book for disabled people is *Yoga for the Disabled* (price £3.95 + 75p postage from Yoga for Health, Ickwell Bury, Northill, Biggleswade, Beds SG18 9SF).

(iii) Renewing your spiritual resources

The third wisdom relates to the 'connection' referred to above. The wisdom says that this connection is real: it is not just an idea. We are part of this huge harmony, and all of our spiritual resources come from it, whether we experience it or not. Some people call it God. Others call it the Universe, Nature, the Great Spirit, simply 'Life'; or feel no need to call it anything at all. Many things cause us to lose contact with this harmony, and given the many ups and downs of life, sooner or later this loss can lead us to feel confused, distressed or simply weary.

The wisdom is that we can speak to this harmony, and let it speak to us. We can receive courage, comfort, inspiration, support and guidance from it. Throughout time, every culture in the world has had ways of renewing its contact with the harmony. The ways may lie through music, dance, prayer, fasting, healing or the silent contemplation of beauty and art. Our own culture has not lost these ways — it has simply scattered them, so there is no longer any single 'way' which everyone can follow. This gives us the freedom to find our own way — but also the freedom to lose our way and to lose the connection. Some then use alcohol or drugs to bring a substitute warmth into their lives, to escape from the cold of daily living. Others simply live with greyness, depression and a lack of freshness or delight in their lives.

To live peacefully, we must find ways of remaking the connection. Once we begin to know that it is there, we can start to speak to it, if we need help or guidance in our lives. Sooner or later, we will find the answers we seek, if we are willing to ask:

> *'I might never have discovered who I really was or have gotten answers to the relentless questions that had driven me to the Cove, without those quiet hours spent in the mountains. I do not know why it is that an intimate contact with wild life and a personal observation of nature helps so much in this self-discovery. But that it is so, I have seen in other people's lives as well as my own. Not that my hometown Asheville was such a large city. Perhaps it is just that even a small city provides artificial distractions which separate us from the roots of our life; even a few bricks and mortar and a little macadam are a shield between us and the wisdom that nature has to give.'*

From *Christy* by Catherine Marshall (Ballantyne).

CHAPTER 10: IDEAS UNLIMITED

TOMMY WILSON'S TALE – Freedom from dull work – Making the most of your community – Skills exchanges – LETSystem – Personal activities – Personal launchpad grants – Other sources of materials – Sports – Local voluntary work – Working with children – Housing issues – Personal care and counselling – Nature conservation and environmental action - Growing your own food – Social, political and economic action – Taking time to read

'But what shall I do with all the hours in a day?' This chapter starts off with the story of one man who has 'gone the whole hog':

TOMMY WILSON'S TALE

'Tommy Wilson's parents think he's daft. He had a steady job as an apprentice jeweller, but gave it up. The money was poor and he didn't like the work. But for a 19 year old from the Gorbals in Glasgow, voluntary unemployment is enough to make his parents' blood boil. But that's Tommy.

'Now he's living off £27 a week dole money and is technically unemployed. He's available for work, as they say. Then again, he's not exactly lying around the house. Six months into his new status, Tommy is a changed man. And it happened for a simple reason: he's got involved in the community.

'That means, along with other things, he's trying to start a community business by setting up a recording studio in the Gorbals, he's behind GOODY (Gorbals Organisation on Development for Youth) and he's helping to set up an advice centre for young people in Glasgow. Then there's the couple of hours as a youth club leader with the unemployed workers centre. For good measure, there's Gorbals Promotions which puts on bands in the Gorbals, playing to audiences of 300 young people.

'So Tommy does not hang around. He's up in the mornings and works well into the evening, planning, organising, going to meetings and getting things done. That's the motivation: trying to help young people in the Gorbals, and giving them a voice so that they can speak to the decision-makers themselves.

'Tommy came into voluntary community work by accident. With his mate, Martin, the plan was to become overnight millionaires, running a recording studio, putting on bands and being kings of the Glasgow music world. They made a good start as budding entrepreneurs, getting all the advice they could and even fixing up premises in the city centre — all without a penny to their name. (Glasgow patter gets you a long way.) That plan, though, has been revised over the past few months as they've talked to youth enquiry staff at the Adelphi Education Centre in the Gorbals. Now it's about setting up a local music centre for local bands as a community business.

' "I realised that there was more to life than personal gain", says Tommy, "and that it should really be for the benefit of the community. It's really needed."

'Tommy admits he's come out of himself in the last six months, learning new skills — like speaking in public, basic administration, and organising — and getting a new outlook on life. He's met lots of local people, officials and anyone who can help young people in the Gorbals. "I've also done more work in the last three months than in two years of working".'

(From *SCAN* magazine, with thanks — see p. 58)

Freedom from dull work – releasing the heart

One of the blessings of unemployment is that it brings a time when you do not have to work at someone else's job, on someone else's terms. So many of us want to live our own lives, free to determine what we do and why we do it. This is one reason why many unemployed people are looking to set up a co-operative or become self-employed. Tommy Wilson has found one way to make his life his own, doing what he really enjoys. This chapter looks at some ways in which you might be able to explore this freedom.

You may find it helpful to look back through Chapters 2 and 3, where we considered the ways in which a solid life can be built up without a full-time job, based on your natural skills and talents. The keys to making the most of your time while you are unemployed are:

- to locate what your natural skills are,
- to locate what your heart wants to be doing,
- to take the opportunity of unemployment to get stuck in. There is no need to wait for a job — there are opportunities all around you.

Making the most of your community

Use this checklist to find out what is happening locally. The library will be a good place to start. Take a notebook and write down all the addresses, phone numbers and other details, so that you have got them when you need them.

Does your local neighbourhood or area have:

A festival .....
Enough playgroups .....
A youth club .....
A drama group .....
A choir or chorus .....
A dance group .....
A good choice of evening classes .....
Facilities for football .....
Facilities for tennis .....
Facilities for badminton .....
A swimming pool .....
Bowls .....
Areas for play safe from traffic .....
An information/advice centre .....
An enterprise agency (see p. 137) .....
A 'Youth-in-Business group (see p. 139).....
A cinema or film club .....
Scouts, guides, brownies, cubs .....
A local rock group .....
A folk club .....
A print workshop .....
Clubs for the disabled and/or housebound .....
Clubs for the mentally subnormal .....
Decent local transport arrangements .....
A holiday playscheme .....

A women's group .....
An environmental action group .....
A library .....
A decent hall .....
Meeting rooms .....
A credit union .....
A street warden scheme .....
A housing action campaign .....
A street market .....
A parent-teachers association .....
A 'Gingerbread' group for single parents ......
Day-time classes for unemployed people .....
An unemployed centre or group .....
Good local dances, discos .....
Regular public meetings to discuss local problems .....
A computers' club .....
A co-operative development agency .....
A community magazine .....
Enough allotments .....
A neighbourhood law centre .....

TOTAL. . . . .

You may be interested to see how your area scores:

- 30–50: Seems like your community is alive and well — so you shouldn't have much difficulty finding things to do.
- 20–30: Your community has woken up, and is starting to do things.
- 10–20: It's just about got the sleep out of its eyes.
- 0–10: Still pretty sleepy.

If your area isn't one of the liveliest, you may be able to help it wake up. See Chapter 5 for ideas.

Skills exchanges

In every community there is a wealth of skills. Those of us who find ourselves unemployed are still rich in skill. Is there a way in which we can use these skills and help each other at the same time? If Dave can turn a useful hand at carpentry, if Kati can turn out beautiful pottery, if Jean can fix a broken exhaust pipe and if Raphael can do a good job at housepainting, and none of us has much money to pay for these things, can't we work out a way to share our skills with each other?

It sounds obvious, but the history of skills exchanges shows that it is not so easy to start one.

One very successful skills exchange was 'Skillswap' in Cwmbran, South Wales. Skillswap was the brainchild of one man, Walter Gould, who provided the leadership necessary to make it a success throughout its life. At its peak, Skillswap had over 400 members with 120 different skills between them. They met weekly in seven separate groups, and had a lively social life, with fundraising for outings and parties. At these weekly meetings they also arranged to do different jobs for each other.

The DHSS ruled that any direct 'trading' of skills was not allowed, forcing the group to develop a 'gift economy', which in fact suited people very well. The only 'rules' were that nobody could give more than six times what she or he received — and all transactions were recorded in a book. The members of Skillswap were not content with just doing jobs for each other, once they got to know each other. They went on to develop a collective greenhouse, a regular woodwork shop for young people run by an older unemployed man, and several infant business ventures. They also did many jobs for free for senior citizens, one-parent families and disabled people.

The group fell apart in the end through a mixture of local bureaucratic incompetence, and a failure to develop leadership in people other than Wally — showing how important it is to develop the kind of supportive 'Network' described in Chapter 6.

Skillswap succeeded because

(1) it built its foundations on a strong social life first, ensuring that people got to know and trust each other and enjoy each other's company
(2) Wally Gould provided strong organisational back-up
(3) he also provided leadership.

The success of a scheme depends on these three factors. Wally's leadership was voluntary, and after a while he had a paid part-time assistant, funded through local sources.

If you want to establish a skills exchange, one recommended path is to form a community self-help group first, following advice in Chapter 5, and then to use the group as the foundation for the exchange. A second path might be to consider establishing a LETSystem (see below).

- *Skills Exchanges: Notes on schemes for unemployed people,* by Maggie Plouviez. £1, from the Volunteer Centre, 29 Lower Kings Road, Berkhamsted, Herts HP4 2AB.
- The *BURN Notes: Unemployed Self-Help in Action* includes a full write-up on Skillswap. £2.50, from CAWTU, Holywell Centre, 1 Phipp Street, London EC2A 4PS.

The LETSystem

A second way for people to share their skills with each other, without the use of money, which is creating much interest in Britain in the late 1980s (although it may fall foul of our ancient benefit rules) is the LETSystem (Local Exchange Trading System). This has been successfully pioneered in several places on Vancouver Island, on Canada's Pacific coast.

A LETSystem is a large-scale community barter scheme, which uses an imaginary currency called the 'green dollar' to record the transactions between people. Very simply, the members of the system describe what skills or goods they have to offer, with the price in green dollars, in a monthly newsletter. When a transaction takes place, they phone a message through to a central answering machine, and the information is recorded on an IBM computer. There are 400 registered members in Courtenay (a small town on the island) where trading has been going on since 1983. In 1985 they were sharing $10,000 worth of trade per month.

The joy of the LETSystem is that in a high unemployment economy, where there is not much money about, it allows people to go on to sharing their skills and enriching each other's lives. The system has been shown to work successfully in practice, but it runs into the same problem as will probably arise here — the welfare authorities treat green dollar income as cash income, which creates a disincentive for unemployed people to use it beyond a certain point. Oh, the delights of our welfare systems, that create such binds around our lives! The LETSystem belongs to the present and future, but we are still bound by the STOPsystems of the past. Maybe the DHSS would agree to allow a limited number of LETSystems to be set up, on a pilot basis.

The paperwork which describes the LETSystem can be obtained by sending £10 to LETSystem, 17 Mackeson Road, London NW3 2LU. The computer software can also be made available.

Personal activities

In the mid twenty-first century, we might look back and realise how much music, literature, film and art was created by 'unemployed' people who used their time to express their creativity. In many towns and cities, creativity is being made a focus of community activity, as a way to let the human spirit write, speak, sing, dance and paint its hopes and fears, its dreams and its distresses. In all of us, there is a creative elf or elverine, waiting to be allowed the space to come out.

For many arts, sports and other activities cost is a consideration. Photographic film and development, paint and paper, musical instruments and equipment all cost money, and this often holds back the creative impulse that could be expressing itself. However, solutions to this problem do appear if we start to think and act collectively:

Personal launchpad grants

In 1984, acting on the intuition that much personal creativity was being held back among unemployed people, Church Action With the Unemployed (CAWTU) pioneered a special scheme in Redcar, on Teesside. They raised £5,000 from the Church of England Board of Finance and gave it away in small 'personal launchpad grants', ranging from £25 to £200, to 79 unemployed people, in partnership with Redcar's 'Impasse' project. Grants were given for such things as silversmithing equipment, rugby football gear, saxophone lessons, computers, canoe kits and sewing machines.

Feedback on the project was very positive, and a report has been written spelling out the practical lessons learnt, with the idea that people in towns and cities around Britain might be encouraged to develop similar initiatives. It is tragic that just when people have the time to begin to develop their own lives, because of unemployment, they are often unable to, because they have no money. Similar projects are now underway in Bristol, Peterborough, and several other places.

For all the practical details, write for: *It Made All the Difference*, price £4.95 postage from CAWTU, Holywell Centre, 1 Phipp Street, London EC2A 4PS.

Other sources of materials

1. A group can tread where an individual fears to tread. . . Many of us would find it difficult to write a personal letter to the local paper asking for arts materials, or cricket gear, but a group can, and people will be happy to give. An arts group can approach the local arts club to discuss the possibility of discounts and other kinds of help. A sports group can approach the council's leisure department. A computer group can approach a firm such as Tandy, Radio Shack or IBM to ask for free equipment.

2. Until April 1988 you can earn £4 a week after expenses, by selling your photography, by gardening once a week for someone, or by teaching someone's youngster how to fish, and the cost of your equipment can count as legitimate expenses. After April 1988 the limit will be £5 (or £15 — see p. 150), and no expenses will be allowed. Group earning schemes will therefore be more important — see p. 55.

Sports

Football, weightlifting, tennis, running, wheelchair olympics, hockey, badminton, swimming, gliding, basketball, athletics, ice-skating — now is a good time to overcome your self-doubts and to take up a sport you have always fancied but never really tried, or to develop one you already enjoy. The library will carry a list of local sports clubs, or know where you can find one. If your council has not already introduced discounts at sports facilities for people bearing UB40s, then pressure them to do so, with supporting letters from, for example, the Trades Council, the Adult Education Department, and local church vicars.

Sport is what you can give, too: many youth clubs long to have someone who will teach swimming, karate or golf to their youngsters. If you don't know where to begin, phone the Youth Service or the Leisure Services Department of the council, and volunteer your services.

Local Voluntary Work

In every town and city, there are handicapped children wanting someone to take them on outings, parents of handicapped children wanting someone to come in for half a day a week to give them a break, and pensioners wishing someone would come and change a light bulb or put up a shelf. Many unemployed people, young and old, have discovered the world of voluntary work, and never looked back. They speak of a new delight and sense of satisfaction that has entered their lives, and of new friends they have made.

In every town and city, you will find either a Volunteer Bureau or a Council for Voluntary Service (see p. vii) which co-ordinates voluntary activity. Amateur radio enthusiasts can run hospital radio stations; would-be teachers can teach English to people whose first language is Urdu or Punjabi. Woodworkers can help local dramatic societies build their stages; seamstresses can help them to make their costumes. There is more going on in the average town than most of us realise.

Working with children

- Pre-school playgroups always appreciate help — you can pick up the skills as you go along, if you have not worked with small children before. The Social Services Department (see p. vii) keeps a list of local playgroups — just get in touch.
- Every summer, holiday playschemes and adventure playgrounds value all the help they can get. This might involve going off on minibus trips, refereeing football matches, or helping children make candles. Social Services Departments will know what's cooking.
- Helping in youth clubs with 9–14 year-olds is a round-the-year activity, where everything goes on from caving and rock-climbing to organising discos and printing T-shirts. The Youth Service (see p. vii) will know where help would be appreciated.
- You can have a lot of fun getting together with other people who have children, who may also be broke and unable to fly off to the Costa del Wherever. Just ride the bus to the end of the line, take a picnic and some cheapo badminton rackets or frisbies and footballs, and you can have a great day. Go one better — your little group of parents can give itself a name and invent a quick constitution. Ask to borrow a minibus from the local school or football club, and you can all go camping in Venezuela (or the nearby hills) for the weekend.

- The art of storytelling is long overdue for a revival. Regular storytelling groups are really appreciated by children; the shared emotions help to nurture warmth and love.

If you live surrounded by concrete in every direction, and you are afraid to let the kids go out to play, are there any alternatives to valium or violence?

> PROBLEMS WHICH SEEM IMPOSSIBLE
> ON THE INDIVIDUAL LEVEL
>
> HAVE SOLUTIONS
> ON THE COLLECTIVE LEVEL

Get together with other parents and start campaigning for an indoor day-care centre to let the kids play together safely and give you a break:

(1) Meet other parents
(2) Discuss your ideas with the Social Services Department, the Community Programme Agency, your local councillor and your Member of Parliament
(3) Use the contacts in Chapter 7 (Women) to help you develop your ideas
(4) Write letters to the local paper, and use your local radio to get support.

Housing issues

For many unemployed people, troubles don't come singly. Lousy housing and living on a lousy housing estate, not to mention the hidden or real threats of violence, heroin or rape, are part of the 1980s package deal which too many people have to put up with.

- The Open University's 'In and Out of Unemployment' pack on '*Group Initiatives*' has a useful sheet, 'Getting Together About Housing', which explains about Tenants Associations, Tenant Management Co-operatives, Housing Co-operatives and Shared Ownership schemes. £1.25 for the pack, from Learning Materials Service, OU, PO Box 188, Milton Keynes MK7 6DH.
- You can get further helpful material and advice from Shelter, 157 Waterloo Road, London SE1 8XF.
- *Tenants Action* (Thames TV, 149 Tottenham Court Road, London W1P 9LL).

Personal care and counselling

Groups such as the Samaritans, who offer support to people feeling suicidal, and the Marriage Guidance Council, who offer relationship counselling to help couples going through difficult spells, depend on volunteers to provide their services. You could train as a volunteer yourself. A phone call to the local group will put you on the way — the addresses are in the phone book.

You can also get involved in one of a growing number of groups in Britain through which people are engaging in personal growth, and supporting each other, for instance, the co-counselling network (see p. 118).

Nature conservation and environmental action

Voluntary groups are planting trees, saving woodlands, protecting threatened species, clearing old beds out of canals, ringing birds, rebuilding dry stone walls, saving old buildings, campaigning to save the tropical rain forest, running urban farms and setting up bottle recycling plants. They all depend on volunteers. In 1914, the posters said 'Your Country Needs YOU'. Today, they need to read 'Your Planet Needs YOU'.

You can find out about local environmental groups, conservation groups and amenity societies by looking out for their notices (eg in the library), or by writing directly to *Friends of the Earth* (377 City Road, London EC1), *Greenpeace* (36 Graham Street, London N1.), *The National Federation of City Farms* (The Old Vicarage, 66 Fraser Street, Windmill Hill, Bedminster, Bristol BS3 4LY), and *The Groundwork Foundation* (27 Mawdesley Street, Bolton BL1 1LN). Ask the library to order a superb book called *Holding Your Ground — An Action Guide to Local Conservation* (£5.95, Gower/Temple Smith)

Growing your own food

If you have a garden but don't yet grow any food in it, you will find other gardeners love to give advice, and libraries have books on gardening. The only cost is the seeds, which you can share with a friend, as there are always more than you need in a packet. Crops can be shared, or sold among friends to pay for next year's seeds (business expenses. . .). If you are drawing unemployment benefit alone, you can legally set up a roadside stall and sell all the veg you can . . . on Sundays. (See Chapter 12, p. 147)

And what if you haven't got a garden?

- Apply for an allotment to the parks department of the council.
- Look around for unused land, owned by British Rail, the Gas Board, the church commissioners, developers, etc, and then get together with friends and ask if you could rent it for a peppercorn on a year-by-year lease, until they need it.
- Could you take a share in someone else's garden? The local volunteer Bureau may know of people who want help with their gardens, who might also let you use some yourself.
- *Working Weekends on Organic Farms* enables you to spend a weekend helping on someone else's farm or smallholding. (See p. 161)

People receiving Unemployment Benefit alone are allowed to earn as much as they like on Sundays...

Social, political and economic action

Here are the addresses of some groups you might want to get involved in. Why not just write for some free information about them, to find out what they are up to, and to ask for the address of their local groups?

- Oxfam, 274 Banbury Road, Oxford;
- Christian Aid, PO Box 1, 2 Sloane Gardens, London SW1, and
- War on Want, 1 London Bridge Street, London SE1, which campaign and raise funds for world development and famine relief;
- Amnesty International, 15 Roberts Place, London EC1, whose members write personal letters of support to political prisoners all around the world and campaign for their release;
- The Conservative Party, 32 Smith Square, London SW1;
- The Green Party, 10 Station Parade, Balham High Road, London SW12;
- The Labour Party, 150 Walworth Road, London SE17;
- The Liberal Party, 1 Whitehall Place, London SW1;
- The Social Democratic Party, 4 Cowley Street, London SW1;
- Friends of the Earth, 377 City Road, London EC1;
- Greenpeace, 36 Graham Street, London N1.

Taking time to read

There is so little time to read, in between working at a job and watching too much television. The break from full-time work offers a chance to catch up and to begin to read a bit, to find out what is going on in the world. Use your local library and bookshop to browse, and see what interests you. Here are 10 titles which we recommend, as they address important issues:

1. *The Aquarian Conspiracy*, by Marilyn Ferguson (Granada)
2. *The Awakening Earth*, by Peter Russell (Routledge & Kegan Paul)
3. *The Gaia Atlas*, ed Norman Myers (Pan)
4. *The Third Wave*, by Alvin Toffler (Pan)
5. *Futurework*, by James Robertson (Temple Smith)
6. *Only One Earth*, by Barbara Ward (Penguin)
7. *Far From Paradise*, by Herbie Girardet and John Seymour (BBC)
8. *The Prophet*, by Kahlil Gibran (Heinemann)
9. *Alternatives* — New Approaches to Health, Education, Energy, the Family and the Aquarian Age (Thorsons)
10. *Our Common Future*, ('The most important document on the future of the World') (OUP)

Finally. . .

Don't forget to leave space for a holiday for yourself. Yes, you did read that sentence correctly! Chapter 13 has some ideas.

CHAPTER 11: HAVING A GO – SELF-EMPLOYMENT AND CO-OPERATIVES

WHAT DO YOU NEED TO SUCCEED? – AM I CUT OUT FOR SELF-EMPLOYMENT? – BUSINESS START-UP RESOURCES – STARTING A WORKERS' CO-OPERATIVE – YOUTH BUSINESS – COMMUNITY BUSINESSES – WOMEN'S BUSINESSES – BLACK PEOPLE'S BUSINESSES

Dreaming of a business

Every week, 1,250 unemployed people or more choose to leave the dole-queue to have a go at self-employment, using the Enterprise Allowance Scheme as a starting block. Seventy per cent of them are still in business 15 months later.

Four new co-operatives start up each week, many of them run by unemployed people. In Scotland there are now over 80 new community businesses set up by local people. In other words, it *is* possible.

The thought of leaving the dole for business can be attractive. It can also be rather scary:

- 'What if I don't make it?'
- 'I'll never be able to handle all the paperwork'
- 'Nobody will want to buy my stuff'

These are common thoughts to run through the minds of people who are starting in business for the first time. A lot has changed over the last ten years, however, and there is plenty of help available if you are willing to look for it. If you are wise, you will use it to the utmost, and avoid the pitfalls that can bring failure, instead of success.

'The majority of business failures are failures before they get underway. The most important way to prevent starting a failure is to do your homework ***before you start up****.'*

(RJH, Douglas Centre for Enterprise Development, British Columbia)

WHAT DO YOU NEED TO SUCCEED?

1. *You need a feasible idea.* You must not be afraid to let go of a favourite idea if it turns out to have no chance of succeeding. You can get advice on how to discover whether it is feasible or not by visiting the local business advice agency (see below).

   Don't let the lack of an initial idea prevent you from searching for one. The achievements exercise in Chapter 3 may show you that hidden within your life lie the seeds of a business. Every area of human activity is a possible business. Even on the remotest Scottish island, or on a huge estate where everyone seems to be unemployed, there is always mail order, offering you the whole country as your market.

   If you are interested in starting a business but don't have any particular business idea in mind, send £1 to Project North East for a useful booklet called '20 Questions To Help You Choose A Business Idea'. (PNE, Marseilles Chambers, 60 Grainger Street, Newcastle upon Tyne NE1 5JG)

2. *You need the practical skills to do the job.* There's no point in trying to repair cars, clean carpets, frame pictures, make clothes, sell computer manuals or babysit for partying elephants if you can't deliver the goods properly. If you have uncertainties about your level of practical skill, enrol on a training course through the Job Training Scheme or at the local college — see Chapter 8. Your excellence at your trade will do more in the long run to make your business succeed than any other factor.

3. *You need the business skills.* Very few people possess business skills when they first think of entering business. If you are foolish you will hope it doesn't matter and plunge ahead anyway. You will get your business skills the painful way. If you are wise, you will enrol on a business skills course and learn how to assess your own strengths and weaknesses, develop your business idea, assess your market, draw up a business plan, keep proper accounts, work out cash-flow projections and do 101 other essential things. These are skills which will be absolutely essential to your future prosperity and peace of mind.

4. *You need start-up capital.* There are very few businesses which need no start-up capital. Don't despair, however — most problems are soluble, especially if you get good advice. The staff at the business advice agency will help you work out what your capital requirements will be and find the people who might lend it to you. Co-operative Development Agencies will do the same for people intending to start a co-operative.

   To get a loan from a bank, you usually need to have collateral — money which you put into the business yourself. Most unemployed people do not own their own houses, or have private resources. Some city councils are beginning to work out loan guarantee schemes to help people in this situation. The local enterprise agency will have the details.

   Under the Enterprise Allowance Scheme you can get a flat-rate allowance of £40 a week for a year (1987 figure). Young people starting in business can also obtain special loans and grants.

5. *You need a network of support around you.* A network of friendly people around you will provide you with contacts, advice, friendship, encouragement and even a practical helping hand when it matters. Some enterprise agencies are beginning to set up business clubs so that people can develop links. There are also moves afoot in some places to develop business clubs for people on the Enterprise Allowance Scheme.

You also need support from your family and friends. Starting a business is very challenging. You may work from home, and you may need to work weekends. Your income will no longer be the same every week. The more your family and friends understand, the more they will be able to support you. In return, take the time to share with them how things are going.

6. *You need the motivation.* The freedom and independence which self-employment or your own co-operative offers may seem to be attractive — but in reality it brings the necessity for hard work, self-discipline and self-motivation. It is exciting, and the challenge can be infectious, but if you have any doubts about *wanting* to do it, then forget it. If you are not 100% behind what you are doing, you will probably not succeed.

7. *You need a picture of yourself succeeding.* Set your goals, and then turn them into a fact in your mind. This is an old secret of success in business, sport, family life or anything else you want to succeed in. Call it 'positive thinking' if you like. By establishing this picture, you create a form into which reality can flow as you work. You begin to manifest what already exists, in your mind.

AM I CUT OUT FOR SELF-EMPLOYMENT?

This questionnaire has been developed by the Douglas Centre for Enterprise Development in New Westminster, British Columbia, Canada, and is re-printed with their kind permission. It will help you consider whether you have the qualities that are necessary if you are to succeed in business. The scoring system has been added by the authors.

	Usually A	Sometimes B	Rarely C
I have the physical energy to work long hours	....	....	....
I have confidence in my own abilities	....	....	....
I can make long-term commitments and work towards distant goals	....	....	....
Money is a major motivation for me	....	....	....
I have a problem-solving orientation; I like to work on difficult tasks	....	....	....
I have the ability to set goals for myself that are challenging, yet attainable	....	....	....
I am not averse to taking calculated risks	....	....	....
I am aware of what I stand to lose should the business fail	....	....	....
Rather than becoming discouraged by failures and setbacks, I have the ability to learn from them	....	....	....

I know my limits; I am willing to ask others for advice when necessary	....	....	....
I have the physical and emotional stamina required to cope with stress	....	....	....
I am able to communicate with others verbally and in writing	....	....	....
I am a good listener	....	....	....
I naturally take the initiative and assume personal responsibility for any task I undertake	....	....	....
Personal accomplishment is more important to me than personal security	....	....	....
I have a high tolerance for ambiguous and uncertain situations	....	....	....
I am competitive in that I strive towards self-imposed standards	....	....	....
I am able to change my immediate objectives as the situation dictates	....	....	....
I have a high degree of commitment to any venture I undertake	....	....	....
I have the ability to find creative and innovative solutions to problems	....	....	....
I have good 'people skills'; I can motivate others to work for me	....	....	....
I am able to analyse situations and take prompt action to resolve problems	....	....	....
I have good organisational skills	....	....	....
I am tactful	....	....	....
I am cheerful	....	....	....
I am considerate yet firm	....	....	....
Subtotals	....	....	

Ticks in column A — 2 points each; column B — 1 point; column C — 0 points, giving a maximum possible score of 52.

Total: ....

Over 45:	You have the capacity to do well — if you do all your homework properly.
36–44:	You have many of the right requirements; if you can work on shifting your 'rarely' ticks into the 'sometimes' column and your 'sometimes' ticks into the 'usually' column, and if you do your homework properly, you can do well.
30–36:	You are not firm enough yet in some of the characteristics you will need to make a success of self-employment.
Below 30:	Forget it — or prove the questionnaire wrong!

BUSINESS START-UP RESOURCES

To find the nearest Enterprise Agency, look under 'business consultants' or 'business enterprise agencies' in the Yellow Pages, or phone the council's economic development department. You can also contact the national link organisation for enterprise agencies, Business in the Community, 227A City Road, London EC1V 1LX, Tel 01-253 3716.

Part-time business start-up courses are run by almost every local college and polytechnic. The MSC runs a full-time Small Business Course for which you can receive a training allowance, and a part-time Self-Employment Course. The enterprise agency will be able to give you details about courses.

The *Enterprise Allowance Scheme* is open to anyone who is unemployed who wants to start a business or become self-employed. If you are accepted onto the scheme, you sign off the dole altogether, and receive a flat-rate taxable allowance of £40 a week (1987) for a full year, on top of which you can earn as much as you like, and also claim Family Income Supplement/Family Credit and Housing Benefit. Details are available at the Jobcentre. The conditions for joining are:

- You must have been unemployed or under notice of redundancy for 8 weeks, and be receiving unemployment or supplementary benefit/Income Support. People who have been on the Community Programme, Voluntary Projects Programme or Job Training Scheme do not have to wait the 8 weeks;
- You must have a potentially viable business idea;
- You must not have already started working on your business;
- You must be able to show that you have at least £1000 for use as capital resources for your business, or that you can raise it by loan or overdraft. This creates problems for people who are unable to get a loan from friends, relatives or the bank. In some areas ways are being found to help, so you should always ask at the Enterprise Agency.

Useful books

- *The Small Business Guide*, by Colin Barrow (BBC Publications)
- *Be Your Own Boss: Starter Kit,* by David Watkins (£7.95, National Extension College, 18 Brooklands Avenue, Cambridge CB2 2HN). This is a workbook, designed to help you assess your ideas, capabilities and possibilities. If you can afford it, worth purchasing.
- *Be Your Own Boss: Growth Kit* the sequel to the *Starter Kit*, provides specialist help for those who have survived their first year and are looking to grow and develop. (£9.95, National Extension College)
- *Creating Your Own Work*, by Micheline Mason (£2.95, Gresham Books, PO Box 61, Henley-on-Thames, Oxon RG9 3LQ). A very enjoyable book, full of case studies

about people who have become self-employed.

- *The Guardian Guide to Running a Small Business*, by Clive Woodcock, (£4.95, Kogan Page Ltd, 120 Pentonville Road, London N1 9JN)
- *Working for Yourself* by Godfrey Golzen (£5.95, Kogan Page)
- *Occupation: Self-Employed*, by Rosemary Petit (£4.50, Wildwood House). More fascinating case-studies.

Kogan Page also publish a series of books on 'Running Your Own. . . ' (Antiques Business, Boarding Kennels, Building Business, Catering Business, Photographic Salon, Pub, Restaurant, Shop, Small Hotel, Arts and Crafts, Wine Bar, Hairdressing Salon).

STARTING A WORKERS' CO-OPERATIVE

The total number of workers' co-operatives in Britain in 1987 rose to over 1500, and an average of four new co-operatives were being registered every week. The new co-operatives are turning out a high success rate, too, and are not dogged by business failure, although wages are not always very high.

A workers' co-operative is a business owned and controlled by those who work in it, for their own benefit. People are attracted to the idea of a co-operative for a variety of reasons. Some want to escape from bosses and supervisors, and work in an egalitarian way. Some want the challenge of starting a business in a new way. Some want to spread particular ideals, such as an anti-sexist or anti-racist approach. There are co-operatives in many different areas of work, from printing and publishing to restaurants, engineering, shoe-making, computer-consultancy, wholefoods and pregnancy advice.

A network of local Co-operative Development Agencies helps groups to develop their ideas, work out business plans, apply for loans, develop good team relationships, and start trading. In some places, where there are no CDAs, help is available through the local enterprise agency or the council's economic development committee. If you have even a loose interest in the possibility of starting a co-operative, arrange a visit to the nearest local Co-operative Development Agency. Once you start talking to people who know about the field, your interest may develop further. Find the address by looking in the Yellow Pages (Business consulting/advice/agencies), or by phoning the council's economic development department. Failing that, write direct to the national Co-operative Development Agency in London, listed below.

- *Introducing Worker Co-operatives*, Open University, Learning Materials Service, PO Box 88, Milton Keynes MK7 6DH.
- *The Workers Co-operative Handbook*, by Peter Cockerton and Anna Whyatt (£4.20, Turnaround, 27 Horsell Road, London N5).
- *Running Your Own Co-operative*, by John Pearce (£4.95, Kogan Page).
- *Industrial Common Ownership Movement (ICOM)*, 7 Corn Exchange, Leeds LS1 7BP, Tel 0532-461737 — a national membership body which promotes co-operatives.
- *Co-operative Development Agency*, Broadmead House, 21 Panton Street, London SW1Y 4DR, Tel 01-839 2988 — a government appointed national agency which promotes co-operatives and local CDAs.

YOUTH BUSINESS

- *Prince's Youth Business Initiative* (8 Bedford Row, London WC1R 4BU, Tel 01–430 0521) is able to provide:

- — bursaries of up to £1,000 for expenditure on capital equipment;
- — small grants for such things as vehicle purchase, training, market research or marketing;
- — low-interest loans of up to £5,000;
- — linked advice from a local business person in most areas of Britain.

- *Livewire* (60 Grainger Street, Newcastle NE1 5JG, Tel 091-261 7856) is a young people's business and community endeavour competition set up by Shell UK which provides regional and national prizes, plus linked business advice.
- *Instant Muscle* (Haymill Centre, 112 Burnham Lane, Burnham, Slough, Berks SL1 6LZ) is a nationwide initiative which helps young people to start businesses.
- *Head Start in Business* (3 Carlton House Terrace, London SW1) run youth business start-up programmes around the UK.
- *Youth Enterprise Centres* There is a growing number of local centres which provide comprehensive support to young people. (Contact Project North East, Marseilles Chambers, 60 Grainger St, Newcastle NE1 5JG, Tel 091–261 7856 for local details.)

Resources and literature on youth business

Special notes for youth workers, careers workers, workers at Unemployed Centres and others who want to develop youth business initiatives:

- The *Education for Enterprise Network* (c/o Paul Moran, Durham University Business School, Mill Hill Lane, Durham DH1 3LB, Tel 0385–41919) creates a link between initiatives, both in schools and among young people. It provides a newsletter and regular meetings to enable people to meet and learn from each other.
- *Education for Enterprise,* ed Tony Watts and Paul Moran is a full report of the network's 1984 conference, including descriptions of key initiatives, including schools' initiatives, and a very thorough resource listing. (£2.60 from CRAC, Bateman Street, Cambridge CB2 1LZ)
- *Guidelines for Youth Enterprise,* produced by David Grayson from the Newcastle Youth Enterprise Centre, for Business in the Community, as a practical guide for staff at Enterprise Agencies, with a resource listing including videos, kits, games and simulation exercises for schools and youth businesses. (£5.50 from The Planning Exchange, 186 Bath Street, Glasgow G2)
- *Youth Enterprise Resources: A Resource Bank,* based on Project North East's experience in the field. £6.00 from PNE, 45 Groat Market, Newcastle NE1 1UG.
- *Work for Yourself: A Guide for Young People*, by Paddy Hall, a humorous practical guide to help young people consider the whole idea of setting up in business (£4.95 from the National Extension College, 18 Brooklands Avenue, Cambridge CB2 2HN).
- *Newcastle Youth Enterprise Centre: From Dream to Reality*, details the practical process of setting up a centre. (£5.50 from Project North East, address above).

COMMUNITY BUSINESS

The community business movement is providing a very valuable contribution to community life, and to our need to do something solid about unemployment. It has developed particularly well in Scotland, as a neighbourhood-based self-help response to local unemployment. A community business is owned and controlled by local people, and run for the overall benefit of the local community, combining both social and economic goals. Businesses range from cleaning buildings (Flagstone Enterprises, Paisley) and providing workspace (Govan Workspace, Glasgow) to home-knitting (Via, Glasgow), to running local shops (Co Chomunn Stafainn, Skye). See Chapter 5.

Resources

- *What Business in the Port?* by Keith Hayton, charts the development of Port Glasgow Community Enterprises Ltd over its first five years (£3.50 from Strathclyde Community Business Ltd, Six Harmony Row, Govan, Glasgow G51 3BA).
- *Little Pockets of Hope,* by Glen Buchanan, tells the story of Govan Workspace, in Glasgow (£2.50 from the same address).
- *Community Business News* (£5.00 pa from Community Business Scotland, at the same address).

WOMEN'S BUSINESSES

Women are starting their own businesses and co-operatives in increasing numbers, and there are a number of useful resources:

- *Enterprising Women* (£1.00 from Greater London Enterprise Board, 63-67 Newington Causeway, London SE1 6BD).
- *A Woman's Guide to Starting Her Own Business,* by Susan Glascok (£2.50, Granada).
- *SWEATSHOP — A woman's guide to self-employment* (£5.95 from Friday Publications, Finsbury Business Centre, Bowling Green Lane, London EC1). Includes information cards and case studies.
- *ICOM Womens Link-Up.* A network of women's co-ops, from ICOM (address above).
- *Women's World Banking* An international initiative to produce financial loans for women's businesses, guaranteed by a special capital fund (c/o Centre for Employment Initiatives,140A Gloucester Mansions, Cambridge Circus, London WC2H 8PA).
- *Women in Enterprise*, a support network, giving advice and information, and running training courses for women who want to start up in business (26 Bond Street, London WC1 2QP).

BLACK PEOPLE'S BUSINESSES

A survey of ethnic minority businesses in the Birmingham area found that there were over 2,000 such businesses, employing over 30,000 people. Some useful contacts:

- *The UK Caribbean Chamber of Commerce*, which is taking various initiatives to encourage more black people to enter business. (Contact UKCCC, 99 Stoke Newington Church Street, London N16, Tel 01–254 4532.)
- *Project Fullemploy* runs business training courses for young people, including a large proportion of young black people. (Contact Fullemploy, 102 Park Village East, London NW1 3SP, Tel 01–387 1222)
- *The Coach House,* a small business training and start-up centre in St Pauls, Bristol, with a strong multi-racial emphasis. (2 Upper York Street, St Pauls, Bristol)
- *'Local Authorities and Black Business Development'* (Free from CRE, Elliot House, 10/12 Allington Street, London SW1E 5EH.)

CHAPTER 12: MONEY

INTRODUCTION – HOW TO GET YOUR BENEFIT – THE 'AVAILABLE FOR WORK' TEST – WAYS OF MAKING YOUR MONEY GO FURTHER – PROBLEMS WITH BENEFIT

INTRODUCTION

This may be the first chapter you have turned to, if your biggest problem about being unemployed is simply the money.

So, a word about what this chapter does and doesn't give you:

- It explains how to sign on and claim benefit (p. 142).
- It describes both the old Supplementary Benefit system and the Income Support system which replaces it in April 1988.
- It shows ways in which you could save money or increase your income (p. 146).
- It offers a stage-by-stage budgeting exercise (p. 146).
- It offers advice on some of the problems that can arise for people receiving benefit (p. 154).
- It tells you where to go for further help and advice (p. 154).
- It DOES NOT spell out all the details of Unemployment Benefit and Supplementary Benefit/Income Support. We realise that in some situations, you will need this detailed information — so we tell you where to go to get it. (p. 154).
- It DOES NOT give actual rates of benefit. These change every April, so any rates we published would soon be out of date.

> The *National Welfare Benefits Handbook* (see p. 154) gives excellent detailed coverage of the system of Supplementary Benefit/Income Support. We strongly recommend that you order the book from the local library, or buy yourself a copy.

The chapter is divided into 3 sections:

In April 1988 Supplementary Benefit is being replaced by a new system of benefit called Income Support. Some aspects of the old system are remaining the same, while other aspects are changing. To cover both systems, we have used the expression 'Supplementary Benefit/Income Support' (SB/IS), where the systems are the same, and described the differences where the two systems are different. The system of Unemployment Benefit is not being changed.

SECTION 1: HOW TO GET YOUR BENEFIT

There are two sorts of benefit for unemployed people — Unemployment Benefit for those who have paid enough National Insurance contributions to qualify, and Supplementary

Benefit/Income Support which is paid to everyone else, including people whose Unemployment Benefit is not enough to meet their basic needs.

1. At the Unemployment Benefit Office

a) As soon as you become unemployed, go to the Unemployment Benefit Office and find the 'fresh claims' desk. (If you have left school and have not had a job before, and are under 18, register with the Careers Service or the Jobcentre before going to the Unemployment Benefit Office.)

Tell them you are unemployed and looking for work, and want to claim benefit. They will give you a claim form called UB671 to fill in and return to them. This is the 'Availability for Work' form, and it is important that you fill it in correctly — see p. 144. They will also ask you a few questions (e.g. whether you have any family, and who your last employer was) and tell you when your signing-on time will be each fortnight.

b) *If you have not worked before* you will not receive any Unemployment Benefit, so you must claim Supplementary Benefit/Income Support. (You will receive a letter in two weeks time telling you that you do not qualify for Unemployment Benefit. This doesn't make any difference to your claim for Supplementary Benefit/Income Support.) Ask for a form B1 to take to the DHSS Social Security Office.

c) *If you have worked before,* take your P45 from your last job or a note of your National Insurance number with you, if you have them. (If you don't, you can still claim benefit.)

- If you are *certain* that you will receive full Unemployment Benefit, but concerned that your benefit will not be enough to cover your basic needs, you can apply for Supplementary Benefit/Income Support to top up your benefit by asking for a form B1. However, you have less freedom to earn extra income from part-time work if you are receiving SB/IS, so consider this factor carefully — see p. 150.
- If you are *not certain* whether you will get full Unemployment Benefit, either because you have not been working for long, or because you did not work all the time for the last two years, then you may receive either no Unemployment Benefit, or less than the full rate. Claim for Supplementary Benefit/Income Support, using the form B1.
- If you think you will get full benefit, but will be very hard up for the next two weeks until your first Giro arrives, you should also apply for Supplementary Benefit/ Income Support.

2. At the Social Security Office

There is usually no need for an interview or visit with a fresh claim for Supplementary Benefit/Income Support. All the necessary information is included on the form B1, so check carefully that you have completed the form correctly to avoid delay in processing your claim. The DHSS will work out how much money you need, according to their rules and rates. These are fixed by law and updated every April.

If the DHSS calls you to an interview and your fares come to more than 80p, you can claim the excess back. You can also claim for fares if you think there has been an error in your payment, or if you are claiming for an Urgent Needs Payment (see p. 159). Ask the interviewing officer.

Take a friend with you to your interview — this often gives people a lot more confidence.

If you are married or live with a partner, either you or your partner may be the claimant. There are various conditions under which you will be better off if one claims and not the other. Ask for advice at the DHSS or the Citizens Advice Bureau. A leaflet called *New Rights to Claim Benefits for Women* is available from Child Poverty Action Group (p. 154).

Savings
Until April 1988: If you have capital savings over £3,000, you will not be able to receive any Supplementary Benefit (see below).
After April 1988: If you have capital savings over £6,000, you will not be able to receive any Income Support. If you have savings above £3,000, each £250 of savings up to £6,000 will count as producing £1 per week of notional income, which will be taken off your benefit.

'Savings' means the total of your savings, less any debts, and less any savings specially put aside to cover bills and other reasonable expenses. Savings includes cash, money in the bank, redundancy payments,and the surrender value of a life insurance or endowment policy (excluding the first £1,500). Guaranteed income bonds held in an insurance company, apparently, do not count as capital savings. Any business assets are ignored. Occasional gifts (i.e. Christmas and birthdays) up to £100 are also ignored.

If you need to dispose of some capital to be eligible to claim benefit, ask the Citizens Advice Bureau (see p. vii) for advice first — the DHSS does not smile on the sudden purchase of a new car, or holidays in Bermuda.

3. Your benefit arrives
Your giro will arrive by post every two weeks.

Unemployment Benefit: Your benefit is made up of a basic rate, plus an addition for any adult dependants. It will stop after a year, when you should claim for Supplementary Benefit/Income Support. You can also claim this while you are receiving Unemployment Benefit if your UB is not enough to cover your basic needs, and SB/IS would pay you more. You will need to claim separately for Housing Benefit (see below).

Supplementary Benefit/Income Support: Your benefit will be made up of a personal allowance for yourself, or yourself and your partner, and for your children, plus (until April 1988) an increase for 'additional requirements' (see below), or (after April 1988) a Premium for families, pensioners, people with disabilities and single parents.

4. Housing Benefit
If you qualify for Supplementary Benefit/Income Support, you will automatically qualify for Housing Benefit. If you are receiving Unemployment Benefit you should apply for Housing Benefit — the forms are in the Post Office, or the Treasurer's Department of your local authority.

After April 1988, Housing Benefit will probably only pay for 80% of your rates. You will be expected to find the remaining 20% from your personal benefit. Check at the Citizens Advice Bureau for up-to-date information.

- If you live in a council house, the money for your rates and rent will be rebated by the council.
- If you are a private tenant, you will be sent a separate giro for your rent by the council.
- If you are an owner-occupier you will receive payment from the Council for your rates and water rates; and a tiny weekly allowance for maintenance and insurance repairs. For the first 16 weeks of claiming benefit you will only receive 50% of the interest payments on your mortgage. This will inevitably create huge difficulties for many people. Seek advice from the Citizens Advice Bureau or Welfare Rights Office. Once the 16 weeks are over, you can get help with paying the additional interest payable on the arrears of interest that accumulated during your first 16 weeks on benefit. (Crazy world, isn't it!)
- If you are an owner-occupier, make an appointment to discuss your situation with your Building Society, and ask them to consider adding any accumulated payments that you cannot pay onto your capital, and furnishing you with figures to

show you how much additional interest you will accumulate on the arrears, so that you can get help paying it off later.

Rights Guide for Homeowners, £3.50, CPAG (Pubs), 4th Floor, 1-5 Bath Street, London EC1V 9PY.

A Guide to Housing Benefit, £4.95, CPAG.

5. How has my benefit been worked out?

There should be a note with your first giro payment explaining how it has been worked out (Form A14N). These are sometimes illegible. To be sure how your benefit has been worked out, write for a proper 'Notice of Assessment' (Form A124).

6. From now on

If you live more than six miles from the nearest Unemployment Benefit Office, you can sign on postally. Otherwise, you now sign on every two weeks, unless you have been out of work for over a year and are over 50, in which case you sign on every 3 months. If you are over 60, you need not sign on at all.

THE 'AVAILABLE FOR WORK' TEST

When you first sign on you will be asked to fill in form UB671, which is a test of your availability for work. This asks questions about the efforts you are making to find work. If you fail to give the right answers, your benefit may be suspended. You will be expected to fill in the form on the spot, or risk suspension.

These are the questions you will be asked, along with the answers you are advised to give in order to avoid suspension:

Qu 1: What are you doing to find work?
Answer: Visiting Jobcentre, searching through newspapers, etc. Give details of the jobs you have applied for.

Qu 2: What job do you normally do?
Answer: Give details of your normal job, and any particular skills or qualifications you have (see Chapter 3). If you have just left college, YTS or training, say so.

Qu 3: What job are you looking for?
Answer: Enter the kind of job you normally do, or want to do, or say you are willing to do anything that fits your skills and experience.

Qu 4: Are you willing to consider any other jobs? If 'no', please give your reasons.
Answer: Answer 'Yes'.

Qu 5: Can you start work today? If not, please say why. When can you start work?
Answer: Answer 'Yes'.

Qu 6: Are you looking for full-time work? If 'no', please give your reasons and write against each day the hours you can work.
Answer: Answer 'Yes'. To receive benefit you must be available for work. Ignore the box detailing days and hours.

Qu 7: How far are you able to travel to work? (for example home town only, within daily travelling distance)
Answer: Within daily travelling distance.

Qu 8: Do you have any adults or children to care for during working hours? If 'yes', can you make *immediate* arrangements for their care if you get a job?
Answer: Either 'no'; or 'yes' to both parts of the question.

Qu 9: What was your weekly wage or salary (before deductions) in your last job?
Answer: Enter the correct amount before deductions. If it was a training scheme such as YTS, state that it was a training allowance. If it was a year or more ago, say which year that wage or salary applied to.

Qu 10: What is the minimum wage or salary (before deductions) you are willing to take?
Answer: Write *either* 'the going rate for the job' *or* the same figure as in 9, *or* the same figure as in 9 'plus an adjustment for inflation'. Don't ask for more than the figure you wrote in 9, unless that was only a training allowance.

Qu 11: If the amount at 10 is more than the amount you have put at 9, please say why?
Answer: Either leave blank or explain that your last income was only a training allowance.

> Qu 12: Please give any other details which you think affect your availability for work.
> **Answer: Leave blank.**

If you give any other answers, you will be referred to an adjudication officer who will review your claim. (Thanks to the Unemployment Unit, 9 Poland Street, London W1V 2DG, for information on this.)

SECTION 2: WAYS OF MAKING YOUR MONEY GO FURTHER

If you are on Unemployment Benefit:	*Tick if yes*	*If no, see number below*
Are you sure you are getting the correct benefit?	.....	No. 1
Have you applied for a tax rebate?	.....	No. 2
Have you applied for Housing Benefit?	.....	No. 3
Are you earning an extra £2 a day or more?	.....	No. 4
Is your partner earning?	.....	No. 5
Have you considered taking a lodger?	.....	No. 6
Have you applied for free prescriptions, etc?	.....	No. 7
Have you applied for free school meals for your children?	.....	No. 8
Have you asked to have your mortgage or HP repayments suspended?	.....	No. 9
Are you paying your fuel bills, etc. in the easiest way?	.....	No. 10
You may be eligible for Supplementary Benefit/Income Support. Have you applied?	.....	No. 11
Have you drawn up a budget of your income and expenditure?	.....	No. 16

If you are on Supplementary Benefit/Income Support:		
Are you sure you are getting the correct benefit?	.....	No. 12
(Until April 1988) Are you receiving any 'Additional Requirements' you might be entitled to?	.....	No. 13
Have you applied for a tax rebate?	.....	No. 2
Are you earning an extra £4 a week (until April 1988) or £5/£15 a week (after April 1988)?	.....	No. 14
Is your partner earning an extra £4 a week (until April 1988) or £5/£15 a week (after April 1988)?	.....	No. 14
Have you considered taking in a lodger, or sub-letting?	.....	No. 6
Have you applied for free school meals, free prescriptions, etc. that you are entitled to?	.....	Nos. 7, 8
Have you asked to have your mortgage or HP repayments suspended?	.....	No. 9
Have you enquired about Single Payments (before April 1988)	.....	No. 15a
or help from the Social Fund (after April1988)?	.....	No. 15b
Are you paying your fuel bills, etc. in the easiest way?	.....	No. 10
Have you drawn up a yearly and weekly budget of your income and expenditure?	.....	No. 16

1. Are you getting the correct Unemployment Benefit?
Phone or visit the Unemployment Benefit Office and ask them to check. If you are still unsatisfied, ask an Advice Centre for help (see p. vii). You can also get help from the Claimants' Union. (See p. 155).

2. Have you applied for a PAYE tax refund?
If you have paid any PAYE income tax since last April 5th, you ought to get some back. After being out of work for four weeks, ask for a form P50 from theTax Office (under 'Inland Revenue' in the phone book) or from the UBO. Your refund will not be paid until next April, or until you return to work.

3. Have you claimed for Housing Benefit?
This is available to anyone on a low income. The easiest way to find out if you qualify is to apply. Phone the local council and ask for the Housing Benefit department. Ask them to post you the forms. Fill them in and post them. (For help with filling in forms, see p. 157.)

Before April 1988: If you are a private tenant, the council will not necessarily take your *actual* rent into account when they work out if you qualify. They will give you benefit on the basis of what they decide is a 'fair rent' for your house. Consult the Citizens Advice Bureau for advice.

After April 1988: A new Housing Benefit scheme is being introduced. If you qualify for Income Support, you will automatically qualify for Housing Benefit, and you should receive all your 'eligible' housing costs. Only 80% of your rates will be paid. Check with the Citizens Advice Bureau for up-to-date advice.

4. Are you earning an extra £2 a day or more after expenses (while on Unemployment Benefit)?
These are the rules about earning money while on Unemployment Benefit:

- You can earn as much as you like on Sundays, as your benefit only covers Monday–Saturday. For possibilities, see No. 14 below.
- You can earn up to £2 a day (after expenses) without losing any benefit. See No. 14 below for a note on expenses.
- You can choose to give up benefit for one or two days, if you find part-time work for those days. If you can earn more than one sixth of your weekly benefit, in one day's work, for instance, it is obviously worth your while to do so. However (you're right, there had to be a snag!), the rules state that if you find work as an employee (as against being self-employed), the work must not be in your 'normal line of work'.

The rules also state that it is not on for you to establish yourself with a relatively well-paid regular job for 2 or 3 days a week, and claim benefit for the other days. This includes Community Programme jobs. And you must still be available for full-time work.

5. The rules about dependants earning money
You can receive a fixed increase of unemployment benefit for a married (or common law) partner, who must declare his or her earnings. If he or she earns *less* than the amount of the increase, the increase is not reduced at all; but if he or she earns an amount *equal* to or *more* than the amount of the increase, the increase is stopped altogether. (This needs some careful thought!) Your own unemployment benefit is not affected.

If you are receiving any Supplementary Benefit/Income Support in addition to your Unemployment Benefit, you will fall under the SB/IS earnings rules, which are quite different (see No. 14).

6. Have you considered taking in a lodger, or sub-letting?
A lodger counts as a non-dependant in your household. The amount you get from the DHSS for housing costs (except water rates) will be reduced by a varying amount (and by none at all in some circumstances) depending on the age of the lodger, and whether he or she is employed. Any income you receive is ignored as a resource — i.e. not counted against your income. If you have three or more lodgers, two thirds of what you charge plus any deduction in your housing benefit is ignored, and one third is counted as income.

If you sub-let part of your home, any profits you make will be completely ignored as income if you use them for capital repayments on your mortgage, provided your available capital does not exceed your outstanding mortgage by more than £500.

7. Have you applied for free prescriptions and other welfare benefits?
With prescriptions at almost £3 a throw, life can get very expensive if you or your children start to fall to pieces. Until April 1988, people on very low incomes and on Supplementary Benefit may receive free prescriptions, dental treatment, glasses, and milk and vitamins for children under school age. After April 1988, only people on Income Support will have an automatic right to these. There is a leaflet in the Post Office or DHSS (Freeline Social Security 0800-666555) which explains whether you qualify for any of these items.

You can get help with fares to hospital if you are receiving Supplementary Benefit/ Income Support, or if the cost of the fares would reduce your income so that it fell within the SB/IS levels. The way to find out is simply to apply, using form H11 (available from hospitals) or to phone Freeline Social Security (0800-666555).

In some areas you may be able to claim a school uniform grant and a clothing grant. Check with the head teacher or educational welfare officer.

8. Have you applied for your children to get free school meals?
Every county and city council has slightly different rules about who gets free meals. The simplest way to find out if you qualify is to phone your Area Education Office (see p.vii), ask for an application form and apply. You may have to persist. People receiving Supplementary Benefit/Income Support or Family Income Supplement/Family Credit should receive free school meals.

9. Have you asked to have your mortgage or HP capital repayments suspended?
Your Building Society and any firms you have HP agreements with may agree to suspend capital repayments until you can find a job again. Write to them, explaining your position. See the *Rights Guide for Homeowners* (p. 144).

10. Are you paying your fuel bills, etc. in the easiest way?

- You can buy stamps for your TV licence and phone bill at the Post Office.
- You can buy stamps for your gas and electricity bills at the Gas and Electricity Showrooms, and also at some local shops or the Post Office.
- You can pay an agreed amount each week or month towards your fuel bills at the post office or by bankers order.
- You can have a slot meter installed if there are no other ways to meet your bills and if there will be real hardship should you be cut off.

If you are under threat of disconnection, see p. 159. See also the *Fuel Rights Handbook*, £4.95 from CPAG (Pubs) , 4th Floor, 1-5 Bath Street, London EC1V 9PY.

11. You may be eligible for Supplementary Benefit/Income Support
Unemployment Benefit levels are very low, and many people will receive more by claiming

Supplementary Benefit/Income Support. To find out if you qualify, fill in a form B1 from the Post Office and post it to the DHSS — but consider the points below first.

If you receive Supplementary Benefit/Income Support, a few things will change:
Positive changes: You will qualify for free school meals, free prescriptions and other welfare benefits (see Nos 7,8).
Negative changes: You will fall under the SB/IS earnings rules, and only be allowed to earn £5 a week instead of £12 or more. If you have any way of earning some part-time cash instead of claiming SB/IS, this may be a better solution. Once you are receiving SB/IS, even if you only receive an extra £1 a week, you fall under their rules, and not the UB rules.

12. Are you sure you are getting the correct Supplementary Benefit/ Income Support?
Freefone the DHSS and ask them to send you a form A124 (Notice of Assessment), and/or ask the Citizens Advice Bureau for their help (see p. vii). If you want to appeal, see p. 156.

13. Until April 1988: Are you receiving any benefit increases for Additional Requirements that you might be entitled to?
Until April 1988, you may be entitled to a regular weekly addition, on top of your normal benefit if you or someone you claim for meets one or more of the conditions listed below. Your claim can be backdated for up to a year. On any medical matters, you will need a doctor's letter, which he or she is legally obliged to provide free of charge.

Additions for heating if:

- A member of your household suffers from ill-health (e.g. bronchitis, rheumatism, arthritis or anaemia).
- Your home is difficult to heat, damp or draughty.
- The heating system on your estate is expensive to run: the whole estate must be designated as having a heating system with 'disproportionately high' heating costs.
- A member of your household is:
  - under 5 or 65 or over, or
  - on a Mobility or Attendance Allowance, or
  - has difficulty in walking.

Other additions:

- If you need more than one bath a week for medical reasons.
- Blindness or recent blindness.
- Special diet (various conditions).
- Domestic assistance necessary (various conditions).
- Hire purchase costs (but not other credit card debts)(various conditions).
- Laundry/launderette (various conditions).
- Special wear and tear on clothing due to mental or physical problems.
- Extra expensive clothing or footwear, falling outside standard sizes.
- Furniture storage (various conditions).
- Regular fares to hospital (various conditions).

If you think you might qualify for any of these, write a letter to the DHSS applying for an Additional Requirements increase, asking for any arrears to be backdated. The easiest way to discover if you qualify is to apply.

After April 1988, Additional Requirements are being abolished. Income Support consists of 'Personal Allowances' and 'Premiums'. Single parents, pensioners, seriously disabled people and children on attendance or mobility allowance, or who are blind, will qualify for premiums.

You are *very strongly advised* to apply for any Additional Requirements you think you may be entitled to before April1988, because the level of Income Support you receive will be based on the level of Supplementary Benefit you received on April 5th 1988.

14. Are you earning an extra £4 a week (until April 1988) or £5/£15 (after April 1988)? Is your partner also earning this?

Until April1988: You can earn up to £4 a week each (after expenses) before you lose any benefit. Anything over £4 each must be declared, and your benefit will be reduced accordingly. You will be expected to show detailed evidence of your earnings; be prepared to argue for your 'expenses'.

Expenses covers anything you have to spend in order to earn your money - child-minding fees, travel costs, playgroup fees, overalls, materials, tools and equipment, private helicopter, and any other reasonable expense. You can also deduct tax and insurance. Travel costs can cover car usage costs as well as petrol — the AA reckon it costs 28p a mile to use a family car. It has been considered quite reasonable to claim £13 expenses in order to earn £15, in the past. If you choose to earn an income through child-minding, two thirds of the income will be ignored. Earnings as a part-time fireman are ignored.

After April 1988: You can earn up to £5 a week each. People receiving the disability Premium, single parents and families who have been unemployed for over two years can earn up to £15 a week each without losing benefit. You can not claim for any expenses.

Ideas? Gardening, casual work, car/bike/gadget/building repairs, odd-jobbing, delivering leaflets, window-cleaning, making things for sale on market stalls, baby-sitting, house-cleaning, car-washing and valetting, etc. Order a copy of *Earning Money at Home* from the library (Consumers Association) to give you ideas.

Chapter 5 contains suggestions about group earning schemes which allow you to enjoy yourself at the same time.

If you earn more than you get on SB/IS, but work less than 30 hours, you keep all of your earnings and receive no benefit (for that week). This is true both before and after April 1988.

15a. Single Payments (before April 1988)

Single Payments are one-off grants paid to people on Supplementary Benefit to meet special expenses where there is a definite need. Your savings must be less than £500, or they would be, if you paid for the item in question.

The payments all have strict conditions around them. You can only get an 'essential furniture grant', for instance, if you need the furniture for a person who is a pensioner, *or* who is chronically sick or mentally or physically disabled, *or* if you are moving home for certain specified reasons.

With these conditions, single payments can cover such things as

- Removal expenses.
- Essential home repairs and maintenance.
- Essential furniture (e.g. cooker, heater, bedding).
- Miscellaneous furniture (when moving home only).
- Clearing an HP debt for essential furniture and household equipment.
- Various housing expenses — returnable deposits to secure a flat, rent in advance, legal fees, survey fees.
- Funeral expenses (comes under the Social Fund).
- Fares (and lodging costs, if need be) to visit relatives in hospital, to visit children in a domestic crisis, or to visit children where custody has not been decided.

- Periods of exceptionally cold weather (average temperature 0 Celsius or lower), if a member of your household is 65 or over, under 2, chronically sick, or mentally or physically disabled.
- A new heating system you are unfamiliar with — half the cost over the first six months if your bill is unpaid when you claim.
- Repairs to a heating appliance, or a replacement appliance.
- Draughtproofing materials (if you cannot do the work yourself, contact the local Volunteer Bureau or Council for Voluntary Service — see p. vii).
- Travel and lodgings costs to search for work.
- Payments which would be 'the only means by which serious damage or risk to health or safety' could be prevented — a safety clause which can sometimes be used to obtain (e.g.) new shoes or payment of fuel debts (under certain circumstances).

You cannot qualify if you have immediate prospects of work (i.e. an actual offer of a job, with an early start date), or if you are a squatter (unless you have permission to live where you are).

If you need to spend money for basic household items, or for a funeral (for instance), visit the Citizens Advice Bureau or Welfare Advice Office. They will know exactly what you can claim for (DHSS Leaflet SB16).

15b. Help from the Social Fund (after April 1988)
The details of the Social Fund are still being ironed out at the time of publication — probably ironed so flat there will be nothing left worth talking about. The Social Fund will make payments (a) for maternity and funeral needs, and (b) for other needs. The overriding principle on which the Social Fund is based is that each local office will have an annual budget, and once the budget is used up, that'll be that.

Both grants and loans will be payable from the Social Fund. If you get a loan, this will be repayable by deductions from your benefit.

Grants will be available to cover funeral expenses. These will be recoverable from the estate of the deceased if possible, but not from the claimant. A flat-rate grant of £80 will be payable for maternity needs. (These began in April 1987.)

'Budgeting loans' (replacing Single Needs Payments) will be available 'to assist an eligible person to meet important intermittent expenses for which it may be difficult to budget.' Don't get too hopeful, though. There is a priority list for people - single people and people without children are designated 'low priority' - and a priority list for 'items', as follows:

- Top priority: a need that, if not met, would cause hardship, damage or risk to the health or safety of the family.
- Medium priority: other items of furniture; redecoration (if the applicant is responsible for decoration); HP and other debts.
- Low priority: includes items which are not covered by the single payments scheme and rent in advance.

Applicants must have been in receipt of Income Support for six months and capital of over £500 will exclude entitlement. Furthermore, there is no guarantee that a need will be met.

'Crisis loans' (replacing Urgent Needs Payments) will be available to meet immediate short term needs in an emergency, or as a consequence of a disaster - if there is a serious threat to the person's health or safety, and if no alternative resources are available. Payments can cover a period of 14 days.

Loans must be repaid within 78, or if necessary, 104 days. The maximum loan payable is £1000; the minimum is £30. There is no interest payable. Repayment will involve deductions from benefit of up to 25% (excluding mortgage interest). A loan can also be recovered from a partner or a person liable to maintain (with important implications for separated spouses and sponsors of immigrants).

Decisions concerning Social Fund payments will not carry any right to appeal — only a right to a review, firstly by a Social Fund Officer, and then by a Social Fund Inspector.

Amendments to these proposals may be published between the publication of this Handbook and April 1988: you are therefore advised to check with your local Citizens Advice Bureau, DHSS or Welfare Rights Office, for final details on the Social Fund.

16. Have you drawn up a complete budget of your income and expenditure, and planned where you could make savings?

Budgeting is never fun, but if you are on a low income, it is essential. Here are some guidelines.

Making up a fortnightly budget sheet (7 steps)

Step 1. Make a complete list of all your fortnightly income (Total 1)

Step 2. Make a list of all your regular financial commitments (bills, etc. not food, etc.)

13 times table:

1	*2*	*3*	*4*	*5*	*6*	*7*	*8*	*9*	*10*
13	26	39	52	65	78	91	104	117	130

11	*12*	*13*	*14*	*15*	*16*
143	156	169	182	195	208

- *Electricity bill:* multiply the last quarter's bill by 2, and then divide by 13. Remember that winter bills are double summer bills. Total: ....
- *Gas bill:* ditto Total:.......
- *Telephone bill:* ditto Total:.......
- *Coal, Calor Gas:* needs its own special calculation. Total:.......
- *Weekly rent and rates:* multiply by 2. Total:.......
- *Mortgage repayments:* multiply your monthly repayments by 6, and then divide by 13. Total:.......
- *Children's school lunches* for 10 days. Total:.......
- *Children's weekly pocket money,* multiplied by 2. Total:.......
- *TV rent and licence* Total:.......
- *Hire purchase* Total:.......

Regular commitments total ....
(Total 2)

Step 3. *Car or Motor-bike.* Work out the annual costs of your

- Road tax: ....
- Insurance: ....
- MoT + services: ....
- AA/RAC membership: ....
- Extra repairs: ....

Total: ....

Divide by 2 and then by 13, to obtain cost per fortnight: ....

Petrol, oil per week: .... cost per fortnight: ....

Total cost of running the car/bike per fortnight: ....

(Total 3)

Step 4. For two weeks, keep a check on all your household expenditure. Make several separate lists, headed food, 'things', papers, bus/train/tube, drink, tobacco, stamps, miscellaneous, cost of being constructively unemployed (evening classes, materials, photocopying, etc.)

Total cost for 2 weeks:............

(Total 4)

Step 5. Make an estimate of the cost of any essential expenditure that is coming up over the next three months, e.g. on clothes, shoes, presents, repairs, etc.

Total: ....

Multiply by 2 and divide by 13. Cost per fortnight: ....

(Total 5)

Step 6. Add together totals 2 to 5:

TOTAL FORTNIGHTLY EXPENDITURE: ....

TOTAL FORTNIGHTLY INCOME: ....

FORTNIGHTLY PROBLEM: ____________

You will probably now need a glass of brandy/week in hospital/hole in the ground to bury yourself in/false beard and passport/new job, as fast as you can.

If (sadly) none of these seems to be realistic solutions to your problems, you have to start making some difficult decisions.

Step 7. Where can you reduce your expenditure? What gets cut out? And, can you increase your income or reduce your expenditure by any of the other measures suggested in this chapter?

Saving money. It is always difficult to recommend ways to save money — everyone is so different, and we all have our different ideas of what is really important, and what can perhaps go. If you belong to a group of people who are also out of work, as outlined in Chapter 5, a general discussion of ways in which you save money would probably yield more ideas than any list printed here would. So just one money-saving idea: form a food co-operative with other local people, and buy your food at wholesale prices, sharing out the work between you.

SECTION 3. PROBLEMS WITH BENEFIT

This Handbook tries to set out the benefit systems as clearly as possible. However, they can be complicated, and you can easily run into problems. Here are some of the more common problems. No. 1 tells you where you can get further help. You are *not alone* with benefit problems — there are people who can help you.

1. Sources of help and advice

• Try to get a clear explanation from the UBO or DHSS by phoning and finding someone who can explain your muddle. Do remember that DHSS staff are undertrained, overworked and underpaid, and that life is not easy on the far side of the barrier. Staff are normally unwilling to give you their names, as they have been personally abused and even attacked in the past, but if you ask for their *extension number* this will enable you to speak to the same person each time, if you find someone helpful.

Writing a letter to the DHSS is often a better way of getting clear answers than phoning. Try to make it polite — the clerks who will be reading your letter did not write the rules. Keep a copy of your letter, plus any replies, for reference. You could also ring Freeling Social Security. Just dial 0800-666555.

• There are two excellent guidebooks which explain the benefit systems better than we can ever hope to. Buy these, or ask your library to order them — they may repay the cost in the form of additional benefits you discover you are entitled to:

National Welfare Benefits Handbook. This covers Supplementary Benefit/Income Support, Family Income Supplement/Family Credit, housing benefits and health and education benefits.

Rights Guide to Non-Means-Tested Social Security Benefits. This covers Unemployment Benefit, Sickness Benefit, Child Benefit and benefits for the disabled.

Both price £4.50 (£2.00 to unemployed people) from Child Poverty Action Group (Pubs), 4th Floor, 1-5 Bath Street, London EC1V 9PY.

- The *Citizens Advice Bureau* (p. vii) can give help and advice. Run by specially trained volunteers.
- *Other advice centres* — you can get help and advice from Centres for the Unemployed, local authority Welfare Advice Centres and Neighbourhood Law Centres. Addresses on p. vii.
- *Claimants Union groups* — these work on a self-help basis, with claimants helping each other. They have found from long experience that if you are prepared to fight for your rights, you will get them, and that it is always easier to do this if you have support from someone sympathetic. Write to the Federation of Claimants' Unions, 296 Bethnal Green Road, London E2 0AG (+ sae) for an up-to-date list of local branches.
- If you are having problems which won't go away, WRITE TO YOUR MP (House of Commons, London SW1). This usually seems to bring pretty quick results. Don't hesitate about doing this — you are doing your MP a service by making him or her aware of the problems faced by unemployed people.

2. 'Voluntarily Unemployed'

If the DHSS decide you are 'voluntarily unemployed' you can be disqualified from Unemployment Benefit for 13 weeks, and/or lose 40% of your personal allowance on Supplementary Benefit/Income Support. (Housing benefit and allowances for children are not affected).

By 'voluntarily unemployed' they mean that you:

- left your job without 'good reason',
- lost your job because of 'misconduct',
- gave up a 'reasonable opportunity' of training 'without good reason' (this includes the Youth Training Scheme, and both Job Training Schemes),
- refused to apply for or take a 'suitable' job, or
- refused to take up a 'reasonable opportunity' of training.

The way to fight the decision is to argue that you had good reason for leaving a job or turning down a training, and to appeal. First ask the Adjudication Officer why you have been cut off (or had your benefit reduced). Then write a formal Appeal stating your reasons. Possible reasons might be:

- dangerous or unhealthy working conditions
- personal health problems, or physical difficulty in doing the job
- a convincing argument that the work or training simply wasn't right for you
- an excessive burden on your marriage or relationship
- you were trying the job out to see if it suited you, and you found it didn't.

If you were dismissed from your job, the UBO will send you a copy of a letter from your ex-employer giving his reasons. You should then give your side of the story. 'Misconduct' means 'blameworthy, reprehensible or wrong' — so argue your reasons well. A strong argument on your own behalf could win you your benefit back. You must appeal within 3 months.

If you, your partner or your child is pregnant or seriously ill, your benefit will only be reduced by 20% if you have less than £100 in savings. They're so kind.

3. You disagree with a decision about your benefit, and want to appeal

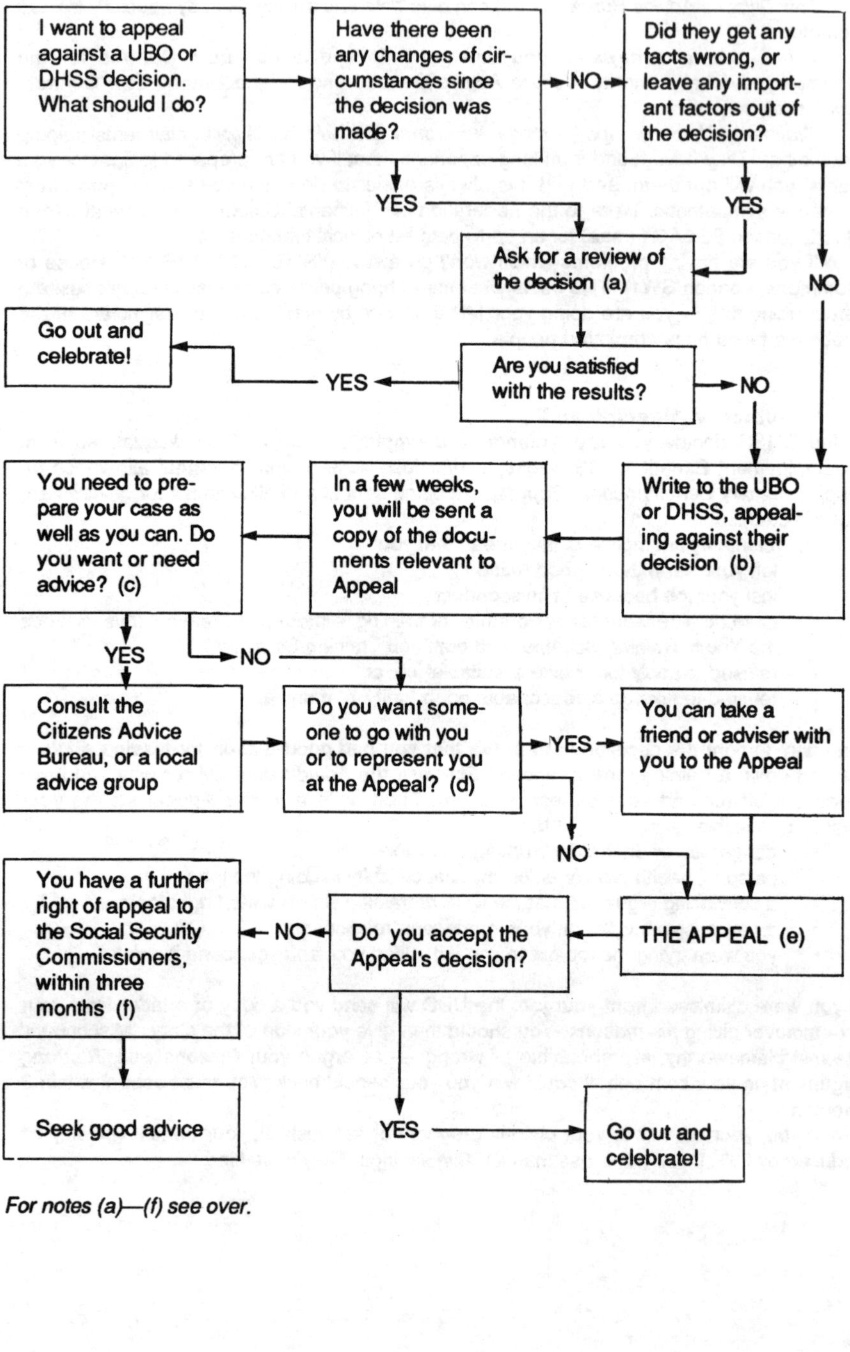

For notes (a)—(f) see over.

Notes

(a) If you can have the decision changed or corrected by review, it will save you going through the appeal.

(b) You have three months in which to make your appeal. Write down why you are appealing in detail, giving your arguments. Your letter will become part of the evidence, so work at it carefully. Get someone from an advice centre (see above) to help you, and keep a photocopy.

(c) The Appeals Tribunal will be fairly informal, but the members of the tribunal can only make a proper decision if they know all the arguments. The DHSS or UBO will be arguing their case, so it is up to you and your adviser to argue yours.

(d) You are allowed to take someone with you to the Appeal, and you are strongly advised to, whether it is a friend or a helper from an unemployed centre or advice centre. You can also ask for someone to attend as a witness to give evidence, if that would help your case. You should all be able to get travel expenses, and claim for meals and loss of earnings.

(e) *The Appeal.* There are no strict rules of procedure. You will be given a chance to put your case, to put questions to the DHSS or UBO officers, and for your adviser or witnesses to speak. You will be told the result of the Appeal within 3-4 days. If you win, your benefit will usually be paid straight away.

Back-payments for *up to a year* can be paid. The DHSS might decide to appeal against the decision, however, in which case you will have to wait until the Commissioner hears the case.

(f) If you lose, you can appeal against the Tribunal's decision, but only on a *point of law.* This can take up to 18 months, and you should always get advice — but it is only by these appeals that claimants' rights get defined, so DO persist if you feel you have been wronged. See the National Welfare Benefits Handbook, and *Social Security Appeals* package (£3 from the Tribunal Representation Unit, 63 Waterloo Road, Wolverhampton WV1 4QU).

4. You want help filling in forms

Don't be embarrassed if you want someone to help you with forms — even university graduates have been known to hide from forms in fright! Get help from a friend or colleague, an advice centre or community centre.

5. Your giro hasn't arrived, or you have lost it

(a) Wait one day, in case it is simply delayed in the post.

(b) Phone the DHSS to see if there is a reason why it has not arrived. If there is a reason, get advice at once from an advice centre.

(c) Phone the Unemployment Benefit Office to report the loss.

(d) Phone the DHSS to report the loss, and visit the office in person. They have instructions to relace the lost giro in full *immediately* if the loss is regarded as genuine and if hardship will occur if you do not get another payment at once.

If you lose a housing benefit giro, or it doesn't arrive, take it up with the local authority immediately. Once they have decided you are entitled to benefit, they have a legal duty to pay you, and that duty is only discharged when you have cashed the giro.

See *Lost giros — how to replace them: a step-by-step guide for claimants*, from Merseyside Welfare Rights Resource Centre, Trade Union Buildings, 24 Hardman Street, Liverpool 1. (£1.50 to organisations, 50p to individuals).

6. Your benefit has been cut under the cohabitation rule

Single women claimants sometimes have their benefit cut if the DHSS get the idea that they've got a man cohabiting with them. If this happens to you, get advice. See No. 1 above.

7. You have been called to a RESTART interview, or the Claimants Adviser wants to see you.
You will be called to a RESTART interview every six months. The interviews have two faces. The face you meet will depend on who is conducting the interview and what efforts you have been making to find a job or a training place.

Seen at its best, RESTART can offer you useful counselling, and a range of practical options (see p. 109). Seen at its worst, it is an attempt to get you off the dole by pushing you into something you may not want.

If you fail to attend, and also fail to attend after a second invitation without giving good reason, your benefit will be stopped, and stay cut off until you turn up for the interview.

When you attend the interview, take with you any evidence you have which shows what you have been doing to find work — a list of jobs you have applied for, letters from employers, etc. If you have any particular problems in finding work (eg a prison record, or physical handicap), make sure you tell the adviser.

8. You want to go on holiday or do voluntary work while on benefit
For a holiday, just ask for a holiday form and fill it in. You will be asked to leave an address where you can be contacted. If you are camping or travelling, leave a contact address. You cannot leave the country without losing benefit.

Voluntary work is a highly important way of keeping up personal self-respect, skill and friendship. As long as you are 'available for work', it is OK to do voluntary work — the government's own Voluntary Projects Programme actually encourages it. Sometimes, if you help at a Playgroup (eg) on a regular basis, a nosy neighbour will phone the DHSS to say you've got a regular job, and you might find your benefit suddenly cut off. Phone up immediately and explain, and get the playgroup organiser to phone too, and it will usually be re-instated just as immediately.

When you sign on for benefit you have to state that you have not done any 'paid or unpaid' work since you last signed on. This actually enfringes Article 23 of the Charter of Human Rights, which states that 'Everyone has the right to work' and work is work, whether it is paid or unpaid. Someone ought to take HM Government to the Court of Human Rights on the matter.

If you have any difficulties regarding voluntary work, write for Information Sheet 4 , The Volunteer Centre, 29 Lower King's Road, Berkhamsted, Herts HP4 2AB.

9. You are having difficulties with regard to Board and Lodging.
For an explanation of the full Board and Lodging rules, see the National Welfare Benefits Handbook (see p. 154). The biggest difficulties have been faced by unemployed young people under 26 who have been refused the right to receive the full board and lodgings charge for more than 2–8 weeks, depending where they are staying.

Young people under 26 are exempt from this rule if:

- you have a child;
- you are pregnant;
- if you have a longstanding illness (a doctor's letter is needed);
- if you have been placed in board and lodgings as part of a programme of rehabilitation or resettlement;
- if you have been 'in the care of the local authority' within the last year;
- if you have been remanded on bail, or under the supervision of the probation or social services department (Social Work Department, in Scotland);
- if you or your partner has been working and not receiving Supplementary

Benefit, while at your present address in the last 6 months;

- if you are under 19 and have no parents and no-one acting as parent;
- if you have left your family home because you believe you are in moral or physical danger;
- if you think you will suffer exceptional hardship by being forced to leave your lodgings.

If your board and lodgings allowance is withdrawn, and you think it should not have been, get advice immediately (see p. 154). Otherwise, you can only receive the full board and lodgings allowance again:

(a) after waiting 6 months from the time you first received the allowance, if you stay in the same area, *or*

(b) if you move to a new board and lodgings area, *or*

(c) if you move to live in a hostel.

It is hoped that these rules will be abolished in April 1989 (or earlier).

10. You are threatened with disconnection

The first thing you *must* do is contact the gas or electricity board and the DHSS. Once you have got in touch, they can discuss arrangements with you. Far too many people leave it until it is too late, just hoping the problem will go away.

There are two things you can do:

- You can arrange a 'Fuel Direct' scheme with the DHSS, so that they take money off your giro to cover the debt and your present consumption of fuel.
- You can arrange to make regular payments every week or month.

You are protected from disconnection by a 'Code of Practice', which states that you should not be disconnected if:

— you have agreed to make regular payments, or to have a 'Fuel Direct' scheme;

— your debt is for a hire purchase debt, not for actual fuel;

— there is real hardship and it is safe and practical to install a slot meter. This would then be set at a higher rate, to collect the debt;

— you are waiting for a decision from the DHSS as to whether they can help you.

11. You need some money very urgently

In an emergency, until April '88, you can sometimes obtain an Urgent Needs Payment. You can obtain a lump sum payment, among other reasons:

- if a close relative or member of your family is critically ill (travel costs, overnight accommodation);
- if a member of your family is stranded in mid-journey (travel costs);
- if you are homeless, and need a deposit for accommodation.

You can obtain an Urgent Needs Payment on a weekly basis, among other reasons,

- if money is lost, stolen or destroyed;
- if you are treated as having income you have not been paid;
- if you are starting work and are paid monthly;
- if your entitlement to benefit is uncertain;
- if your benefit has been suspended, pending a decision by an adjudication officer, tribunal or Commissioner;
- if you are one of a couple, and your partner is not supporting you;
- if you have suffered a disaster (eg a fire or flood — having one of those 'disastrous days' doesn't count).

In some circumstances, you may be asked to repay an Urgent Needs Payment if, for example, you later receive backdated benefit.

From April '88 onwards, Urgent Needs Payments will be replaced by Social Fund loans (see p. 151).

12. Starting work

When looking for work, remember that you may be able to claim Family Income Supplement/Family Credit and Housing Benefit if the job is low-paid. Seek advice from an advice centre to see if you qualify.

Until April '88 When starting work (or on the Enterprise Allowance Scheme or Youth Training Scheme), if you have been receiving Supplementary Benefit you can claim a Single Payment to help with clothing you need for work. You can also receive benefit to cover your first 15 days at work, before your pay arrives. Ask for form A7 from the DHSS, get your new employer to stamp it, and return it to the DHSS at once. You can also get a grant for basic tools and work clothes, and fees for a driving licence and medical examination, if they are essential and your employer will not pay, up to a maximum of £35. You can also get your travel expenses paid in full for 15 days.

After April '88 You may be able to get a loan from the Social Fund for these same things (see p.151).

For help available while looking for work, see Chapter 13.

Points not raised in this chapter

The *National Welfare Benefits Handbook* contains 250 pages of detailed advice about the benefits systems. This chapter has omitted 90% of the detail, and some of these details may affect you. We have not covered, for instance, details about separations and divorces, buying and selling houses, special disability payments, or detailed payments for heating problems.

If you are unemployed, £2 will buy you a copy of the book. It is also available in local libraries. We recommend it.

A final word

Many people experience great difficulty with the benefits systems. The only way to be sure of your rights is to struggle and fight for them. You may often feel justifiably angry, but do remember that benefits offices themselves have suffered from heavy cuts, and staff are often young and inadequately trained. If you have difficulties with benefits offices, contact the local branch of the Civil and Public Service Association, either directly or through the local Trades Council.

With unemployment here to stay, it would seem, something better *must* be developed. Local 'Consultative Councils' would help to represent and protect the consumer — i.e. you. Such bodies could lead to better trust and understanding between claimants and benefits officers, and enable practical improvements to be made in the benefits service locally.

There is plenty that a local action group could do to improve matters, in addition to giving individual benefits advice: local (and national) annual prizes — and publicity — for the best and the worst benefits offices; monthly awards for the most friendly and helpful benefits clerks; organising demonstrations when nothing else works — civil servants hate having the Press, TV and local MPs making a noise outside their offices; and challenging benefits office staff to friendly football and cricket matches, to build up better relationships. No-one else is going to change this world apart from us.

CHAPTER 13: HOLIDAYS! AND TIME TO UP AND GO?

Countryside ideas – International Workcamps – Working holidays – Low budget holidays, together – Holidays to raise your awareness – House-swap holidays – TIME TO UP AND GO – Moving away to another area – Moving house – Leaving home – Moving to London – Looking for work abroad – Rural resettlement

You need a break to recharge your batteries and get things into perspective? . . . a new place . . . new sights . . . new faces? . . . get away from the city to green fields . . . the seaside . . . months in the Bahamas sipping cocktails by the poolside? . . . Ah! It would be so wonderful, if only . . .

But — what about the MONEY?

It may need a bit of creative thinking, careful planning and seeking out of information, but there *are* low cost ways of getting a break. And unemployed people *do* need a break. You know full well that being unemployed is not one perpetual holiday. Why not get together with friends and brainstorm some ideas? Then each person go and check out how one of the ideas could be made into a reality. (See Chapter 5 for instructions on brainstorming.)

The benefits situation is quite straightforward: you simply ask the DHSS (or the UBO) for a holiday form and leave an address where they can contact you, in case they suddenly decide to offer you a job. You don't have to sign on while you are away, and you pick up your benefit when you return.

This chapter offers you some ideas to start with. Please write to us c/o the NEC with other ideas you may have found, and we can publish them in the next edition.

Countryside ideas

1. Working Weekends on Organic Farms (WWOOF)

Joining WWOOF lets you in on a network of farms where you can work (often with other friendly WWOOFers) at weekends or for longer periods, in return for free board and lodging. A perfect way to lose some flab, overdose on fresh air, and sample organic turnips and real ale. To join, send £5 to WWOOF, 19 Bradford Road, Lewes, Sussex BN7 1RB.

2. British Trust for Conservation Volunteers (BTCV)

Another way of feeling virtuous and enjoying yourself in the fresh air is to go on a BTCV working week or weekend. Send off for their free brochure on Conservation Working holidays, which lists hundreds of opportunities from rebuilding the footpath to Dylan Thomas's boathouse at Laugharne, Carmarthen, to repairing the coastal path near Lulworth Cove, in Dorset, and the erection of rabbit-fencing on the island of Hay, Orkneys.

You have to pay a donation towards food and accommodation of between £14 and £20 per week. Accommodation varies from camping to comfortable bedrooms in Field Study Centres. Age range 16–70! You can try it out for just a weekend or a day, by contacting the regional organiser. There are also some 3-month placements, (but you have to go off benefit), and opportunities overseas in Northern France, or Iceland if you have experience.

For details, contact BTCV, 36 St Mary's Street, Wallingford, Oxfordshire OX10 0EU.

Dreaming of a holiday

A similar but smaller programme of working holidays is organised by the **National Trust**, on their own properties, generally for younger people: Acorn Camps, National Trust, PO Box 12, Westbury, Wilts BA13 4NA.

3. Walking/Cycling holidays

An extremely cheap means of transport! Why not think about doing part (or all) of one of the nine Long Distance Paths in Britain? As well as the Pennine Way, these include the Somerset and North Devon Coast Path, South Devon Coast Path, North and South Downs Way, Cornwall Coast Path, Cleveland Way, Pembrokeshire Coast Path, and Offa's Dyke Path. You can get details of all of these from the Countryside Commission, John Dower House, Crescent Place, Cheltenham, Glos GL50 3RA.

There are guide books for each section — libraries should have a selection. Look out too for *The Footpaths of Britain — a Guide to Walking in England, Scotland and Wales,* by Michael Marriot (Queen Anne Press). You will also find the following helpful:

- **The Youth Hostels Association**, Trevelyan House, St Stephens Hill, St Albans, Herts A11 2DY. (All ages.)
- **Backpackers Club**, 20 St Michaels road, Tilehurst, Reading, RG3 4RP.
- **Ramblers Association**, 1–5 Wandsworth Road, London SW8 2LJ.
- **Cyclists Touring Club**, Cotterall House, Meadrow, Godalming, Surrey.
- **Camping Club of Great Britain & Northern Ireland**, 11 Grosvenor Place, London SW1W 0EY.

Consider getting people to sponsor you and raise money for your favourite charity (or your unemployed centre), as well as having a holiday, perhaps doing a long distance path — or even walking around 100 Jobcentres (choose a scenic route!). A sponsored walk/ride will need careful planning and good promotion, to be sure of covering your costs and raising money. Do some research on strategies that other groups have used successfully locally. (The backing of a chain of pubs, a major firm or a TV personality is always helpful.)

4. Sport and Activity holidays

Canoeing, tennis, football, aikido, potholing, dance, photography — these kinds of holidays are listed in *Activity and Hobby Holidays*, from the English Tourist Board (4 Grosvenor Gardens, London SW1). Most of these cost lots, but if you got ideas first from the brochure, you could then (a) fundraise as a group to go on such a holiday, (b) write a well-written letter asking if they have any reductions for unemployed participants, maybe in return for some extra help? (c) write as a group to ask for a booking at one of the well-equipped centres at a reduced rate, out of season, and then fundraise.

The **Sports Council** (16 Upper Woburn Place, London WC1H 0QP) is very keen to help unemployed people get involved in sports, and they may be able to help out, for instance if you want to organise a local 'Try A Sport' week, or gala event. They are also a good source of information on sporting opportunities.

5. Alternative Holidays

This is the title of a free publication from SCEC, 2 Canning Street, Edinburgh EH2 8EG, detailing cheap holiday ideas at home and abroad.

International Workcamps and Exchanges

Put aside the awful visions of forced sewing of mailbags that the phrase 'workcamps' conjures up. You can meet some fascinating people from all over the world.

I (Jane) went on a United Nations workcamp building a children's playground in a tiny village in the Auvergne in France and ended up making Polish, Danish, Moroccan, German and French friends, several of whom I later visited for low-cost foreign holidays.

With IVS (see below), once you have done a workcamp in Britain, you can attend camps in Europe, although, alas, the benefit rules do not allow you to receive any benefit if you declare that you are leaving the country. Most workcamp projects last 2–3 weeks, and cost you nothing apart from your membership fee to join the organisation, and the cost of getting there. Some ask for a contribution towards food and accommodation.

- **International Voluntary Service (IVS)** (53 Regent Street, Leicester LE1 6YL) provide the largest number of camps each year, mostly at Easter and in the summer, Write for their brochure in good time each year, and apply early. If you get a job and can't go, you can always apologise and back out.
- **Quaker Workcamps** (Friends House, Euston Road, London NW1 2BJ) organise 15–20 camps a year in Britain and Northern Ireland.
- **Concordia** (8 Brunswick Place, Hove, Sussex) organise fruit-picking work-camps.
- **Winged Fellowship for the Disabled** (Angel House, Pentonville Road, London N1 9XD) need volunteers for their holiday schemes with the disabled in Nottingham, Surrey and Essex. They will pay half of your travel expenses, up to £20, (except in July, August and September), and your board and lodging is all provided free. Good opportunity!

- **The National Youth Bureau** (17 Albion Street, Leicester LE1 6GD) provides a free annual listing of opportunities all over Britain (excluding IVS camps) called *Sparetime Sharetime — A Guide to Voluntary Work*, covering everything from excavating medieval villages to tree-planting to helping on holidays for handicapped children. Just send a large stamped addressed envelope. Ask also for their leaflet *Workcamps — Why Bother?* which may dispel any misgivings or inertia.

Exchanges
An unemployed youth group in Ardrossan, Scotland, arranged an exchange visit with a group in Holland. Another Scottish youth group, from Findhorn, arranged an exchange with a group of native Indian youngsters from Winnipeg, Canada. Plenty of fundraising is involved, but there's also plenty of advice available. Write to **SCAN** (see p.58) for their special broadsheet, *Your Passport to International Exchanges* (Nov. 85), Atholl House, 2 Canning Street, Edinburgh EH3 8EG.

Working holidays

Working holidays involve signing off benefit, and earning some money (never very much) at a temporary job, usually in the summer. There are some very useful directories, which tell you all the details, and start you dreaming. Be sure to apply in spring (or earlier) for summer jobs, as they go quickly.

- **The Central Bureau for Educational Visits and Exchanges** (Seymour Mews House, Seymour Mews, London W1H 9PE) produces *Working Holidays*, covering Britain and abroad. Yearly editions. Also *Volunteer Work Abroad*, and *Working as an Au Pair*, which lists reputable au pair agencies in 13 different countries.
- **Vacation Work** (9 Park End Street, Oxford OX1 1HJ) produces a range of publications, including (1987 prices)
  - *Directory of Summer Jobs in Britain* £4.95
  - *Directory of Summer Jobs Abroad* £4.95
  - *Adventure Holidays Britain and Abroad* £3.95
  - *Work Your Way Around The World* £6.95
  - *Kibbutz Volunteer* £4.95
  - *Summer Employment Directory of the US* £6.95
  - *Working in Ski Resorts — Europe* £4.95
  - *International Directory of Voluntary Work* £5.95
  - *Directory of Work and Study in Developing Countries* £6.95
  - *Hitch-Hikers' Manual — Britain* £3.95
  - *Europe — A Manual for Hitch-Hikers* £3.95
  - *The Travellers' Survival Kit* series, covering separately Europe, the East, USA & Canada.

These should all be available in libraries, and should be required reading in all Unemployed Centres! If they're not (as with all other books) ask the library to order copies or write direct to Oxford. (Send 75p postage if ordering direct.)
P.S. These make excellent Christmas presents for friends who are unemployed!

If your imagination is fired, and you are beginning to think about the idea of a year spent travelling, broadening your horizons through voluntary and paid work, *A Year Off, A Year On* (£2.25, CRAC, Bateman Street, Cambridge CB2 1LZ) has a lot of relevant information.

- **Community Service Volunteers** offers long-term voluntary work places to 18–35 year olds. Details on p. 00. So do the **Cyrenians**, working with homeless people — details in the *Working Holidays* book.

There are several Christian organisations, which offer full-time voluntary service opportunities to young people in sympathy with their beliefs. **Time for God** (2 Chester House, Pages Lane, London N10) provides board, lodging and pocket money for 17–25 year olds, and opportunities to work in churches, community centres, etc. **Careforce** (130 City Road, London EC1V 2NJ), offers 8–12 months' service to 18-23 year-olds.

Low budget holidays – together

If you are less ambitious, or tied by children or relatives, try arranging a cheap camping or self-catering holiday with a few others. It usually works out a lot cheaper in a group. You can fundraise together to cover the costs. Several groups have already had a lot of fun in this way. People from Newcastle's Centre for the Unemployed have organised their own off-peak holiday camps. An unemployed group in Bridport, Dorset spent two weeks camping in the Brecon Beacons, raising the money by jumble sales and street theatre. Some unemployed youth groups have spent up to a year raising funds to go to Spain or Portugal together.

The Holiday Care Service (2 Old Bank Chambers, Station Road, Horley, Surrey RH6 9HW, Tel 0293–774535) provides free advice and information for people on low incomes, or with special needs, such as being handicapped, or a single parent. They have lists of cheap self-catering accommodation, camping sites and sources of financial help — some charities occasionally give grants to people in particular need, when recommended by a social worker or church minister. Send a stamped addressed envelope for their lists.

One-parent families can find holiday help through a special group called **SPLASH** (Empire House, Clarence Street, Swindon, Wilts SN1 2PL, Tel 0793–613220).

There are a few low-cost holiday centres exclusively for women and children, offering friendly informal accommodation. *Spare Rib* (see p. 00) often carries advertisements. One well-established centre is **The Women's Holiday Centre**, The Old Vicarage, Horton-in-Ribblesdale, Settle, N. Yorks. Guides covering facilities for people with disabilities are listed in Chapter 7.

Holidays to raise your awareness

There are now a wide range of centres and groups offering weekend and longer breaks for people interested in personal growth, meditation, natural medicine, different kinds of therapy — or just (!) raising their awareness. Many are expensive, but an increasing number of groups offer a sliding scale of prices, in order to allow people on very low budgets to attend. Even when special rates are not advertised, groups may offer a bursary, if you write an honest letter explaining your circumstances. It is always worth trying.

The publications listing this type of centre and holiday are:

- *Human Potential Resources Quarterly* (£2.50 p.a. for unemployed people, 35 Station Road, London NW4 4PN). Carries articles and listings of courses.
- *Open Centres Magazine* (50p per copy from Cara Voelcker, Avils Farm, Lower

Stanton, Chippenham, Wilts SN14 6PA). Lists meditation groups, and news about spiritually oriented centres where people can stay.

- *South-West Connection* (43 Oriel Grove, Southdown, Bath BA2 1JE). Quarterly guide to activities in the south-west. (Free, donation for postage).
- *People in Sheffield* (74 Bower Road, Sheffield 10) Newsletter listing weekends, evening courses and occasional weeks of activity such as massage, creative dance, and healing workshops in and around Sheffield.

Some of the Centres which offer courses are:

1. **Lower Shaw Farm**, Shaw, Swindon, Wilts SN5 9PS. They run regular Easter, May and New Year celebration weekends, weekend courses on topics such as Growing and Using Herbs, Spring Stretch, Yoga, Meditation and Massage, and a regular week in summer called 'Looking at Alternatives'. They also organise free working weekends, and offer their space at low price to groups — another chance for a self-organised group holiday. Children generally welcome.
2. **Monkton Wyld Court**, nr. Charmouth, Bridport, Dorset. A community which runs a wide programme of personal growth events, also regular play weeks for parents with children under 6.
3. **Centre for Alternative Education and Research** (CAER), Rosemerryn, Lamorna, Penzance, Cornwall. Runs a programme of personal growth events, and also welcomes people to stay for weekends at some times of the year.
4. **Laurieston Hall**, Laurieston, Kirkudbrightshire, S.W. Scotland. A large community of people, running courses including music-making, women's weeks, and children's weeks.

For each of these, write for their free programmes of events, and see what attracts you.

There are a number of Retreat Centres where you can arrange to spend a week or weekend if you need a peaceful atmosphere, or a chance to step back and think, or rest. For most places, you do not have to be a committed Christian (or Buddhist, in Buddhist centres), but you should respect and have an interest in the retreat house you are visiting. For Christian-based retreat centres write to: **The Association for Promoting Retreats**, St Martin-le-Grand, Colney Street, York YO1 1QL, or enquire at your local church or chapel. For Buddhist retreats write to: **Friends of the Western Buddhist Order**, Lessingham House, Surlingham, Nr Norwich, Norfolk, or the **Buddhist Society of Great Britain**, 58 Eccleston Square, London SW1V 1PM.

House-swap holidays

The idea here is that you swap houses with a family or individual living in another area.

- **National Housewives Register**, 245 Warwick Road, Solihull, West Midlands B92 7AH, arrange such schemes, and Unemployed Centres could easily do likewise, if two Centres were to twin together, e.g. in a city and in a rural area.
- If you have any special hobby, whether bird-watching or bell-ringing, try advertising in the specialist journals or newsletters for a swap — then you will be dealing with like-minded people.
- **Servas,** 77 Elm Park Mansions, Park Walk, London SW10 0AP. Set up in 1949 to link individual people working for peace around the world. Approved travellers can receive lists of Servas hosts in different countries and in their own country, and then you write a polite letter to the people you want to visit. Guests can stay two nights, are invited to pay for meals and lend a hand. By joining Servas you can

act as both a host and a traveller. If you are a host, you will meet fascinating people from all around the world, and make good friends. A mattress on the floor and a friendly approach is all that is needed. Write for details, and it costs £10 to join, once you are approved.

So — just a few ideas to set your mind thinking about holiday possibilities. Why not take a risk? Holidays do not always have to be conventional seaside trips. We all need a change of scenery and a break from day-to-day routine, every so often.

TIME TO UP AND GO?

Moving away to another area

Finding out about jobs

1. Your local Jobcentre will have details of some jobs in other areas, but not a complete listing. You can ask the Jobcentre to forward your name to the Jobcentre in the area you want to go to, or to give you the address so that you can write yourself. They may be able to let you know what's available.
2. Obtain copies of the local papers in that area. Go to your nearest large library and ask for the *Advertisers' Annual* (which lists all the local and regional newspapers) or the Yellow Pages for the relevant area (under 'Newspaper and Periodical publishers'). Write to the head office of any local or regional papers, sending 45p for a copy of an issue which carries a lot of job advertisements.
3. Write to the employment agencies listed in the Yellow Pages for the area in question.

Moving House

1. Home owners

If you own your own house, and are receiving Supplementary Benefit, you are allowed to be absent from your house for up to 6 months if you need to be, while in transition, without it being counted as capital. So your benefit will not be affected. In general, you'd do well to buy a copy of the *Rights Guide for Home Owners* (£3.50, CPAG [Pubs], 4th Floor, 1-5 Bath Street, London EC1V 9PY)

Being unemployed, you have an opportunity to save yourself quite a sum of money if you do your own conveyancing. If you spent a full 3 weeks studying the form, learning the lingo, and doing all the bits and pieces, you might save yourself around £600 on your solicitor's bill. See *The Legal Side of Buying a House* (Which/Consumer's Association, 14 Buckingham Street, London WC2N 6DS).

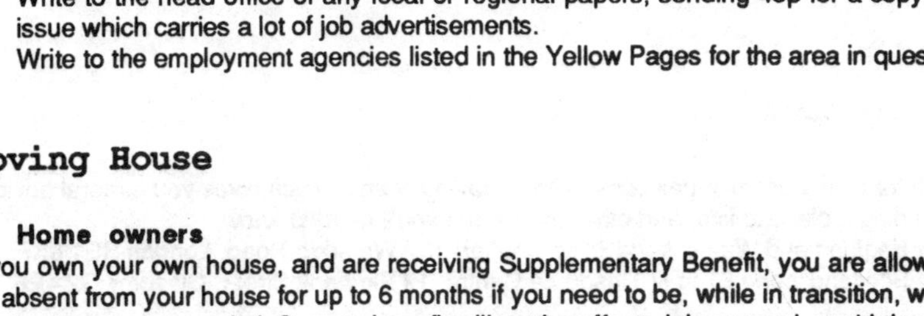

Moving house

2. Council house tenants

If you are a council house tenant, and you want to move to a council house in another area, get in touch with your local housing department as a first step, for their advice. They will tell you about the National Mobility Scheme. You may also want to advertise your house in the local paper of the town or area where you want to move to for three weeks. (See above for addresses of local papers. The *Advertisers' Annual* will also list small ad. rates.) If there is a Neighbourhood Advice Centre of any kind in the place you want to move to, ask their help and advice. Small postcard advertisements in newsagents' windows will help, as well.

3. Private tenants

If you are on Supplementary Benefit/Income Support you may be able to claim for two rents (one in your old area and one in the new) for a short time if you *have* to pay both.

Advice on finding a flat or house to rent is really beyond the scope of this Handbook. Some areas are lucky enough to have housing advice centres, which can help. Get in touch with the Citizens Advice Bureau to find out if there is one in the area you are moving to and to ask their general advice on finding a place to rent.

If you want lodgings, the social services department should keep a list of good lodgings in the area you are moving to — or be able to obtain one for you. The housing department might have a list too. (But they don't usually bother much about single people.) The addresses of YMCA and YWCA hostels in England, Scotland and Wales can be obtained from the YMCA (National Office) at 2 Weymouth Street, London W1N 4AX. The Jobcentre can also help you to find temporary lodgings, since they keep lists of suitable lodgings for people going on their Job Training Scheme courses. (If you are under 26 see p. 00)

Leaving home

Write off for a very useful small book called *Leaving Home*, which gives you general advice about finding a place to live, and other things that you'll need to know.

For England and Wales, send £1 to Shelter, 157 Waterloo Road, London SE1 8XF.

For Scotland, send £1 to IT Resource Centre, 19 Elmbank Street, Glasgow G2 4PB.

Moving to London

There are more jobs available in London and the south-east than elsewhere, but there are also more people chasing them. London has 400,000 unemployed people — more than any other European city. It also has a *very severe* housing problem, and life can be very unpleasant if you don't find somewhere to live quite quickly. There is no romance in dossing on a dirty floor.

- *A Job to Move — the Housing Problems of Young People*, by Jean Conway and Ewan Ramsay (£4.95 from SHAC, 189a Old Brompton Road, London SW5 0AR) spells out the difficult details.

If you are set on going, do plan carefully:

- Write off for the *Leaving Home* booklet, before you set out, and also for a *free* leaflet called *Coming to London?*, available from LCWWG, 57 Great Russell Street, London WC1B 3BD, Tel 01–430 1524.
- Write to the *Alone In London Service* to ask for their advice. (38 Mount Pleasant,

London WC1, Tel 01–278 4224). They offer personal advice and counselling on a drop-in basis to young people aged 16–21.

- In order to claim benefit in London, you must have some proof of identity with you. The DHSS will accept the following as 'proof':
    - Current full driver's licence
    - Passport
    - Birth certificate (but not if recently issued)
    - Bank account plus bank card
    - Wage slips (unless very recent)
    - National Insurance number or card, if backed up by tax certificates
    - Council rent book
    - Fuel bills

  but *not* medical cards, travel passes or private rent books.
- The many hostels in London are nearly always fully booked, so you simply have to have the persistence of a mule and go on phoning and visiting until you find an unexpected vacancy. You should write for the directory called *Hostels in London* (£2 from LCWWG, 57 Great Russell Street, London WC1B 3BD)
- If you stay in bed and breakfast, until you can find a place in a hostel, the DHSS will only pay a set amount towards the daily cost, which will be less than what it actually costs you.
- If you are under 26, you will only be allowed to receive benefit in the London area for 8 weeks (under the 1987 DHSS rules). After that, you will not be allowed to receive benefit again in London for 6 months.
- The *Piccadilly Advice Centre* (100 Shaftesbury Avenue, London W1, Tel 01–434 3773) can give sound advice about accommodation and other matters to people of all ages.
- The *Soho Project* (142 Charing Cross Road, London WC2, Tel 01–836 8121) also gives advice to young people.
- *Centrepoint Nightshelter* (65a Shaftesbury Avenue, London W1, Tel 01–434 2861/2) can give emergency accommodation to young people (16–19) without any money. Phone before 4 pm, during the day.
- *The Housing Advice Switchboard* (01–434 2522) deals with housing advice of all kinds.
- Capital Radio run a special free *Jobfinder Service*, with an information centre in the foyer. Capital Radio, Euston Tower, Euston Road, London NW1.
- *Workout* (previously Capital Jobmate) (8 Strutton Ground, London SW1, Tel 01–222 0222) will pair young people up with an adult 'Jobmate', to help them survive unemployment and find work. This has proved itself to be a very popular and successful scheme.

Looking for work abroad

The best source of information about jobs in Europe and overseas is the daily newspapers — the *Sun*, the *Daily Mirror* and the *Star*, etc. for skilled manual jobs, and *The Times*, the *Guardian*, the *Daily Telegraph* and *The Independent* for skilled professional jobs.

Some of these advertisements are from agencies, so make sure the terms are right before setting off for Germany or Saudi Arabia. Magazines such as *Construction News* also carry advertisements. Jobcentres operate a central clearing house for jobs abroad, if you ask about this. Over the page are listed a few books which will also help you in your search.

- *Directory of Jobs and Careers Abroad* gives precise information about skills and qualifications in demand in countries overseas, both in Europe and further afield. It comes out every year, from Vacation Work, 9 Park End Street, Oxford OX1 1HJ (£9.95).
- *Directory of US Summer Employment* (£6.95 from Vacation Work, address above)
- *Emplois d'Été en France* (£5.95 from Vacation Work, address above)
- *Internships - On the Job Training Opportunities in the USA* (£9.95 from Vacation Work, address above)
- *Working Abroad: The Daily Telegraph Guide to Living and Working Overseas*, by Godfrey Golzen and Margaret Stewart (Kogan Page) gives advice on how to get a job overseas, what kind of salary to expect, cost of living comparisons, moving house, money matters, etc. with a country-by-country survey of the job situation. (Kogan Page, 116a Pentonville Road, London N1 9JN)
- *Working in the Federal Republic of Germany*, a special booklet, should be available at the Jobcentre.

British citizens are entitled to go to any other member country in the Common Market to look for work. Special work permits are not required. Check in advance with each embassy, however, to discover how their systems work, and what kind of paperwork is required.

- *North Sea oil* — Jobcentres have an application scheme for all North Sea oil work. Word has it, however, that the only reliable way to get work there (unless you have a special skill that is needed) is to go up to Aberdeen, be prepared to make do for a few weeks (sleep in a van, etc.), and presistently foot your way around the offices of the oil companies every day. This way, if you are in an office when a vacancy comes up, you might be lucky. You have to be very determined to get a job. There is demand for all sorts of workers, from kitchen staff to barbers, etc. as well as for labourers.

Rural resettlement

Some people might want to take the opportunity to move out of the city, and into a rural area. The *Rural Resettlement Handbook* is a superbly thorough book designed to help people who wish to live and work in rural areas. Coverage includes moving house (and council house swaps), looking for land, smallholdings, subsistence farming and gardening, job opportunities, self-employment, practical experiences, planning permission, finance, etc. Price £4.95 post-paid from Lighthouse Books, 27a Sydney Street, Brightlingsea, Essex CO7 0BG.

CHAPTER 14: LOCAL COMMUNITY STRATEGIES

NATIONAL PROGRAMMES AND POLICY CHANGES – BUILDING AN INTEGRATED STRATEGY, LOCALLY – A ZODIAC STRATEGY: TWELVE ZONES OF INTEGRATED ACTIVITY – IN CONCLUSION: THE POLITICS OF THE FUTURE – RESOURCES

In the late 1930s, the preparations for World War Two put an end to the unemployment of those years. In the late 1980s, we need something equally drastic - of a peaceful nature. In this chapter, we consider the wider question: 'How can we begin to eliminate unemployment?'

It is an urgent question. Morale is low, often very low, in areas where unemployment is high, and more is needed than just endless temporary schemes which dump you back on the dole a year later.

NATIONAL PROGRAMMES AND POLICY CHANGES

Changes in government policy can make a big difference. The following 12 changes would be a good shopping list, for a start:

1. A programme of major investment in city renewal, channelled through both local authorities and Development Corporations including a programme of financial assistance to enable councils to replace tower-blocks (where unemployment is often double what it is elsewhere locally) with good quality, human scale houses;
2. Major new investment in our schools, colleges and universities, to create solid foundations for the future, and a major increase of funding for non-military scientific and technical research programmes;
3. A major national programme to eliminate illiteracy within ten years;
4. Funding for regional development agencies in the North-East, North-West, West Midlands and South-West (and anywhere else that needs one), equivalent to the Scottish and Welsh Development Agencies;
5. The necessary reforms to encourage long-term loans and venture capital for local investment and investment in new local businesses by the high street banks, and to make the government's loan guarantee scheme more accessible to small beginners;
6. A guarantee of 50% funding over a 15 year period for all local agencies concerned with economic regeneration (e.g. Enterprise Agencies, Youth Enterprise Centres, Co-operative Development Agencies);
7. A programme of funding for local worksharing agencies (as described below);
8. A scheme to allow people who *want* voluntarily to live on the dole for up to a year to do so without hassle;
9. A guarantee that no-one need ever be out of work for more than a year, through a variety of opportunities, including various changes to the Community Programme (see below, p. 45), and an effective personal 'new directions' programme, offering assertiveness training, life-planning and careers advice to unemployed people (Building on 'Restart');
10. Reforms to the national benefits system to remove its objectionable features, to bring respect and dignity to claimants, to create local benefits consumer councils and to introduce a sliding scale earnings rule;
11. A national 'Post-YTS' scheme in addition to 'Restart' and JTS, to help young people to

move towards self-confidence and self-reliance;

12. A major change of policy as to the way public money is used, moving away from defence expenditure and towards post-industrial regeneration, to secure our economic and educational foundations for the next century.

We are not dealing with the need for a repair job on the industrial age: it is the 2050s we need to plan for, not the 1950s. We have to *create* the future that we want, just as people created the industrial age in the first place. We have a lot of 'creative leaps' to make, in order to get across the gap and reach the post-industrial age successfully (see Postscript). The only thing that will happen if we do nothing, will be nothing. The Portuguese tried that route at the very beginning of the industrial age. They were powerful and prosperous in the pre-industrial age, but instead of moving with the times, they chose to sit back on their assets:

Portugal	Britain
One of the world's most powerful nations in the pre-industrial era	One of the world's most powerful nations in the industrial era
Discovered major assets in the form of Brazilian gold	Discovered major assets in the form of North Sea Oil
Lived off their assets instead of building an industrial future	Lived off their assets instead of building a post-industrial future
Became one of Europe's poorest societies over the next 300 years	?

We are not a world power any more. Every penny we spend on maintaining a nuclear defence policy helps to dig our post-industrial grave. We need all the resources we can find to invest in post-industrial regeneration, to eliminate unemployment and to build a new and different Britain.

BUILDING AN INTEGRATED STRATEGY, LOCALLY

Government action can achieve a lot. The main thrust of this chapter, however, is on what can be achieved at the *local* level in the cities and towns and areas where we live. Governments can help or hinder that work, but the work itself will always have to be done locally.

> *'We've got to find a way to get round these people who are in power, and get on with the job of creating a new economy.'*
>
> David Hopson, UNET

Since the beginning of the 1980s (after an initial period when people buried their heads in the sand, hoping the whole problem would simply go away), many local initiatives have been established. These cover everything from business start-up agencies and ITeCs (Information Technology Centres) to unemployed centres and training centres, all of which have had a positive impact on unemployment locally, some more so, some less so. For those involved, the 1980s have been a hardworking, often frustrating, but very creative time.

At first, these initiatives were independent of each other, as many still are. In the mid-80s, however, the emphasis shifted to embrace co-operation and integration. Thus in Barnsley, the local authority established a one-stop centre to meet many of the needs of unemployed people locally — business advice, an ITeC, a Centre Against Unemployment, a co-operatives office, a training team and a policy and research team. Similarly, in Kent, Swale Work Initiation Measures (SWIM), an independent initiative in which local people from many different areas are involved, embraces a local enterprise agency, a Community Programme scheme, the Youth Training Scheme, a youth business initiative, a local investment fund and a drop-in centre.

There is no limit to what can be achieved locally by a mixture of creativity, co-operation and hard work (though the lack of funds is a constant hindrance). Experience during the 1980s has shown us what works and what doesn't work, and has begun to awaken a vision of what is possible. The next stage is for communities to pull together the various strands of activity into a coherent integrated local strategy. This might sound like a lot to hope for, but it is already happening in several places, such as Hammersmith and Fulham (London), and Minneapolis-St Paul (Minnesota, USA) — where the city faces similar problems of post-industrial transition, and where the Mayor's Office has launched a drive to create a 'home-grown economy' by local economic development activity.

The need in our communities is for new vision and new long-term goals — 25 year goals, intermediate goals, and intentional policies and plans to reach them. Without vision, people perish — and people *are* perishing .

Stage 1: *'Let's just hope this problem disappears soon.'*
Stage 2: *'Let's start a project!'*
Stage 3: *'Let's work out how our projects can work together, and support each other.'*
Stage 4: *'Let's establish an integrated strategy, to bring our different areas of work together into a coherent whole, to give strength to our shared vision.'*

So what might such an integrated strategy look like?

A ZODIAC STRATEGY – TWELVE ZONES OF INTEGRATED ACTIVITY

Every town and city will develop its own individual response to its problems. Many problems are similar, however, and there is a lot of borrowing of good ideas and practice going on.

The strategy diagram (Figure 11) shows twelve areas of activity which are essential if a local strategy is to succeed. The diagram also contains a central co-ordinating body and a network linking the people involved in the strategy.

Without the network, misunderstandings, 'keep-off-my-patch' jealousies and other muddles can arise. Good communications and regular face-to-face contact are the oil without which things grind to a halt.

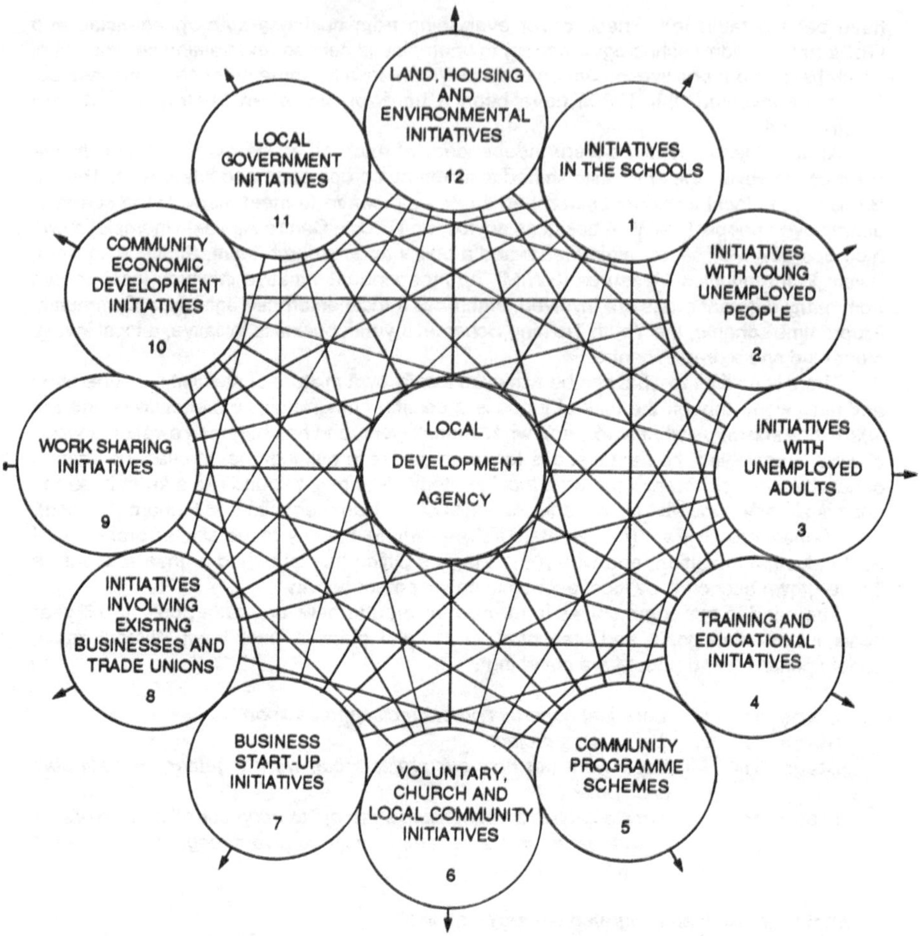

Figure 11: Integrated local strategy to tackle unemployment

Holding the centre

The central body provides the leadership, and holds the overall purpose and direction. This function can be provided by the local city or borough council, or by an independent development agency, as is the case with SWIM, in Kent, or the Royal City Development Association in New Westminster, British Columbia (Canada). There is not space to go into the work that is happening around the world, but readers would be astonished — and, I hope, delighted — to learn what is developing. Without great fanfares or trumpeting, a new vision of community economic development is being born.

A guiding principle behind this vision is that 'we are all in this together'. Everyone has a part to play, from the council, to the business community, to the churches, to the unemployment groups, to the labour movement.

A second principle is that 'top down' and 'bottom up' approaches must be combined so that the resources of government, business and local institutions are combined with the resources of individuals and voluntary and community groups. This is easier said than done. Bureaucrats can be impatient of the intrusion into their empires that such a partnership involves; people outside bureaucracies can be impatient of the regulations and committees that have to be satisfied. For an integrated strategy to succeed, everyone must be included.

1. Initiatives in the schools

Initiatives are needed in schools which encourage teamwork, co-operative skills and an active approach towards life. The schooling system which was adequate for the industrial age is disastrously inadequate for the post-industrial age:

- It generates 'failures' through an exam system which was specifically designed to locate the minority destined for higher education, and to consign the rest to unskilled factory and farm work. As long as there were unskilled vacancies, and an incentive for children to obey what they were told, the system 'worked'. Initiatives such as TVEI and CPVE, 'Records of Personal Achievement' and the Scottish '16-plus Action' now give a chance for a different kind of learning and assessment to take place in which young people are invited to be active, to make decisions, and to solve real problems.
- It expected young people to learn what they needed by passive absorption, and failed to teach skills of initiative and enterprise. Initiatives in which young people set up and run their own companies, co-operatives and community enterprises can produce a remarkable change in attitude. Young people are given the freedom to experiment and to make mistakes without being judged for them. With this they learn responsibility.
- It fails to teach teamwork skills, except in the sports, and it actually punishes mutual support as 'cheating'. The post-industrial age needs teamwork and group methods, both in the workplace and in the community.

2. Initiatives with young unemployed people

The need here is for:

- High quality YTS schemes which are relevant to the future needs of the local economy and which embody action-learning, teamwork and self-governing methods, and
- A proper 'post-YTS' strategy for unemployed 18-25 year olds.

The former needs research into the local economy in the form of a 'community profile', so that the community can perceive its future needs. It also requires local employers and colleges to be involved with the MSC in planning YTS schemes.

The post-YTS group of youngsters who are still unemployed provide one of the biggest headaches for most towns and cities. Defeat, disillusion, despair, and a lack of any substantial practical experience create a lot of unhappiness in this group.

A relevant strategy requires the following components:

1. *Personal one-to-one encouragement* from a supportive adult who can provide help with jobhunting, and practical encouragement for young people to get the most out of their lives while they are unemployed. 'Workout', in London, (previously known as

Capital Jobmate) has developed a very successful working model of this support.

2. *A broader working definition of 'success'* that does not depend on the acquisition of a full-time job or a place at college, which will allow young people to build up a positive self-image while 'unemployed' (see Tommy Wilson's tale, Chapter 10).
3. *Access to facilities* for the development of personal skills, hobbies, sports, artistic and community activities, including the provision of satisfactory places to meet socially.
4. *The provision of a wide range of 21 hour courses at local colleges*, including separate courses with creche facilities for young women, who are often intimidated by dominantly male projects and activities.
5. *The development of an integrated youth-in-business programme*, involving training courses, support, start-up finance and sheltered workspace (See Chapter 11).
6. The development of the Job Training Scheme in a way that provides a solid, relevant training which is respected by local people.
7. *Young people's own involvement* in the development of initiatives.

There must be a collective framework through which all this can happen. The development of this approach has training implications for everyone involved.

3. Initiatives with unemployed adults

The experience of the last five years has shown that when there is backing, training and support from local agencies, successful initiatives can be started by unemployed people themselves. These take the form of self-help groups, local action initiatives, benefits take-up campaigns, drop-in centres, women's projects and community workshops. Without that backing, such initiatives have an uphill struggle, and are easily defeated. The Community Education Service in Irvine, Strathclyde, has developed an excellent training approach which empowers selected unemployed people to set up local projects, and then gives them the back-up they need (See 'Unemployment — Communities Take Action', p. 58).

A local strategy needs to involve specific initiatives for unemployed people who have personal disabilities. The Southwark Disabilities Employment Section incorporates initiatives aimed at improving the employment prospects of disabled people into the mainstream economic strategy of the Borough. Southwark employs full-time development officers to do this, as does MENCAP through its 'Pathway' projects, whose staff persuade local employers to set up sheltered employment openings for people who have a mental handicap.

If goodwill is to be generated locally, which is essential for the success of a strategy as a whole, it is essential that the relationship between unemployed people and the local DHSS be improved, through the establishment (for instance) of local consultative committees including claimants, the issuing of 'codes of conduct' from the regional DHSS office to encourage good practice and polite relationships, and the establishment of more schemes such as 'Stand-by' (see Chapter 5) which allow unemployed people to earn money and store it as credits while on benefit.

Many unemployed people lose hope because they lose their sense of direction in life when they are without a job. Personal counselling and life-planning work is really necessary, to help people assess what they want from life, what their own natural skills are, and what their immediate goals are. The MSC's 'Restart' initiative could provide this if funding were sufficient for people to receive support over a period of weeks or months, individually and in groups.

4. Training and educational initiatives

What is required here is:

- Good co-ordination between staff from the different agencies which provide courses, namely the MSC, REPLAN, local colleges, schools, adult and community education departments, the Workers' Educational Association, the Open University and College of the Air organisers.
- The provision of a service which enables people to develop personal learning plans.
- The provision of more and better free courses for unemployed people.
- The proper distribution to all unemployed people of easy-to-follow information about courses.

'Learning Links' in Gillingham, Kent, has tackled part of this agenda (the co-ordination of information about courses) using a computer data bank situated in the foyer of the local Jobcentre. It also incorporates information on informal learning situations, such as local clubs and self-help groups.

5. Community Programme schemes

Moving on through the Zodiac, the Community Programme is with us to stay, and energies must therefore be devoted to ensuring that schemes provided are of the highest quality. Most CP schemes have been developed in an isolated 'Stage 2' context (see p. 173) without relation to other local initiatives or to any overall community strategy.

A good Community Programme scheme must meet the needs of unemployed people for skill development, and provide good training. It should also provide counselling and life-planning courses, so that people can use the opportunity which CP schemes offer them to develop their lives. The quality of personal attention and counselling given on a scheme can make the difference between 30 per cent or 70 per cent of CP workers going on to get jobs or full-time college or training places, when they leave.

If CP Agencies are to play a full role in an integrated local strategy they must develop more democratic governing frameworks. Local people should feel that an agency is 'our agency', and not experience it as a large and sometimes alien body. This implies the encouragement of smaller agencies and the scaling down of larger ones (some of which have become mini-empires) and a requirement by the MSC that workers from schemes and unemployed people should be included in agency decision- making.

Projects also need to be given longer timetables; longer assured lives; longer notice of policy changes; clearer guidelines; more realistic staff wages; more staff continuity; higher wages for older workers and workers with families; funding for development work to improve the quality of projects; and greater provision for the development of new skills.

6. Voluntary, church and local community initiatives

Some of Britain's most exciting initiatives to tackle unemployment have come from these sectors of the community — 'the ordinary people'. The worst problems of unemployment are often concentrated in the larger city housing estates, and if community groups are not involved in the overall strategy, there will be little chance of success. These estates should be encouraged to build up their own local economic culture, and establish their own enterprises, overcoming the historically-induced climate of poverty, welfare dependency and oppression.

There are plenty of examples of what can be achieved at the voluntary and community level, such as the church-based 'Impasse' centre in Redcar, the community businesses and other activities set up by the Easterhouse Festival Society in Glasgow, the Coventry Workshop set up by the Bitteswell Employment Alliance, or the Broadwater Farm Youth Association Co-op, in Tottenham.

However, for every community initiative which succeeds there may be ten which fail to realise their potential. For a community to draw on its huge untapped resources, there is a need for community skills and resource banks; for Community Initiatives Funds to cover the cost of feasibility, research and planning exercises for new initiatives; for training; for easy single door access to council departments; for council bureaucracies to adapt to accommodate community groups whose members often have no experience of the legal and financial intricacies beloved by officials; and for more local authority Section 137 funding (the 2p rate) to provide resources.

7. Business start-up initiatives

During the industrial age, it was left up to the entrepreneurs to start the businesses that other people depended upon for their livelihoods. No-one thought to help the entrepreneurs: they seemed to do well enough on their own.

Since unemployment became a major problem, communities have begun to recognise that much can be done to help people start new businesses, and to help them develop once they are going. The core of the process is the local enterprise agency and the co-operative development agency, which give the direct one-to-one help people need to get going. 'No town should be without one'. However, this is only the beginning, as Figure 12 illustrates.

Figure 12 shows the range of business support systems which have been pioneered in Britain over the past ten years. What is happening is the beginning of a huge and silent transformation of business. The range of business support initiatives outlined below have all been shown to bring results. The authors argue that a proper business start-up and support strategy will avail itself of *all* of them, in a fully integrated manner.

1. *Enterprise workshops* provide homes for a number of new businesses, usually in old converted warehouses or schools, on easy-in, easy-out terms. By sharing facilities, a community of support builds up, which provides an enjoyable and supportive environment to the people who are running their businesses in the shared space.
2. *Business training courses* of all shapes and kinds — taster courses, evening and weekend courses, idea development courses, full-time courses, courses for people on the Enterprise Allowance Scheme and special courses for people who want to start co-operatives and community businesses.
3. *Community marketing and design facilities.* New businesses and co-operatives cannot usually afford to employ marketing or design consultants, so it makes sense to set up arrangements to meet their needs collectively. The success of the New Work Trust in Bristol, which provides marketing assistance for local businesses, shows how it can be done.
4. *Training and development courses.* Once established, businesses need to grow and develop. New methods of management, group work, participation and involvement, profit-sharing, production and systems-management (for instance) do not just grow on

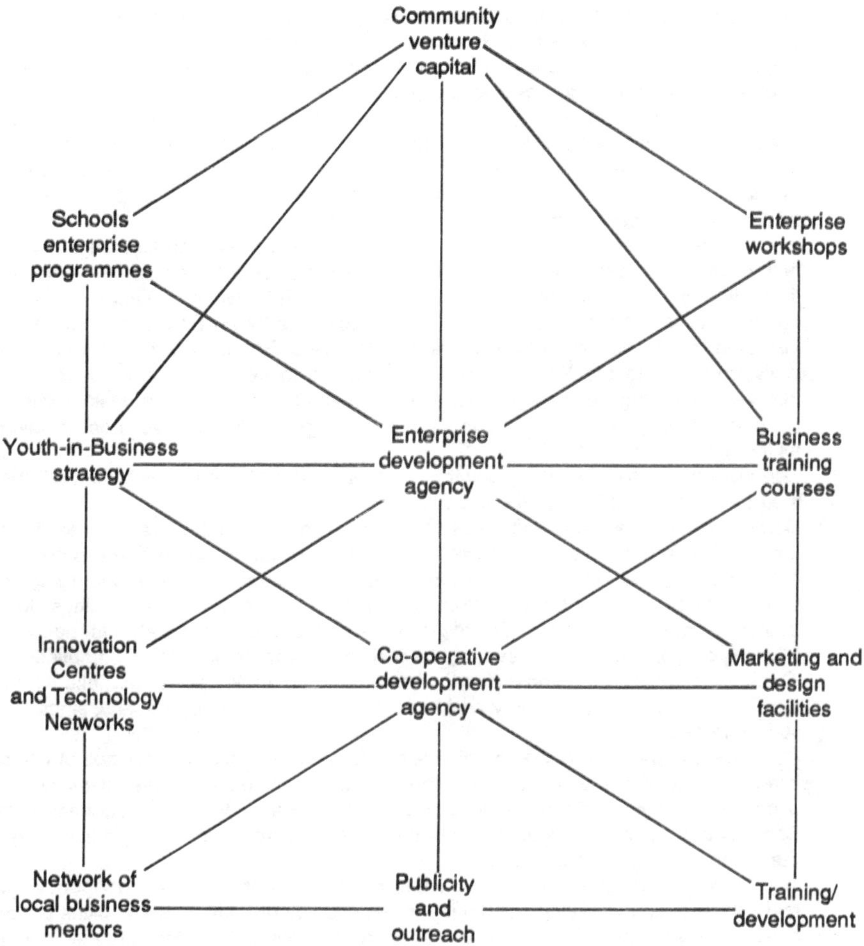

Fig. 12: Community-based business support systems

trees. They need to be introduced systematically. The local community can collectively become a 'change-agent', through its colleges and enterprise agencies, and deliberately choose to sow the seeds of change with local firms, to encourage them to innovate and to grow.

5. *Publicity and outreach*. In its early days, Project North East (Newcastle-upon-Tyne) made specific business start-up excursions to periferal housing estates, using a mobile exhibition. Radio, newspapers and local business competitions can also be used to reach out to people who do not traditionally think of themselves as being able to run a business.
6. *Networks of local business mentors* to give support and advice to people who are starting up.

7. *Innovation centres.* The skills and resources of local colleges and polytechnics can be drawn upon to provide help with research and development, which is beyond the financial reach of most people who are just starting. This is being done in London's Technology Networks, for instance, and in the Calderdale Business and Innovation Centre, at Dean Clough in Halifax. In Chicago, the Illinois Inventors Council gives specific assistance with patents and business development to help investors turn their ideas into practical job-creating possibilities. In Minneapolis-St. Paul, the city employs an inventor to teach inventiveness to seven-year-olds, so that they start thinking creatively at an early age.
8. *A youth-in-business strategy* integrating the many strands of action that are needed to help develop successful youth businesses. The evidence for success lies with initiatives such as Liverpool's 'Into Business' project, which trains 240 young unemployed people a year to become self-employed, Newcastle's Youth Enterprise Centre and Glastonbury's Facility for Arts and Crafts Enterprises (FACE), which builds business skills training into the YTS and enables trainees to become independent craftspeople on finishing the course. To make the most of young people's desire for independence through business, a complete strategy needs to be developed, involving all the agencies concerned.
9. *Schools enterprise programmes* with pupils learning the ropes early by establishing their own mini-companies and co-operatives.
10. *Community venture capital initiatives.* People who do not own their own homes do not usually have any collateral to secure a loan. The community can tackle this problem collectively by setting up special loan guarantee funds and by encouraging the establishment of community venture capital funds. In several British cities, local authority-based Enterprise Boards have been set up to meet this need. In Minneapolis, in the private sector, 10 insurance companies have established a 'Community Initiatives Consortium', through which they have channelled loans totalling £2 1/2 million to minority and hard-to-borrow business operations, since they started in 1981.

    Local people have hundreds of thousands, or even millions of pounds of capital invested around the world through their various pension schemes, bank deposit accounts, savings schemes and investment bonds, even in the poorest communities. Some of this money needs to start rolling locally, to allow people to begin investing in the future of their own communities.

    At the centre of a web such as this needs to lie the Enterprise Agency, the council's economic development office, or an equivalent body. In some cities people concerned with business start-up and support have begun to fill this strategic role, in addition to their all-important work of hands-on business start-up advice and support.

> *'Enterprise Agencies need to use their position as private and public sector partnerships to initiate the preparation of business plans for their communities. For only through the production and carrying through of such plans can the regeneration of communities be achieved.'*
>
> Jeff Pride, Director of MADE
> (Merthyr–Aberdare Development Enterprise Ltd)

INTERLUDE

Some thoughts about business

In the industrial age, business was seen as a private affair, looking after its own interests, in which it was wrong for society to interfere. Trade unions were only grudgingly accepted after a bitter historical struggle, which has now started up again. Free market economics still operates — fatally — on this premise.

In the post-industrial age, business will be seen as a community affair, with it being in the community's interest to see that successful businesses are created and sustained. In return, communities will begin to expect new codes of conduct from the businesses they help to create, to ensure that these businesses do not create ecological disturbances; that they involve their workers both in the running and the profits so generated; and that they develop an ethic of social responsibility, both locally and globally, and do not exploit either the poorer countries in the world or the poorer communities in this country. (In Easterhouse, Glasgow, one of Britain's most neglected communities, Ladbrokes extract their greatest profits in all Europe through their bookies shop, stealing the money away from the Easterhouse community and giving nothing back in return.) The fact that business has been run in a certain way for the past 150 years does not mean that it will go on being run in the same way for the next 150 years.

To continue around the Zodiac:

8. Initiatives involving existing businesses and trade unions

For instance:

- Active intervention in troubled companies to assist with company restructuring, developing new products, finding new markets and assisting possible worker-buyouts — the kind of activity pursued by the Greater London Enterprise Board (GLEB).
- Organised activity to help workers made redundant by plant closures to establish new businesses.
- Challenging local businesses to double their turnover by improving their business methods and developing three year plans, which the agency BASE (Bathgate Area Support for Enterprise) in Scotland is doing.
- Co-ordinating the development of local businesses and bringing skilled business consultancy to bear on their future plans, as the network of co-operatives in Mondragon (Spain) does through Ularco, one of its secondary co-operatives.
- Establishing local partnership arrangements to foster business development, as the Neath Development Partnership does, with involvement from local companies, the county and borough councils, the Welsh Development Agency, the Wales TUC, the trade union AUEW and the private job creation specialists, PA Management Consultants.
- Encouraging local companies to embrace the latest advances in management and technical design and to invest more in research and development.

9. Worksharing initiatives

Worksharing is a major area of untapped potential in Britain. The term 'worksharing' is used here to refer to a portfolio of different options which might be available to workers. There is accumulating evidence that many workers want the freedom to do *less work for less pay.* Up to 40 per cent of workers, according to some surveys, want to reduce their worktime with proportional reductions in pay. In Canada, 31 per cent of all working people and 64 per cent of women professionals stated a preference for worksharing, if it were available. One Canadian estimate (from Frank Reid, in the University of Toronto's economics department) suggests that unemployment in Canada could be cut from 11 per cent to 6 per cent (1986 figures) if reduced work hours could be made available to all who wanted them. A US Department of Labor survey found that 60 per cent of those interviewed favoured worksharing, corresponding to a 4.7 per cent reduction in total worktime. In Europe, Frank Reid suggests, a 4.7 per cent reduction in worktime would produce a 2 per cent increase in the number of people in jobs, which translates into 420,000 new jobs.

Worksharing initiatives are complex affairs, requiring careful negotiation between workers and employers. In North America, there is a 'Network for Work Time Options' with 18 member organisations, such as California's 'New Ways to Work' and Michigan's Work Options Resource Centre. A properly resourced local centre can generate change by co-ordinating four types of activity:

1. Briefing employers and unions about new work options
2. Tracking and promoting current examples
3. Education programmes for the general public
4. Assistance to individuals in negotiating new work schedules with their employers.

The 40 hour week/48 week year no longer suits the majority of the population, but for the lack of alternatives, many working people are trapped into working hours they dislike, which decreases productivity, increases absenteeism and sick leave, and is frustrating, when so many people have no work at all. New options are emerging, which need to be encouraged:

1. *Deferred salary leave plans.* In Winnipeg, Canada, the teachers' union and employers have negotiated a scheme which allows teachers to plan ahead for a year off work, with their jobs guaranteed when they return. A calculated proportion of the teachers' salaries is put aside in a special tax-free savings fund, sufficient for them to live on during their year off. The negotiators arrange that a fixed number of teachers take a year off through the leave plan every year. There were just 20 in 1985, as the scheme is still young. Knowing that there will be 20 'vacancies' every year, the employers have taken on an additional 20 full-time teachers.
2. *Jobsharing*, where two people share one job. Barclays Bank already has 2,000 jobsharers in Britain. The potential for development is restricted by the lack of local jobsharing registers, which could put potential jobsharers in touch with each other and assist them in job applications.
3. *V-time* is currently available in 14 state agencies in California. V-time is a time/income trade-off arrangement, which allows employees to take 'x' numbers of days off per month, in the form of shorter working days, shorter weeks or blocks of time added to vacation time.
4. *Compressed and modified workweeks,* in which work is compressed into four 10-hour or three 12-hour days, often alternating with a normal work week.
5. *Flexitime,* which allows employees to choose their starting and ending times, and as a side-effect, reduces absenteeism by 40 per cent and overtime by 50 per cent, as well as reducing employee turnover and raising morale.
6. *Banked overtime,* which gives employees the option of taking time off at a later date instead of being paid for overtime hours. Full-time relief staff are hired to cover for banked overtime absences.

In Britain, *New Ways to Work* (309 Upper Street, London N1 2TY, Tel 01–226 4026) encourages worksharing, especially jobsharing, but as with the local Co-operative Development Agencies, tangible results will not begin in earnest until each city or district begins to set up its own local Worksharing Agency.

Worksharing is an effective way of creating new jobs. At the same time, it represents a practical creative leap out of the '40 hours/48 weeks/48 years' strait-jacket of the industrial age. Details about the options listed above are available from New Ways to Work.

10. Community economic development initiatives

Research in Baltimore, USA, showed that in a prosperous part of the city, a dollar could circulate up to 8 times locally, being spent in local shops and businesses, stimulating trade and activity, before it left the local economy; in a poor area, it might circulate only once. Community economics is the art of making people develop ownership and involvement in their own local economy, and of maximising the retention of money in that economy, in order for it to be available as spending power to local people to encourage trade.

Various types of initiative are being developed around the world to achieve this end:

- *Import replacement policies.* Jane Jacobs argues very clearly in *Cities and the Wealth of Nations* that historically, city-regional economies which have grown successfully have done so by substituting local manufactures and production for imported goods and services. The province of Manitoba, in Canada, developed its own car insurance business ('Autopak') to offer a better service to local people and to prevent the massive outflow of dollars to Ontario, where Canada's insurance companies are all based. Those dollars remain available locally to finance further economic activity.
- *Local authority purchasing policies.* The city of Glasgow gives precedence to local businesses if their bids for tender are within 5 per cent of the highest bid, and if they will reduce their prices accordingly.
- *Energy policies.* Ten times more energy has been 'created' in the USA by energy saving measures since 1979 than by any other method. Many American cities are now developing energy programmes to increase efficiency and save costs. This also saves on the amount of local money exported to pay for fuel, heat and light, money which is lost to the local economy. Amory Lovins' work (see p. 188) is probably the best in the world on this subject.
- *Recycling policies.* Ever-increasing sums of money are spent importing raw materials and then disposing of the waste afterwards. Community recycling policies save on this expenditure, conserve the Earth's scarce resources and create local jobs. In Britain, Oxfam and Friends of the Earth have both developed local recycling initiatives. In Manitoba, the Manitoba Waste Exchange lists waste materials generated by 78 local companies, including such items as waste newsprint, battery acid, scrap glass, brass, copper, zinc, freon, gypsum, restaurant fat, solvents, felt, vinyl and horse manure, and offers them for sale to a mailing list of 1,100 people.
- *Biomass sustainability programmes.* These ensure that the long-term sustainability of the natural economy (the gross nature product) is maintained, through the health of the surroundings topsoil, plant cover, tree cover, water supply, wildlife and species variation.
- Launching *community currencies* such as the LETSystem (see Chapter 10), which encourage local people to trade with each other sharing their skills and resources, without need for money, which is often in short supply among unemployed people.
- *Community banking.* In Mondragon (Spain), the existence of the Caja Laboral Popular enables people's savings to be retained locally and recycled as new local investment. This has been a critical factor in the success of the Mondragon co-operatives.

Historically, a nation will decline if there is a shortage of risk capital to invest in its future. The same is true of a community. The major industrial owners of the past raised risk capital to put into their factories, shipyards and workshops. Today, communities have to do it for themselves. There is money around, even in the poorest communities — but there are no channels which allow local people to choose to invest their savings in a way that will secure the future of their children. So, we have to create those channels.

- *Encouraging local ownership of businesses* through expanding the community business and the co-operative movements and by encouraging firms to develop 'ESOP' policies (Employee Stock Ownership Plans). Another success factor in Mondragon is the rule that workers must purchase shares in the co-operative they work in, and must also sell them if they leave, so that ownership never leaves the area. Policies that give the community and employees a stake in local enterprise help to build community cohesion.

11. Local government initiatives

For an overall community strategy to work, the elected members and the administrative staff of the local council must both be involved and feel involved, without trying to take it over. In New Westminster, British Columbia (Canada), the Mayor, several councillors and the chief planner all sit on the steering committee of the Royal City Community Development Association, which is proceeding with a community-based economic development strategy for the city. When the Association decided to carry out a detailed profile study of the city's economy, the city planners were able to help immensely, and did not feel that such an activity had to be 'theirs'.

There are many ways in which local authorities can assist a community strategy, in addition to pursuing traditional policies such as industrial prospecting and giving support to the activities referred to above. Further measures can include:

- The use of superannuation funds to invest in local companies.
- The establishment of loan guarantee funds to provide security for business ventures by people and groups who have no collateral, or who the banks are shy of lending to.
- Equal opportunities policies to ensure the fair distribution of jobs to women, ethnic minorities and disabled people.
- Pay equalisation policies to eliminate men's and women's earnings differentials.
- Establishing Enterprise Boards to provide grants, loans and consultancy to businesses and co-operatives.
- Undertaking a range of measures to support:
    1. co-operatives (as detailed in *Worker Co-operatives: How Local Authorities Can Help*) — see p. 187
    2. economic development in general (as detailed in *Effective Economic Development: A Discussion of Local Authority Organisation, Management and Training*) — see p. 188
    3. voluntary and community initiatives (as detailed in *Joint Action — The Way Forward*) — see p. 187
- Encouraging the process of 'popular planning' in communities to assist people to dream, think and plan for the kind of future they want in their neighbourhoods. This has been done in the docklands of London, but the community's own dreams were overruled by the superior power of the London Docklands Development Corporation.

12. Land, housing and environmental initiatives

- In Swansea, the City Council is persuading building societies to release mortgages to unemployed people, to allow them to build their own homes.
- In Brixton, the Black Roof Housing Co-operative, a voluntary group of mainly black and homeless young people, has converted short-life properties, and bought two houses and a church, which they are converting into flats to provide themselves with a place to live.
- In Macclesfield, unemployed people working with a community architect have renovated the houses in the terrace where they live, and transformed their local environment.
- In Glasgow, the council has assisted the formation of tenant management co-operatives in some blocks of flats. This allows residents (many of whom are unemployed) to do their own repairs and maintenance. The council is now planning to sell 2,500 houses in poor repair to groups of tenants forming community ownership co-operatives.
- In the Pleck, Walsall, the Pleck Community Association is assisting block-dwellers to take over block management agreements and run their own retail services.
- On the Broadwater Estate in Tottenham, and elsewhere, the Priority Estates Project approach, which involves tenant participation, is resulting in the reappearance of local pride and community self-help.
- In Bristol, youth workers in the south of the city drew up plans with the Abbey National Building Society for a block of flats to be converted into accommodation for young single people.

Transform your local environment

In many parts of Britain, problems of housing, community development, environmental development, economic development and unemployment go hand-in-hand. New approaches are clearly possible. Major land development and environmental schemes are likely to be part of many community strategies, if new visions of what localities could look like begin to take hold. Community tree-planting schemes, urban farms, wilderness areas, murals, play areas, footpaths, locally created parks, car-free streets and similar initiatives all help in enabling local people to experience ownership and pride in the neighbourhoods where they live.

Our traditional planning processes need to be put through a 'creative leap', in order that people should be able to participate actively, and with excitement, in the dreaming and the creating of the future of their own communities. 'Popular planning' has made a good start on this process. Traditional planners can be very threatened by the challenge to their power that such participatory developments bring. A new generation of planners is emerging which is open to participatory approaches.

THE POLITICS OF THE FUTURE

The kind of politics involved in this 'community strategy' approach to unemployment is neither simply left wing or right wing. It fosters the qualities of enterprise, self-reliance and initiative, as well as the qualities of co-operation and mutual support. Initiatives around Britain are being started by Socialists, Greens, Conservatives, Liberals, SDP members and Communists, as well as by people who don't care about politics at all. Traditional business types are beginning to think in terms of 'community profit', while traditional community types are beginning to think in terms of sound business practice and commercial viability. It is an enormously healthy marriage of right and left. In this sense, the approach is 'transpolitical'. With only one wing, you cannot fly - you just go round in circles. There is not much room for dogmatists, of either right or left, in this process.

This could be a measure of the way in which politics in the post-industrial age is going to develop. In place of the left-right contrast, the important contrast in the future may be between those who believe in *government by administration*, by which people at the centre do things for other people (the way government has traditionally been run), and those who believe in government by *animation*, where the role of government workers is to enable people to find out for themselves what they want to do, and assist them to do it. All the technological developments of the present time point us in this latter direction, as does the success of initiatives such as schools enterprise projects, self-help schemes and business start-up programmes, which help people realise their own dreams.

To make government by animation work, administrators have to be cured of their desire to minister, and inspired by the desire to animate. How do we train them to understand the processes of creativity and dream-fulfilment? Maybe by beginning with their own lives, so that they discover that long forgotten dreams can be awoken, and made to live. For all of us, this is the hope: that dreams be made to live.

In conclusion: the creative leap

Britain is facing a considerable crisis, even if to many people living in the south it seems invisible. As the Industrial Age collapses, the visions that inspired it are collapsing too: all that we are left with seems to be a fetish of money-making.

But life itself never collapses. Its visions and stuctures only collapse to make room for new ones, expressing new visions. To reach them, we have to make a creative leap:

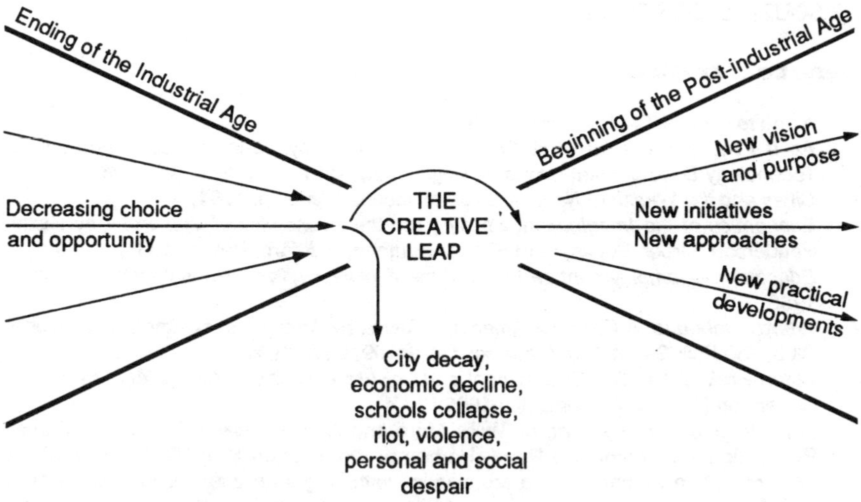

Fig. 13: The Creative Leap

This leap does not mean just 'trying harder', or pouring more money into the old system:

- It means opening up our lives to new dreams and new possibilities, and granting a new recognition to the importance of the human spirit, the carrier of our dreams.
- It means rethinking the ways we organise our working lives to give us more choice, more self-expression and more involvement in what we are doing.
- It means helping our young people to learn in ways which engage their whole sense of being.
- It means finding new ways of organising our schools, colleges, trade unions, businesses, arms of government and many other major institutions, to allow greater involvement and creativity.
- It means finding new ways to organise our economies, locally, regionally, nationally and globally, so that we overcome the misery and waste of unemployment, the destruction of our living environment, the holocaust of famine and the risk of nuclear destruction.
- It means reaching our eyes towards new visions. The age of nationalism, economic greed and selfishness is over. We must choose to work for something different.

A generation of people is growing up who are still young, and not yet in positions of real power, who for the first time in history have understood a forceful truth: that we belong together and must learn to live together on this one rather small planet.

In Chinese the word for 'crisis' is *wei-chi*. *Wei* means 'danger' and *chi* means 'opportunity'. The crisis of unemployment is twinned with the crisis of the planet as a whole. Both crises bring us many dangers. Both crises also bring us opportunities to rethink, to dream new dreams and to rebuild our economies on new principles.

The thinking, dreaming and building must be done for the Earth as a whole. There is an awful lot to be done.

RESOURCE LISTING

General books

- *A Job to Live*, by Shirley Williams (Penguin, 1985)
- *As If People Mattered — A Prospect for Britain*, by John Davis, (Intermediate Technology Development Group, 9 King Street, London WC2E 8HW, 1986)
- *Cities and the Wealth of Nations*, by Jane Jacobs (Penguin, 1984)
- *Economics of the Imagination: Spelling out the Economics of Tomorrow*, by Hazel Henderson (Green Books, Ford House, Hartland, Bideford, Devon, 1987)
- *Education, Unemployment and the Future of Work*, by Tony Watts (Open University, 1983)
- *Energy Unbound: A Fable for America's Future*, by Amory and Hunter Lovins (Sierra Club, 730 Polk Street, San Francisco CA 94109, USA, 1986)
- *Futurework: Jobs, Self-Employment and Leisure After the Industrial Age*, by James Robertson (Temple/Gower Smith,1985)
- *Long-term Unemployment*, by Willie More and Andrew Howell (£5.00 from Pepar Publications, 50 Knightlow Road, Harborne, Birmingham B17 8QB). An excellent practical guide for people who are working with long-term unemployed people on a daily basis, written by the organisers of Birmingham's Job Change Project, and based on seven years of experience in that area.
- *New Ideas in Ecology and Economics*, the transcript of the excellent CBC broadcasts, May/June 1986. ($5.00 Canadian from CBC Enterprises, PO Box 6440, Station A, Montreal H3C 3L4, Canada)
- *Nice Work if You Can Get It — How to be Positive about Unemployment*, by Guy Dauncey (NEC, 1983, £3.95)
- *Paths to Paradise: On the Liberation from Work*, by Andre Gorz (Pluto, 1985)
- *Previews and Premises*, by Alvin Toffler (Pan, 1985)
- *Sleepers Wake! Technology and the Future of Work*, by Barry Jones (Wheat- sheaf, Brighton, 1982)
- *The Future of Work*, by Charles Handy (Blackwell, 1984)
- *The Living Economy — A New Economy in the Making*, edited papers from the 1984 and 1985 TOES (The Other Economic Summit) conferences (RKP, 1986)
- *The New Economic Agenda*, papers from the Findhorn new economics conference (Findhorn Press, The Park, Nr Forres, Morayshire, Scotland, 1985)

Books and papers concerned with practical developments

- *The LEDIS sheets*, (Local Economic Development Information Service), The Planning Exchange, 186 Bath Street, Glasgow G2 4HG (send for sample sheets; £25 per year subscription)
- *Initiatives* magazine, £17.50 per year from Longmans, Sub Dept, 4th Avenue, Harlow, Essex CM19 5AA.
  (These two publications provide the best ongoing coverage of practical initiatives and development.)
- *Making Unemployment Work*, by Michael Moynagh (Lion, 1985)
- *Beating Unemployment — A Practitioner's Handbook* (Centre for Employment Initiatives, 140A Gloucester Mansions, Cambridge Circus, London WC2H, £2.50)
- *Joint Action — The Way Forward.* Report of a joint Local Authority Association/ NCVO Working party (NCVO, 26 Bedford Square, London WC1B 3HU, 1984)

- *Long-term Unemployment: Action for a Forgotten Million,* by Peter Ashby (Bedford Square Press, £2.95). Takes a very positive and imaginative approach, arguing for a flexible programme of support combining opportunities for personal development, community development and skills development.
- *Worker Co-operatives — How Local Authorities Can Help,* by Alan Taylor (ICOM Co-Publications, 245A Coldharbour Lane, London SW9, 1983)
- *Effective Development: A discussion of Local Authority, Organisation, Management and Training* (Planning Exchange, address above, 1984)
- *BIC Post,* the newspaper of Business in the Community (Free from BIC, 227a City Road, London EC1V 1LX)
- *A User's Guide to the Manpower Services Commission,* by Alastair Thomson and Hilary Rosenberg (Kogan Page, 1986)
- *Local Economy.* A serious practical and theoretical quarterly magazine (£19.50 pa from LEPU, South Bank Polytechnic, Borough Road, London SE1 0AA)
- *Summary of the Economic Renewal Project* ($1 from Amory Lovins, Rocky Mountain Institute, Post Office Drawer 248, Old Snowmass, Co. 81654, USA)

Organisations

- *ACTION on long-term unemployment* is a national charity that is concerned with the plight of Britain's one and a half million long-term unemployed people. It is working to encourage changes in popular attitudes to long-term unemployment, to develop a programme of action-research, to encourage innovations in local schemes for long-term unemployed people.
  Contact: ACTION, 79 Prince George Road, London N16 8DL.
- *Business in the Community* (BiC) is a partnership between businesses, voluntary, professional and educational organisations, chambers of commerce, the trade union movement, and central and local government. Its purpose is to promote corporate community involvement. BiC provides the co-ordination for the large network of Enterprise Agencies throughout Britain, and acts as a 'sharp edge' for the business world's thought and action in the field of local economic regeneration.
  Contact: BiC, 227a City Road, London EC1V 1LX, Tel 01-253 3716.
- The *Centre for Employment Initiatives* is an independent organisation which provides a practical focus for local economic regeneration. Its staff assist and advise on numerous community-based initiatives in Britain and around the world.
  Contact: Centre for Employment Initiatives, 140a Gloucester Mansions, Cambridge Circus, London WC2H 8PA, Tel 01-240 8901/2/3.
- *Charter for Jobs* is a national employment campaign focusing on the need for new national policies to create jobs — a one-year job guarantee for the long-term unemployed, a substantial rise in public spending to generate employment, and a cut in taxes on jobs.
  Contact: Charter for Jobs, South Bank House, Black Prince Road, London SE1 7SJ, Tel 01–735 0777.
- The *Community Projects Foundation* is a national community development agency, receiving its core funding from the Home Office. It runs innovative projects around Britain in conjunction with local authorities and other bodies.
  Contact: CPF, 60 Highbury Grove, London N5 2AG, Tel 01-226 5375.
- *The Planning Exchange* is an independent, non-profit organisation which acts as a centre for information, research and education in the fields of environmental, economic and social planning.
  Contact: The Planning Exchange, 186 Bath St, Glasgow G2 4HG, Tel 041-332 8541.

POSTSCRIPT

In his book *The Prophet**, the Lebanese author Kahlil Gibran writes about the day when Almustafa, 'who was a dawn unto his own day', is to leave the city of the Orphalese, where he has lived among the people for twelve years, and return to his native land.

The people are sad to see him go, for they have loved him much. Before he goes, the seeress Almitra begs him to share with them his truths. These words are not in Kahlil Gibran's book, but had he lived in the 1980s, perhaps they would have been.

> *Then a man stood forth from the crowd and said, Speak to us of Unemployment.*
>
> *And he answered:*
> *When you have no work, are your souls truly without work? Your souls never sleep. Not until your smallest dreams are fulfilled will your souls rest.*
>
> *At times when there is no work, when idleness threatens to consume you, know that there is still meaning and purpose in life.*
> *Use your days with joy, asking only how to be true to yourself and to your people, pausing not to have self-pity or to wait in helplessness.*
>
> *See your unemployment as a blessing, a time of rest and rekindling. Many do not know that the Earth we dwell on is one with the heavens above, and that behind every action there lies purpose. Nothing is without meaning, even when you choose to say 'This has no meaning'.*
>
> *And when you suffer doubt, remember this: many times, in the long unfolding of the world, there have been difficulties and changes. It is only natural to experience uncertainty. But do not let your uncertainty cause you to lose heart, or to lose the knowledge of who you really are.*
>
> *You have been given a gift — a time to find new paths, wherein your soul will drink sweet water. Enjoy your gift. For even as one door closes, others await your knock.*
>
> *You are part of Life, as everything else is. Go out and see what can be done — for there is much to be done before the Earth is finally built in the light of Heaven.*

THE END

* *The Prophet*, by Kahlil Gibran (Heinemann)

Index

STOP PRESS: August 1987

- The Government is proposing policy changes which will deny benefit to all 16 and 17 year olds who refuse a place on the *Youth Training Scheme*. If implemented, this will have a number of negative effects. Details of this and other issues concerning young people are published quarterly in *'Youth Training Update'*, free from National Youth Bureau, 17 Albion Street, Leicester LE1 6GD.

  An active campaigning approach to issues concerning young people and youth training is taken by *Youthaid*, 9 Poland Street, London WC1, Tel: 01–439 8523.
- If the new *Job Training Scheme* takes off successfully, it is probable that young people aged 18–24 will be discouraged from taking places on the Community Programme.
- The *Community Programme* may become a scheme only for over-25 year olds. The system of payment for the Community Programme is due to change to a 'benefit plus' basis (i.e. the rate of benefit you receive plus £20, or some equivalent figure).

Further information

- In Wrexham, a **Social Security Consumers' Committee** has been set up (see Chapter 12). A free leaflet is available (*Give Claimants a Say*), also a report on their first year's work (*Consulting Claimants*, £2.50), from the Welsh Consumer Council, Castle Building, Womanby Street, Cardiff CF1 2BN.
- **The Open College** is now broadcasting a variety of practical skills training programmes on Channel 4 (1-2 pm initially); other TV channels will soon follow suit. There are over 100 student support centres to give back-up support. Write for details (no stamp needed) to The Open College, Freepost, Manchester M3 8BA.
- **Prestel** offer an educational service including information on educational advice centres and details of higher education course openings. Available in larger libraries if you've not got it on your TV.

Books and leaflets

- *Facts about Jobhunting*, send a large SAE to Jobs, Consumer Association, PO Box 44, Hertford SG14 1SH.
- *Debt: A survival guide*, including a six step action plan. Free from public libraries and the Office of Fair Trading, HMSO.
- *A Year Off. . . A Year On — a guide to jobs, voluntary service and working holidays during your education* (£2.55 from CRAC, Bateman Street, Cambridge CB2 1LZ). Covers paid work, work camps, travel and expeditions, working in France, and personal stories.

New addresses

- *Friends of the Earth*, 26-28 Underwood Street, London N1 7JQ, Tel: 01-490 1555.
- *War on Want*, 37 Great Guildford Street, London SE1 0ES, Tel: 01-620 1111.

A REGULAR 'NEW UNEMPLOYMENT HANDBOOK' UPDATE SERVICE is going to be available electronically through UNET (see p. 57). Anyone possessing a personal computer and modem will be able to access this regularly. Relevant information from the Feedback Sheets will be included in this service. Details from UNET, Holywell Centre, 1 Phipp Street, London EC2A 4PS.

Many thanks to everyone who has helped.

Without vision, people perish
Without anger, people perish

HANDBOOK FEEDBACK SHEET

We encourage you to write in with corrections, comments, criticisms, new information and new ideas, whether it is a change of post-code or a scheme for unemployed people to colonise the Moon. Please use the space below (and over), and then simply fold the sheet in 3, seal it with sticky tape, and pop it in the post.

fold 2

CUT ALONG HERE

fold 1

Your name and address:

Thank you!

NO
STAMP
NEEDED

The New Unemployment Handbook, Freepost,
National Extension College,
18 Brooklands Avenue,
Cambridge CB2 2HN

Please use this space for your comments and reactions.